LANGUAGE AND LITERACY SERIES

Dorothy S. Strickland, Celia Genishi, and Donna Alvermann SERIES EDITORS

ADVISORY BOARD: RICHARD ALLINGTON, KATHRYN AU,
BERNICE CULLINAN, COLETTE DAIUTE, ANNE HAAS DYSON, CAROLE EDELSKY,
JANET EMIG, SHIRLEY BRICE HEATH, CONNIE JUEL, SUSAN LYTLE, TIMOTHY SHANAHAN

---

* Volumes with an asterisk following the title are a part of the NCRLL set: Approaches to Language and Literacy Research, edited by JoBeth Allen and Donna Alvermann.

(Continued)

teaching**media***literacy*.com

A WEB-LINKED GUIDE TO RESOURCES AND ACTIVITIES

Richard Beach

TEACHERS COLLEGE PRESS

Teachers College, Columbia University
New York and London

The *New York Times* September 5, 2005, article by Daniel F. Barry, "Texas Way Station Offers a First Serving of Hope," is discussed in Chapter 4 in the section by Martha Cosgrove entitled "A Teaching Idea–The Opportunity Disaster Provides: From Non-Fiction to Literary Theory to Poetry." Copyright © 2005 by The New York Times Co. Reprinted with permission.

Published by Teachers College Press, 1234 Amsterdam Avenue, New York, NY 10027

Library of Congress Cataloging-in-Publication Data

Beach, Richard.
  Teachingmedialiteracy.com : a web-linked guide to resources and activities / Richard Beach.
    p. cm. – (Language and literacy series)
  Includes bibliographical references and index.
  ISBN-13: 978-0-8077-4744-5 (pbk. : alk. paper)
  1. Media literacy–Study and teaching. I. Title.
  P96.M4B43 2007
  302.2307–dc22   2006025552

ISBN-13: 978-0-8077-4744-5 (paper))

Printed on acid-free paper
Manufactured in the United States of America

14 13 12 11 10 09 08 07   8 7 6 5 4 3 2 1

Contents

Acknowledgments

I wish to thank the following people for their assistance with this book: for his ideas on innovative ways of integrating the web into teaching, Thomas Reinartz; for helpful, insightful reviews of initial drafts, Renee Hobbs, David Reinkings, Marjorie Siegel, and Scott Sullivan; for his careful, thoughtful editing of drafts, Michael Greer; for his thorough copyediting, Karl Nyberg; and for her ongoing, spirited support of this whole project as acquisitions editor, Carol Collins. For assistance in designing and maintaining the Website: Scott Hatch, Beth O'Hara, Tamela McCartney, and Joel Swanson. And for their teaching ideas, all of the students who have taken my media studies methods course over the many years, some of whose activities are included in this book, I am most grateful; as teachers, we learn much from our students.

Introduction:
The Book and the Website

THIS BOOK IS DESIGNED primarily as a resource book to assist you as a teacher in teaching media literacy through use of the extensive resources available on the web, resources that are transforming how and where media literacy is taught.

ADVANTAGES OF USING THE WEB

Much of the material in this book is based on a graduate-level course for teachers offered at the University of Minnesota—"*Teaching Film, Television, and Media Studies*"—that I have taught for the past 30 years. In the past I was limited to studying visual images, showing video clips, and looking at copies of magazines or newspapers, within my own physical classroom. Now my students can readily access visual images, video clips, magazines, and newspapers on the web anytime and anywhere. I can then create media lab activities in which students may work in groups to dissect media texts available on the web, work that is not limited to my classroom. And in their own classrooms, they and their students can access these same texts, often projecting them on a screen or whiteboard for class discussions.

The many advantages I have enjoyed in using web resources with current and future teachers of media literacy will, I hope, prove equally valuable for other educators, whether in universities or in secondary classrooms. What follows is a brief rundown of activities made possible by the vast resources of the web. These activities, as well as the resources themselves, are explored more fully in the chapters of this book and in my associated website, which provides ready access through its thousands of links to the sites described in these pages.

Accessing Current Digitized Media Texts. One limitation of many media studies textbooks and curricular materials is that the media texts in these books and materials date quickly. Media content that is even several years old may no longer be familiar to students or have much interest to them. One value of using the web as the source of media texts is that students can easily access digitized media texts, and much of the content on the web is relatively current.

Sharing Responses Online. In my course in the past, discussion of media texts was often limited to my classroom. Now my students share their responses in online discussions outside class. For example, students may share a video clip of a movie trailer and, in an online chat, critique the film techniques employed in the trailer.

And students are not limited to just their peers' responses. By participating in blogs or in chat rooms, they can share their responses with larger audiences beyond the classroom.

Studying Audiences' Online Responses. Students can also use their access to online audiences' responses to media texts to conduct their own media ethnography studies of how these online audiences construct the meaning of media texts. For example, they can study how and why members of a television program's or rock group's fan site enjoy a particular program or group.

Constructing Digital Media Texts. A central approach of media literacy instruction is that students best learn the characteristics of media texts by creating and sharing their own. Students can use web-based digital design tools to create digital video productions, blogs, wikis, podcasts, websites, and digital storytelling as texts. In creating these "new media" texts, they are learning a range of digital literacies, for example, how to make hypertextual links between existing media texts. And they can readily share these texts with larger audiences beyond the classroom, enhancing their motivation to create them.

Critiquing the Web Itself. The web and the digital literacies associated with using the web have become a central focus for media literacy instruction. Through active use of the web and production of web-based media texts, students learn to critically examine the effectiveness and usability of websites as well as the ideological assumptions inherent in and institutional forces behind ideas presented on these sites.

Accessing Lessons, Curriculum, and Links. The web also serves as a vast repository of lessons and curricula available on all aspects of the media so that you do not have to reinvent the wheel in creating your own curriculum. Moreover, in constructing your own lessons, you can draw on web-based materials and media texts. For example, in studying differences in global news coverage of an event, you can ask students to go to online newspapers from around the world to compare their coverage of that event.

CRITICAL ANALYSIS OF THE MEDIA

While the web has transformed media literacy instruction, the basic goal of that instruction has not changed: to foster critical analysis of the media. Given the centrality of media use in society, students need to learn to analyze and critique film, television, radio, magazines, newspapers, and websites. However, with the current narrowing of the school curriculum to a focus on test preparation, you may need to justify the value of studying media in schools; this is the subject of Chapter 1.

To help students learn to critique media texts, this book summarizes various critical approaches for analyzing media texts, media representations, and media genres, as well as methods for helping students appreciate and critique the use of media production techniques. The book also provides methods for helping students analyze their own uses of the media as audiences constructing the meaning of media texts.

Learning to critique the media also involves an understanding of the larger economic and institutional forces shaping them. This book provides methods for critiquing how advertising reflects and fosters a consumption society and how print, television, and radio news are often shaped by corporate ownership.

Finally, the book ends with a discussion of ways to consider integrating media into the literacy curriculum, by identifying those literacies involved in understanding and producing both media and print texts, rather than teaching media as a separate, isolated component of the curriculum.

Throughout the book, to illustrate the application of the ideas presented, I have included teachers' descriptions of their own media literacy instruction, in the form of classroom activities.

USING THE BOOK'S WEBSITE

An essential component of this book is its accompanying Website: **http://www.teachingmedialiteracy. com**

This Website contains thousands of links to informative sites, which are referenced in the book according to a triple numbering system (chapter.topic.link), along with a description of each site. (In many cases, due to space constraints, the Website will contain more extended descriptions of the linked sites than is possible in this book.)

If, as you are reading, you want more information on any topic or link, you can easily access the numbered link on the Website and go to the source of the information. For example, a citation in the book of (8.3.2) refers to the second link in Chapter 8 on topic 3; you can go directly to this link on the Website, or, should you want to know more about how "Advertising drives content," go to any of the 8.3 links. At the start of each chapter, there is a key to the topics discussed in that chapter in order to make the correspondence between the structure of the book and the Website even more transparent.

To navigate the site, first go to the chapter table of contents in the column on the left or click on a chapter number along the top of the page. Click on a chapter to open up the specific topics in that chapter. Then click on the links to sites listed for that topic. The Website also contains suggested readings for these topics, as well as some units devised by students taking the media literacy course at the University of Minnesota.

All links on the website are continually checked to ensure that they are current. Dead links will be removed or replaced. When new links are added under relevant topics, they will be noted as "new".

I will also provide new ideas and resources for teaching media on my blog, **http://teachingliterature.typepad.com/teachingmedia/**

You can contribute your own ideas as comments on this blog or to a Media Literacy Wikibook written by teachers at **http://teachingmedialiteracy.pbwiki.com/MediaLiteracyWikibook**.

Goals for Media Literacy Instruction

A S A TEACHER OF media studies, you may often face the challenge of having to justify the inclusion of media studies in the curriculum. With the current trend in the United States toward an increased emphasis on basic skills, course offerings in media studies–as well as art, music, social studies, and second languages–are being reduced, particularly in larger urban districts where schools are under scrutiny to improve test scores.

Because media studies is still widely perceived as peripheral to "teaching the basics," few states have any distinct media studies curriculum strand (Kubey & Baker, 1999; 1.1.4; for a map developed by Kubey and Baker with each state's media literacy standards, 1.3.11a), although there are general media literacy standards formulated by organizations such as Mid-Continent Research for Education and learning (MCRE) (1.1.6–7). One exception is Texas, where the curriculum framework (*Viewing and Representing: Media Literacy in Texas*, developed by Renee Hobbs and others [Education Service Center Region XV]) revolves around critically analyzing media representations focusing on topics such as crime reporting, romances, politics, and the culture of celebrity (1.1.8). However, many states and districts are now devoting more attention to teaching it, leading them to adopt state standards related to it (Schwarz & Brown,

2005). The Website contains examples of some of these standards and justifications for inclusion of media literacy in the curriculum (1.1.9–14).

Unfortunately, teachers often do not receive adequate training in teaching media literacy (1.1.15); there is also significant parental opposition to media education as a "frill" (1.1.16). And No Child Left Behind testing mandates have often narrowed the curriculum focus, excluding attention to media and digital literacies (1.1.17).

In other countries, including Britain, Australia, and Canada, media studies, by contrast, assumes a central role in the curriculum. In Ontario, Canada, media education has been required in grades 7–12 since 1987 (1.1.2). In Britain, there is a nationwide curriculum and students take national exams in media studies, including a portfolio in which they must demonstrate their ability to critically analyze the media and the role of media industries in shaping media content (1.1.3).

In Australia the curriculum itself has, in certain provinces, been redefined to focus on the importance of media literacy. For example, The Queensland "New Basics" Project organizes their K–12 curriculum around the realities of students' lives in contemporary society (1.1.1). Within the curriculum focus on "multiliteracies and communications media," students address the question, "How do I make sense of and communicate with the world?" through "blending traditional and new communications media." Much can be learned from these efforts abroad.

JUSTIFYING
MEDIA/FILM STUDY IN THE CURRICULUM

Consider these comments made by a school board member in Eden Prairie, Minnesota, who complained that teachers in the district were using videos and DVDs inappropriately:

> To me, showing movies is a pretty low skill level. I would rather that teachers use the skills they have to get students involved in reading and discussing topics. . . . If we're showing a lot of videos in the classroom, then I view it as a problem. We do get parents calling us, saying: "Why are they showing *Schindler's List*? Why are we showing *Pippi Long-stocking*?" (Draper, 2002, p. 1a)

If you were a teacher in the Eden Prairie district, how would you respond to this school board member's perception of the problem of showing films in class? What assumptions is this school board member making about the role of media literacy in schools? How does media studies fit into the school curriculum? Is it simply a marginal add-on—something that involves "low skill levels," as the school board member argues—or is it something that should be more central to the school curriculum, given its important role in the culture? To assist you in formulating a rationale for teaching media studies in the curriculum, this chapter reviews some basic justifications for including media studies in the school curriculum.

Building Upon
Students' Active Use of the Media

The marginalization of media in the curriculum ignores the centrality of media in our lives; one study found that on an average day, people spend about two-thirds of their waking hours interacting with media, more time than they devote to sleeping, eating, or work (Center for Media Design, 2005). This is particularly true for students. A 2005 study found that students in grades 3–12 spend an average of 6 hours and 21 minutes daily engaged with some sort of media, compared to about 50 minutes of time devoted to homework (1.2.1; 1.2.2). Children and ado-

lescents have grown accustomed to multitasking in their bedroom media cultures, engaged in IM-ing, blogging, video games, online sites such as MySpace, music on iPods™, DVDs, and cellphones. Nearly half (46%) of children and adolescents with TVs in their rooms do at least half of their TV viewing on that set; 75% report multitasking while watching TV (Knowledge Networks/SRI, 2003, 1.2.3). A 2003 survey by Grunwald Associates found that more than 2 million American children ages 6–17 have their own personal websites (1.2.4). From these experiences, students acquire a range of digital literacies associated with the use of digital tools—for example, their ability to combine images, music, sounds, and texts together in a hypermedia production. Or they acquire social literacies through the use of email or computer chat, mastering synchronous and asynchronous chat involving high levels of thinking, learning, and social development (Choi & Ho, 2003; 1.5.3).

In producing and sharing online texts, students are using texts to communicate their ideas and construct their identities. Digital tools allow students to construct their own personal mix of media texts (for example, their own playlists on an iPod) or to display their digital literacy competence and agency to peers (for example, by sharing video clips on cellphones). Based on his research with disengaged high school students' high levels of engagement in a high school media literacy project, David O'Brien (2003) argues that adolescents often use media text—internet chat rooms, web pages, computer games, film/video, music—to display high levels of competence in using these media texts (1.5.4).

Some neurologists (Restak, 2003) and cognitive scientists (Clark, 2003) posit that this multimediating in the bedroom culture has changed the neural networks in kids' brains so that they prefer to learn in new and different ways. Through this engagement, they acquire a range of digital literacies required for successful participation in the online, networked social world of the mediasphere. It is also the case that this multimediating requires active, as opposed to passive, uses of the media. Simply watching a TV drama in the bedroom is a very different experience from actively formulating messages in writing a blog. One study found that 3rd graders with a TV and no computer in their bedrooms scored the lowest in math and language arts tests, while those with a computer and no TV scored the highest on these tests, suggesting that active use of computers influenced their school performance (Borzekowski & Robinson, 2005).

Moving Digital Literacies
from the Bedroom to the Classroom

One central justification, therefore, for incorporating media studies in the classroom is to extend the active participation in and construction of media in the home to the classroom. A primary goal of media education is to foster active, critical response to media as opposed to passive participation. This entails creating classroom activities that involve students in critically analyzing and producing media texts in ways that build on their multimediating experiences.

As they move from this multimediating experience in their bedrooms to the classroom, students then often perceive learning decontextualized "reading skills" with only print texts as anachronistic and not engaging, particularly in classrooms devoted exclusively to traditional literacy instruction (Street, 2004). One primary justification for including media studies in the curriculum is the need to create a curriculum that will engage students in their learning. If students are highly engaged with outside-of-school multimediating, then the curriculum needs to build on that experience in ways that enhance their uses of the media. If, for example, students are writing daily in their personal blogs, then writing instruction in school can capitalize on that experience by providing ways to improve that writing through, for example, linking to other blogs, as opposed to simply teaching traditional writing forms. Or, if students are learning to "read" websites or blogs in terms of how to search for certain information, then they need to learn how to critically assess the validity of that information.

The Eden Prairie school board member would probably respond to all of this by arguing that students still need to learn basic reading and writing skills to perform well on tests (O'Brien & Bauer, 2005). While this argument presupposes narrow notions of what constitutes reading and writing, counterarguments can be offered in the same vein. Some research indicates that incorporating media education into the curriculum can enhance the development of reading and writing skills (Hobbs, 2006; Hobbs & Frost, 1999, 2003). Eleventh-grade students in an English class received media literacy instruction that was designed by English teachers and integrated into their curriculum over the course of school year. Students in this course improved in their reading, viewing, and listening comprehension of print, audio, and video texts, message analysis and interpretation, and writing skills to a greater degree than did students in a control group (1.2.7). Placing critical reading of both print and media texts as central to the English language arts curriculum leads students to improve in both areas (Hobbs, 2006). When students are actively engaged in media literacy activities that include uses of reading and writing for definite purposes, those students can also improve in basic skills.

You could also consider ways to draw on the digital literacies associated with active engagement with video games, virtual reality systems, and interactive computer programs (Gee, 2003) by devising equally engaging experiences for the classroom. Students' learning of traditional print literacies can be enhanced through participation in virtual, interactive, or game-like activities. As will be discussed in Chapter 2, students playing video games are learning in highly interactive ways that are quite different from the often passive modes of learning in schools (Gee, 2003). However, none of this should be framed as an either/or opposition; schools *are* exploring new ways of fostering learning that incorporate new forms of media, as evident in work being done at the MIT Media Lab on new forms of learning (1.2.8).

Helping Students Learn
to Communicate in Multimodal Ways

In arguing that films do not belong in the English classroom, the Eden Prairie school board member presupposes a distinction between print literacy as involving high-level skills, and film literacy as a low-level skill unrelated to teaching reading. Such a hierarchy fails to recognize that engagement with media or technology involves literacy practices similar to those involved in understanding or producing print texts: comprehending messages, interpreting social purposes, defining connections or links, critiquing assumptions, formulating ideas, and so forth.

The school board member is also assuming that there is a clear distinction between print and non-print texts and that schooling should be focused on teaching students to learn to read print texts. However, many media hybrid texts (Stroupe, 2000), such as webpages, chat sites, IM-ing, and so forth, involve complex reading strategies (Lewis & Fabos, 2005), as well as literacies involved in producing media texts (1.3.1). Not only are students highly engaged in multimediating, but they are also learning to communicate in multimodal ways that combine print with visual, sound, and tactile new media digital texts (1.3.2–3). In writing a blog or posting a profile on MySpace, they include visual images, hypertext links, and audio or video clips. This requires that students learn how to move texts from one mode—for example, images from print texts—into another mode, inserting those images into an iMovie™ video production (Kress, 2003, p. 36).

Helping Students Engage with and Evaluate Texts

Audiences experience high levels of pleasure in responding to texts as forms of entertainment that evoke emotions of suspense, admiration, intrigue, fear, power, envy, and so on. In arguing for the need to focus exclusively on the reading of print texts, the Eden Prairie school board member fails to recognize the importance of choosing texts—whether media or print texts—that will engage students to the extent that they actually want to learn how to read them. Too often, students have little interest in improving their reading because they have little interest in the texts they are required to read. In some cases, viewing a film adaptation based on a text that engages them serves to enhance their interest in reading a text; generations of student interest in reading Shakespeare's *Romeo and Juliet* was sparked by the 1968 Zeffirelli film adaptation.

Audiences also gain pleasure from acquiring new information and ideas from popular culture texts that capture characteristics unique to their own or others' cultures (1.4.1–9). They experience aesthetic pleasure through engaging in well-developed stories and characters or innovative cinematic, production, or sound quality.

A key aspect of the pleasure gained from media texts has to do with judging the quality of texts, particularly by devotees of a particular genre or type of film. People who enjoy horror films acquire criteria for judging what they perceive to be a well-made horror film. English teachers devote considerable time to teaching "literary appreciation" of literary texts, which suggests a corollary need to help students learn to recognize and appreciate the artistic and aesthetic aspects of film, television, or media (Bordwell & Thompson, 2003; Giannetti, 2004; Zetti, 2004). This is the topic of Chapter 3.

Students also need to be able to judge media texts according to criteria unique to a specific media type or mode. For example, students may judge a film as superior to a novel without considering that these are two different forms; a film succeeds according to cinematic techniques while a novel succeeds according to the use of language. In discussing film adaptations in Chapter 10, I examine ways of helping students judge the effectiveness of film adaptations according to criteria specific to both film and literature.

Helping Students Understand How Media Constructs Reality

Another rationale for studying the media in school has to do with helping students understand and critique the role of media in constructing or mediating reality (De Zengotita, 2005; Freccero, 1999; Ogdon, 2001; Simon, 1999). Studying media representations of gender, class, and race (1.5.1) helps students recognize that these are social and cultural constructions that are shaped and influenced by media texts. For example, advertisers construct notions of what it means to be masculine or feminine in order to sell products associated with being or becoming what the culture considers to be masculine or feminine (1.5.2). Helping students understand the fact that the realities of their lives are constructed encourages them to critique these constructions, for example, racist constructions of people of color.

Students need to understand the degree to which media constructions or representations function to create a common, shared culture. With the rise of a mass media during the 20th century accessible to millions of people came a common set of media experiences and the concomitant construction of a mass popular culture. For example, during the 1950s, most Americans had access to mass-circulation magazines such as *Life, Look, The Saturday Evening Post, Colliers, Time*, and *Reader's Digest*. These magazines contained articles and ads portraying Americans as active consumers, particularly in terms of gender roles. Men were shown driving new cars with large fins and a lot of chrome; women were shown cooking in their kitchens with a lot of new appliances. These media images functioned to construct a shared sense of a mass culture based on practices associated with being an active American consumer (Marling, 1996; Young & Young, 2004).

Unfortunately, much of this construction of mass media by large media conglomerates such as Disney, Time Warner, and Murdoch's News Corporation ignores or misrepresents unique features of local cultural practices—of Maine fishing villages or rural Appalachian towns, for instance—as well as large swaths of the U.S. population, including African-American, Latino, Asian-American, and Native American cultures. Like the Disney World exhibits (1.5.3) about different global cultures, which often homogenize unique cultural features by portraying them through a Western, White perspective (Giroux, 2001), many mass media representations reflect stereotypical representations: for example, portraying predominately African-American or Latino urban neighborhoods as dangerous and crime-ridden. Given the importance of helping students examine their cultural heritage, it is important that they learn to critique these media representations as reflecting the invisible norms of White, middle-class American culture. One of the potential fears of school board members in a largely white Midwestern suburb such as Eden Prairie might be that newer media texts may challenge these norms through portrayals of the increasing diversity in American culture.

Students also need to be able to infer how media constructions or representations reflect ideological agendas, a topic discussed in Chapter 4. For example, Hollywood films of the 1930s through the 1950s often represented the world in terms of traditional White, male ideological constructions of gender, class, and race. Western media representations of African, Middle Eastern, and Asian societies portrayed these societies as backward, uncivilized, and unsophisticated relative to European or American value systems. Unpacking the ideological assumptions and biases behind these representations provides students with an understanding of how media texts mediate their perceptions of the world, the subject of Chapter 5. For example, by studying hip-hop media culture, students explore alternative cultural perspectives (Rice, 2003a, 2003b). (For an extensive discussion of literacies associated with hip-hop culture, see Morrell, 2002 [1.5.4], and the curriculum, *Flipping the Script: Critical Thinking in a Hip-Hop World* [1.5.5].)

One of the underlying ideological agendas of many media texts is to create representations of the "other" in ways that will foster fear or resentment. In Michael Moore's *Bowling for Columbine*, he argues that the sharp media focus on potential dangers related to terrorism, crime, economic decline, diseases, or natural disasters serves to create a sense of fear that is then used by politicians to build resentment toward people of color as the "other" (Siegel, 2006). In my media studies class, we discuss how sensationalized television news stories about urban crime foster fears in the public that translate into regressive public policies (1.5.6). This leads to a discussion of the ways in which media representations foster the development of a consumer

culture in which private, commercial, and individual needs and the values of White, middle-class America take precedence over the larger public good related to a sense of shared, multicultural society.

In critiquing media texts, it is important for students to recognize that the meanings of these texts do not actually lie "in" the text, but rather in how audiences construct the meaning of media texts within specific social contexts (Buckingham, 2003). For example, the meaning of a video game often revolves around players' uses of that game for social purposes; players share their game experiences in online chat rooms in order to construct their identities and status as game experts. Students can study the practices and stances that define the meaning of media texts in social contexts, the subject of Chapter 6. All of this helps students understand how their purposes, needs, knowledge, attitudes, and social agendas serve to construct the meaning of media texts.

Critiquing media texts, particularly films and television shows, also involves analyzing the value assumptions constituting the prototypical roles, settings, storylines, conflicts, and themes of certain genre texts, the subject of Chapter 7. For example, in critiquing the reality TV genre, students may examine how the competitive conflicts between participants reflects a conservative ideological discourse of individualism as opposed to a conception of society in which people value the larger common good.

A TEACHING IDEA

ANALYZING MEDIA COVERAGE OF DISEASES AND EPIDEMICS

One of my goals as a teacher is to create awareness that the news is not objective. In this particular activity we look at news coverage of the AIDS epidemic and consider what is included in stories about AIDS, what is not, and why media shapes the stories as they do.

I have found that students are more open to discussing and delving into critical issues that could force them to reconsider their views of the world if we (1) look at parallel situations in history and (2) use drama as opposed to group discussion. It seems that this gives students the distance they need to critically examine their world.

With this in mind we read the novel *Fever 1793* (Anderson, 2002) which is about the yellow fever epidemic in Philadelphia and the fact that the epidemic was basically ignored until the upper-class citizens began to get sick, and that immigrants and the poor were blamed for the spread of the disease. We then read chapters on AIDS from *When Plague Strikes: The Black Death, Small*

Pox, AIDS by James Cross Giblin (1997). We divided into groups and students created miniskits in which they developed dialogues between the people and groups with opposing views on AIDS, for example, a drug addict had a conversation with a news reporter or a parent of a child with diabetes had a conversation with a scientist about which diseases should be chosen to study.

Since we had already explored the idea that yellow fever was a legitimate topic only after the upper class was afflicted, students found it relatively easy to create skits showing the same idea as it pertained to AIDS. When students assumed these roles, we made it clear that they were presenting the opinions of another person and not their own. Students are much more willing to make these various positions clear when they feel like they do not need to put themselves on the line by voicing their own opinions. After these miniskits, we identified the tensions related to objective reporting of new and formulated statements about these tensions. For example, one set of tensions revolved around the fact that TV stations want news stories to boost ratings, like stories about AIDS, but parents and religious groups don't want to see gay men and drug users on their TVs, so they persuade companies who advertise on TV that they won't buy their products, and the companies won't give money to the TV stations unless they stop talking about AIDS.

Finally, we read the chapter in Giblin's book entitled "A Normal Happy Teenager," about how the media portrayed AIDS in relation to Ryan White, a child with AIDS who was not permitted to attend school. After his death, Congress passed the Ryan White Act to prohibit such discrimination. We created a miniskit that showed how Ryan's status as opposed to any new information about AIDS changed people's opinion and thus affected what was allowed on the news. At this point students were comfortable with the idea that there were many factors that affect the news and that it does not tell an objective story that contains all facts and points of view.

Mary Ballsrud,
Hidden Oaks Middle School, Prior Lake, Minnesota

Helping Students Recognize Forces Shaping the Media

The ways in which media texts construct and represent the world are driven by certain status-quo power structures and economic interests (Giroux, 2001, 2004; hooks, 1996). Often the mainstream media may be reluctant to challenge those in power; in some cases, they may actually perpetuate those in power. During the initial attempts to justify the invasion of Iraq by the Bush administration, the *New York Times* printed several stories containing misinformation promulgated by the Bush administration about the existence of weapons of mass destruction in Iraq. That misinformation was then used by the administration to promote its public relations efforts for going to war.

As will be discussed in Chapter 4, to identify the ideological forces driving the media, students need to reflect on how media representations position them to adopt certain ideological stances (Ellsworth, 1997). Stuart Hall (1993) describes three alternative positions audiences may assume relative to the text: 1) a "dominant-hegemonic reading" in which audiences may simply accept or identify with the dominant value stance without challenging that stance; 2) a "negotiated reading" in which audiences struggle with or negotiate the disparities between their own and the text's implied value stance; and 3) an "oppositional reading" in which audiences resist, challenge, disagree with, or reject the dominant stance. In studying an oil corporation ad that portrays the corporation as "doing everything it can to protect the environment," students could consider how they are being positioned by the oil corporation's attempt to portray itself in a positive light. Students may assume an oppositional reading by examining the negative impacts of oil consumption and carbon dioxide emissions on the environment in terms of pollution and global warming.

On the Website, I include a large number of different critical pedagogy organizations and resources that provide examples of specific methods for engaging students in analysis of the ideological forces shaping the media (1.6.1–31). Many of these organizations have developed curricula and resources for engaging students in critical pedagogy.

A central focus for critical pedagogy analysis of the media involves analysis of the increasing conglomeration of the media industry that serves to squeeze out small, independent media producers who are more likely to produce media about local popular cultures. Because large media conglomerates such as Time Warner™ (CNN/AOL), Disney™ (ABC), the News Corporation™ (Fox), GE/Vivendi™ (NBC), Viacom™ (CBS, MTV), The Tribune Company™, and Clear Channel™ are primarily concerned with bottom-line profits and advertising dollars, they often produce only programs or texts that will appeal to large, mass audiences. They are therefore less concerned about examining specific local popular cultures. They are reluctant to produce texts that may alienate a large segment of their audiences or challenge the status quo, for example, stories critical of the companies who advertise in their newspapers or on their shows or hard-hitting documentaries about powerful local political or economic players.

This conglomeration of the media industry also limits the number of different sources providing news or information, so that a city with only one newspaper has only one perspective on issues facing that city. Because media organizations are owned by larger corporations, the owners of those corporations often have little interest in producing quality media and focus primarily on profits. As a result, to reduce costs, television network news companies have cut the number of reporters, replacing news coverage with a focus on celebrity stories and "uninformed punditry and pointless prognostication, an inexpensive and entertaining way to maximize profit, but nothing remotely close to journalism" (Nichols & McChesney, 2005, p. 24).

Because print and television news mediate our understanding of the world, it is essential that students learn to critique how these ownership issues influence news and documentaries, particularly in terms of their objectivity, depth of coverage, and political perspectives, the subject of Chapter 9. And students need to examine how corporations use public relations and branding techniques to promote their agendas by identifying instances of brand names, logos, and promotional materials in their school and community and then identifying how these images and materials are being used to promote corporate agendas (Graydon, 2003, 2004; Moore, 2004; 1.6.32).

A Word About Media Effects

Finally, certain ideological agendas influence media education itself, as well as larger beliefs and attitudes about education. In my course, I use examples such as that of the Eden Prairie school board member to have my students discuss how these beliefs and attitudes shape perceptions: in this case, of the ideal literacy curriculum. I also have my students examine some of the ideological assumptions associated with debates about the influence or effects of the media on behavior or attitudes, particularly in terms of portrayals of violence and sexuality and the need for censorship, filtering programs, parental monitoring, and ratings.

Drawing on research on media effects, some media educators cited on the Website advocate the need for increased control over the portrayal of violence, sexuality, and antisocial behaviors in the media (Postman, 1985; Walsh, 1994; 1.6.33–34). These educators and others (1.6.35–51) cite research findings showing negative effects for excessive television viewing on children's development and social participation:

- viewing at ages 1 and 3 was associated with parental reports of attention disorder symptoms at age 7 (Christakis, Zimmerman, DiGiuseppe, & McCarty, 2004).
- viewing of television violence is related to less perspective-taking and moral reasoning (Krcmar & Vieira, 2005).
- obesity rates increased with each extra hour of viewing for low-income multiethnic preschoolers (Dennison, Erb, & Jenkins, 2002).
- individuals who are sensation-seeking, verbally aggressive, and argumentative experience higher levels of preferences for violent media and report higher levels of violent behavior than individuals without these traits (Greene & Kramar, 2005).

In contrast, other media educators point to the fact that viewing of children's programs has positive educational benefits (Anderson, Bryant, Wilder, Santomero, Williams, & Crawley, 2000). Perhaps more importantly, they also note the positive influence of media instruction. In one study, 3rd and 4th graders who were given instruction in media literacy watched less television and played fewer video games, and also reduced their use of verbal and physical aggression as judged by their peers (Robinson et al., 2001).

Some educators note that attempts to control the media will shortchange students' ability to use media in a responsible, mature manner (Gitlin, 2001; Kellner, 2000). As Henry Jenkins (2004a) notes:

> Too often, media literacy advocates depict kids as victims. We are told that advertising is "killing us softly," that we are "amusing ourselves to death," and that the only real alternative is to "unplug the plug-in drug" (to quote a few phrases often bandied about). These approaches emerged from an era dominated by top-down broadcast media. Increasingly, kids are demonstrating the capacity to use media to their own ends and adult authorities are holding them accountable for their practices. (p. 2)

One major limitation of much of the media effects research is that it assumes a direct cause/effect relationship between viewing and adopting certain attitudes or behavior. (For a critical review of this research, see Freedman [2002], Kirsch [2004], and Sternheimer [2003]. Assuming cause/effect relationships fails to consider what readers or viewers bring to media texts as central to the construction of the meaning of that text. A reader's or viewer's beliefs, attitudes, and behaviors are more likely to be shaped by their family, peer group, or school than by the influence of individual texts. Research shows not only that media education can have positive influences on students uses of the media (1.6.52), but also that parents' intervention in the home through shared viewing and discussion of media has a positive influence (1.6.53–54).

Media texts reflect the beliefs and attitudes of a larger society, and people are socialized to adopt those beliefs and attitudes. Cynthia Selfe (2004) argues that violent video games, rather than being the cause of violent behavior, might be a reflection of a society that itself values or is characterized by violence. Based on her interviews with adolescents playing games, Selfe notes that far from focusing on the violence in the games, adolescents themselves describe how they are using the games to develop certain literacies, learn about other cultures, and work online with others.

For further reading on issues of the influence of the media on behavior, see the 2003 Yearbook from the International Clearinghouse on Children, Youth and Media, *Promote or Protect? Perspectives on Media Literacy and Media Regulations* (1.6.55), The National Institute on Media and the Family, which advocates for more parental control of television viewing practices (1.6.56), the Center for Research on the Effects of TV (1.6.57), MediaScope, which advocates for constructive depictions of health and social issues in the media (1.6.58), Teen Health and the Media (1.6.59), TV Turnoff Network, which advocates less TV viewing (1.6.60), links on research on the negative effects of television (1.6.61), Kill Your Television (1.6.62), and Websmart Kids, which focuses on children's uses of the Internet (1.6.63).

SUMMARY

In summary, there are a number of different arguments that you could make to justify the value of teaching media literacy in schools to critics like the Eden Prairie school board member.

- *Building upon students' active use of the media.* We need to recognize that today's adolescents are actively involved in participating in and constructing media, and that schools and teachers must be instrumental in helping students build on and further develop these various literacies.
- *Moving digital literacies from the bedroom to the classroom.* Rather than perceiving students' vast interactive experience as peripheral or irrelevant to the reading of print texts, we need to help transfer

these multimediating practices to the classroom, and in the process improve reading and writing instruction and learning. This involves reframing the English language arts curriculum in terms of the literacies underlying understanding and producing both print and media texts, literacies necessarily for functioning in today's world.

- *Helping students communicate in multimodal ways.* Given the ways in which people in contemporary society communicate with others in highly multimodal ways, students need to learn ways to combine print and media texts to engage audiences. This requires that students learn how to analyze the semiotic meaning of images as well as the underlying cultural codes constituting the meaning of those images.
- *Helping students engage with texts and evaluate them.* We need to recognize the importance of student engagement in learning; if students are not engaged in school, they will not be motivated to learn what is taught. Students are often highly engaged with media texts; the practices involved in interpreting and evaluating media texts can be applied to the reading and writing of print texts.
- *Helping students understand how media constructs reality.* Given the enormous influence of the media on everyone in our culture, students benefit from an examination of how media shapes their self-perceptions and perceptions of others, especially in terms of gender, class, and race differences. As members of an increasingly diverse society, we need to be able to critique stereotypical representations and how those representations position us to adopt certain beliefs and attitudes.
- *Helping students critique ideological and economic forces shaping the media.* As future citizens whose votes will influence public policies, students should be able to critically examine how media representations reflect the influence of ideological and economic forces—and to understand how the increasing concentration of media ownership limits portrayals of alternative political perspectives.

As the foregoing summary suggests, it is not enough simply to insert media studies into the traditional school curriculum framework; the curriculum framework itself needs to be transformed in ways that recognize the centrality of media/digital literacies in students' lives. Developing an alternative framework involves identifying these literacies and teaching activities designed to promote these literacies, the purpose of this book.

WEBSITE RESOURCES
FOR TEACHING MEDIA LITERACY

Keeping up with new developments in media can be overwhelming for teachers interested in integrating media into their curriculum. As I noted in the Introduction, the web provides extensive resources for you and your students. You can access many of these through the Website connected to this book. You can also acquire up-to-date daily links by subscribing to the Media List listserv at media-l@nmsu.edu.

In addition, you can research specific topics yourself, using search engines such as Google™ or Yahoo™. Other resources and lessons are available from media literacy organizations such as the Alliance for Media Literate America (1.7.1); Frank Baker's extensive Media Literacy Clearinghouse (1.7.2); the Media Awareness Network (1.7.3); the Center for Media Literacy (1.7.4); the New Media Literacies organization (1.7.5); Reel Action: Teen Media, a site sponsored by the Proscenia Organization (1.7.6); the Media Literacy Online Project (1.7.7); the National Telemedia Council (1.7.8); the New Mexico Media Literacy Project (1.7.9); Project Look Sharp (1.7.10); Media Ed: UK's Media Education Site (1.7.11); Media Literacy Review at the University of Oregon (1.7.12); MediaStudies.com (1.7.13); and the Action Coalition for Media Education (1.7.14).

Because most of students' media use occurs in home contexts, there is a strong need to assist adults or parents in ways to critically engage students in media use (Hogan, 2001; Strasburger & Wilson, 2002). Thus it would be valuable whenever possible to involve parents in assignments associated with critically responding to or producing media texts. In an issue of *Cable in the Classroom,* "Thinking Critically About Media: Schools and Families in Partnership," educators describe ways of helping parents foster discussions with adolescents through co-viewing the same media texts, recognizing that adults and adolescents often deliberately choose different texts, and recognizing the need for active mediation over unproductive restrictions (1.7.15). You can also send home instructions or information about classroom activities that involve media production so that parents can assist with those production activities. And you can provide parents with copies of the *Cable in the Classroom* articles, as well as materials from other sites: Media Literacy 101 (1.7.16), Center for Media Literacy: Parents, Kids, and the Media (1.7.17), Smart TV Viewing Tips (1.7.18), and Alliance for a Media Literate America, which challenges opposition from many quarters to media education, opposition often based on misconceptions of media education (1.7.19).

The Website for this book also contains a link to my older, previous version of the Website with modules that are similar to the material in this book, although some of the links may be dated or dead (1.7.20). There are also links on the new site to examples of various district, state, and organizations' media curriculum frameworks (1.7.21–30), as well as material for evaluating the effects of media education (1.7.31–32).

For each of the topics in this book, it is important that you continually return to consider the larger goals and purposes outlined in this chapter to justify inclusion of these topics in the curriculum. To do so, you can refer to the testimonies noted on the Website acquired by Mike Gange of Fredericton, New Brunswick, Canada, who asked his high school students at the end of his media literacy course to address the following questions in their journals: "How have you become more media literate? How have you changed since the beginning of this course?" (1.7.33). Or better yet, you can canvass your own students about the value of media literacy instruction and draw upon their testimony.

CHAPTER 2

Digital Media Tools

Key to Topics

IN THIS CHAPTER, I discuss some of the ways in which digital media tools are transforming or "remediating" (Bolter & Grusin, 2000) traditional media, forcing them to adopt more interactive, online modes of delivering news, video, audio, and music content.

ADOLESCENTS' USES OF NEW DIGITAL MEDIA

A number of different studies by the Pew Internet and American Life Project and other organizations listed on the Website have found that adolescents are increasingly engaged in the multimediating uses of digital media tools (2.1.1–36a). One survey found that 87% use the Internet, 51% go online daily, 81% play online games, 76% obtain news online, 75% of online adolescents use instant messaging, and 33% have used a cellphone to send a text message (Lenhart, Madden, & Hitlin, 2005). Through these uses of digital tools, adolescents are shifting from passive consumption of

media: for example, constructing their own versions of movies instead of "going to the movies."

Through uses of digital tools such as blogs, wikis, instant messaging, online chat, website production, digital video production, digital music tools, and video games, students are acquiring diverse literacies: making connections between texts and experiences; adopting different persona and voices; employing problem-solving and inquiry-based skills; and communicating ideas to others. Students are also learning specific digital literacies through the use of digital tools (Manovich, 2001; Street, 2004). For example, learning to read a website to determine which icon to click on involves learning to read for relevancy of information consistent with one's needs, a very different process of reading from the linear left-to-right manner associated with reading print texts (Kress, 2003).

It is also the case that ways of accessing and viewing media, particularly television and music, have been transformed by digital media. Audiences no longer need to organize their viewing around the set television schedule, but can view downloaded video when they please, as well as fast-forward through the ads. Moreover, given the rise of Internet TV, independent producers can bypass traditional network control to air their content (for a list of different Internet TV broadcasters, see 2.1.37–56).

LITERACIES ACQUIRED THROUGH USE OF DIGITAL MEDIA

From their active use of digital media, students are acquiring a host of different literacies (for a discussion of these literacies by theorists such as Lev Manovich, see 2.2.1–3). In this chapter, I describe these different literacies and then illustrate how you can use several key digital tools to help students acquire literacies through creating blogs/wikis, engaging in video games, participating in online personal sites, and acquiring inquiry-based thinking through use of webquests.

LEARNING TO MAKE CONNECTIONS

One essential literacy involves learning to make connections between different texts as a means of constructing knowledge (Myers & Beach, 2004). Digital media texts invite audiences to make links between texts, images, and video/sound clips to construct connections that afford new understandings of the world (Landow, 2006). Jay Lemke (2003) notes how audiences learn to make these links between viewing films, playing games, and going to the films' or games' websites (2.3.1–11). In contrast to reading static print texts, readers of digital texts use hypertextual links to make connections to a vast network of digital material. For example, students can read hypertext digital literature developed through use of Storyspace™ (2.3.12–14) or create hypertext reports based on research on American history and culture (Patterson, 2000; 2.3.15). To organize, categorize, or create maps to visually portray relationships between the texts, they can employ digital tools such as Inspiration™ (2.3.16), Tinderbox™ (2.3.17), NoteTaker™ (2.3.18), NoteBook™ (2.3.19), and OneNote™ (2.3.20). And in engaging in digital storytelling productions, they create narratives through making links between photos, videos, texts, and music about their past autobiographical experiences (Hull, 2003; 2.3.21–24).

Students can also use digital tools to engage in inquiry-based critical literacy to examine issues facing society, adopting the kinds of inquiry-based approaches illustrated on the University of Illinois Inquiry Page site (2.4.1) for using digital tools to frame issues for addressing social problems (2.4.2–4), for example, the problem of the consumption of resources in a consumer society (2.4.5). Students can also explore issues of crime, housing, transportation, employment, and so on, facing urban planners and residents through formulating solutions on the game Simcity (2.4.6). They can share their critical perspectives about issues such as gender equity through writing e-zines (2-4.7–9). And they can study how museums mount digital art collections that also address contemporary social issues (2.4.11–23).

BLOGS, VLOGS, AND WIKIS

Two powerful digital tools that foster the use of these hypertextual links and inquiry-based learning in teaching writing are blogs and wikis. Blogs are highly personal, diarylike websites that are readily shared with a handful or millions of readers (Kline & Burstein, 2005; Sifry, 2004). Wikis are more collaborative sites for use by groups of students creating shared texts. One advantage of having students create blogs and wikis rather than websites is that students do not need to be concerned with learning web design to create blogs or wikis. Moreover, in contrast to websites, blog and wiki sites are highly interactive, building around either local or world-wide audience comments and contributions.

However, the most important feature of blogs and wikis is that, in contrast to listservs, email, or IM-ing exchanges, they encourage students to continually construct hypertextual links to other blog postings or wiki documents. While students can certainly include hyperlinks in their Word or PowerPoint documents or websites, blogs have the additional feature of automatically searching for links to other blogs, as well as news feeds from various online syndication services. These automated searches are driven by what is called RSS, or Really Simple Syndication. Rather than having to read separate blogs, students can use aggregators such as Bloglines or NetNewsWire that collect RSS feeds from different blogs that one subscribes to and then display postings for further sorting. And wikis are organized around links between "WikiWords" associated with a vast network of wikitexts or the Wikipedia.

Students may also want to explore the use of vlogs—blogs with video content—to convey their messages by linking text with video clips for sharing on sites such as Google Video™ (2.4.76). For more on vlogs and vlog hosting sites, see 3.4.77–97.

Using Blogs in the Classroom

Setting up blogs in a classroom is a relatively easy process (for suggestions, see Gosney, 2004; Hill, 2006; Meloni, 2006; Richardson, 2006; Warlick, 2005). You can use any number of free or lost-cost (about $40–$60 per year) blog hosting services such as Blogger (2.4.24), Typepad (2.4.25), MSN Spaces (2.4.26), Yahoo 360 (2.4.27), Wordpress (2.4.28), Edublogs: free blogs for teachers from Wordpress (2.4.29), Movable Type (2.4.30), Radio Userland (2.4.31), Angelfire (2.4.32), Xanga (2.4.33), Dairyland (2.4.34), or Easyjournal (2.4.35). For specific advice on setting up a classroom blog, go to Mike Hetherington's How to Set Up a Student-Centered Blog (2.4.36) as well his classroom Room 613 Student Blog (2.4.37).

A key consideration in setting up a blog has to do with your purpose for using blogs—whether you want your students to focus primarily on using their blog for academic work—for responding to your specific writing prompts or tasks—or for sharing their own personal, diarylike reflections on both school and outside-of-school topics. In either case, as in responding to journal writing, you can then post your own comments to students' blogs to foster further reflection (Glogoff, 2005). To insure active student use of blogs, you should require that they frequently create a certain number of posts and comments to other students' blogs, as well as follow guidelines for appropriate use of language and avoiding plagiarism. (For some further specific advice on using blogs in education, see 2.4.38–42).

This leads to a further consideration—whether to have students make their blogs accessible only to the class or to the larger public. One advantage of restricting access to the blogs is that students could then share personal information that they might not want to divulge to the larger public. One advantage of sharing blogs with the larger public is that students may then garner comments from readers worldwide who have expertise on the topics addressed in their postings. In the process, students are learning to participate in a larger community of practice beyond the classroom (Ferdig & Trammell, 2004).

One good place to begin is to have students analyze others' blogs. On the Website, I've listed some blogs related to using digital tools in education and teaching writing, as well as some blogs on media literacy

(2.4.43–71). They first need to understand the various elements of the typical blog page that appear when not in an posting/editing mode: the title or name of the blog, an author's byline/bio, a blogroll of favorite blogs, archives organized by categories or dates, a calendar, links to websites, lists of favorite books or films, the posts, and comments to posts.

The fact that writers employ links to a range of other texts reflects the fact that hypertextual writing is highly collaborative—that rather than privilege single texts and the single lone author, hypertext writing consists of networks of texts in which the author herself is a part of a network (Landow, 2006). Rather than construct single, autonomous texts, writers are collaboratively creating texts within a nexus of linked texts. This requires students to not simply read posts as single texts, but rather to explore the ways in which posts are linked to a range of different, linked texts.

Thus, analyzing arguments in individual posts requires an awareness of the positions formulated within a larger blog community in which people are responding to one another's postings. Through analyzing links, students are learning to scour sites to find a relevant topic and then filter posts to judge useful, credible content that serves as the basis for posting reactions or their own ideas (Blood, 2002). By tracing links across these different postings, students can note instances of agreement or social consensus as well as instances of disagreement or dissonance. To help students recognize the centrality of connections in writing blogs, you can have students examine the ways in which writers use links to other postings to frame their own posts.

Once students are in the posting/editing mode, students then need to consider the use of a title that summarizes their post that is linked to the category archive; a time and date stamp; the post itself, which includes hotlinks; the comment box for eliciting comments; and a "trackback" option for linking one blog to another blog.

Keeping a blog requires a high level of persistence in posting material on a frequent basis. Students need some strong reason to want to write in their blog. One of the limitations of blogs is that the dialogue on blogs consisting of comments to posts and countercomments can be more artificial compared to the more informal, less definitive exchanges on listservs or online chat rooms (Krause, 2004).

However, blogs can be an appealing alternative to essay or journal writing in that they engage students in making hypertextual connections within the blogosphere and social connections to a worldwide audience. The essays about the social aspects of blogging on the Website (2.4.72–75) points to their social appeal for writers seeking a large virtual audience.

Setting Up a Wiki in the Classroom

One alternative to blogs is wikis. Wikis differ from blogs in that they involve multiple writers collaboratively composing, revising, and editing the same online text (Ebersbach, Glaser, & Heigl, 2005). Creating wikis requires that students learn to work collaboratively with others to generate text.

Wikis can be used in the classroom for collaborative writing projects, for example creating reference manuals or glossaries, a class statement or letter to the editor, a Wikibook textbook or handbook on the topic they are studying, or a service learning/inquiry-project report (Barton, 2004; Moxley, Morgan, Barton, & Hanak, 2005). (For examples of high school students' collaborative wiki writing, see 2.4.98). For example, students could create an informational guide for students new to your middle or high school, providing 6th or 9th graders with information about how to cope with the challenges of being in a new school, a text that could be revised by the new students regarding the usefulness of the advice. Or students could create study guides for individual novels read in your class, guides that would be updated with new interpretations.

One primary characteristic of wikis is that writers organize their writing around specific topics, or WikiWords (Morgan, 2004), the central organizing feature of the widely used Wikipedia (2.4.99). As Morgan (2004) noted, "On a wiki, we don't write in just words, sentences, paragraph, parts, but collect those units into topics and arrange those topics in various ways." This requires that students organize their thinking around linking together key concepts or ideas in their writing that represent a range of linked texts.

Collaborative writing of a wiki text requires that students establish a division of labor based on the roles each student is assuming in the collaboration (Ede & Lundsford, 1990). Each student can agree on what material they will be contributing to the text or what topics they will be addressing in the text. Students can also take responsibility for revising or editing one another's text or a section of a text. From making these decisions about who is responsible for what aspects of a text, students are learning to work collaboratively with one another.

Because wikis provide a paper trail document history of all of the changes made, both you and the students can be consciously aware of revision processes (Digital Media Center, 2005). Students can also create task lists, outlines, or deadlines as documents to provide further information for evaluating student work. This means that in evaluating student work, you can determine which students contributed certain text or made certain revisions. You can also use wikis to engage in explicit instruction about the revision process by projecting a wiki on a screen and asking students to react to whether or how certain revisions served to enhance the quality of a text. (For some further suggestions on using wikis in the classroom, see 2.4.100–120).

To set up a wiki in your classroom, you can use one of many free wiki hosting sites or "wiki farms" that are listed on the Website, 2.4.121–130. (You should also check on whether your school provides for a wiki on the school server.) Each wiki program has a particular style guide for creating, formatting, and revising text. For students to practice using a wiki, they can go to the Sandbox option to experiment with writing in a wiki. To create new pages, students click the EditText or Edit link and create a new page by identifying a WikiWord title as a word with at least two capital letters, a combination of upper/lower-case letters, and no spaces between words. Then click on Save to create a page based on the WikiPageWord. That page will now show up with a question mark after the WikiWord, indicating that it is an empty page with no text. Students then click on the question mark to begin creating text.

In creating text, students create links to other pages in a project by typing WikiWords being used in the program. By clicking on page titles, students can review other pages in the project that link to the page they are working on. Students can also create links to other websites by creating hypertext links.

You may want to have your students create a collaborative Wikibook, with groups of students writing different sections of the book (for sample Wikibooks, see 2.3.131).

VIDEO GAMES AND PROBLEM-SOLVING STRATEGIES

Through engaging in video games, an increasingly popular form of media (Mandese, 2004), students acquire various problem-solving strategies (Gee, 2003). The level and nature of problem-solving varies according to the type of game; "fighter"/"shooter" games involve mostly defensive, survival strategies, while "God games" involve improvised ways of coping with more complex problems. For example, the Atari game *RollerCoaster Tycoon* involves designing amusement parks in ways that avoid accidents for people on the park rides. These God games evolved from popular older games such as *Myst,* in which players can move through a vitual environment and note clues for solving certain puzzles, often by selecting to go through certain secret doors, but largely without interacting with others. (For a discussion of *Myst* in the evolution of game design, see 2.5.1).

In participating in games, students are also acquiring different scenarios or narratives for coping with challenges or conflicts (Jenkins, 2004b). In attempting to successfully complete an arduous quest or solve a crime, they are acquiring various genre narratives familiar to readers of fantasy and mystery novels. The graphic portrayals of violence in many of these games have led to charges that playing games may cause adolescents to engage in violent behavior or become immune to the effects of real-world violence. However, as Henry Jenkins argues in his discussion of myths about games on the Website (2.5.2), participating in the vicarious world of gaming does not necessarily transfer to lived-world contexts. Moreover, both Jenkins and James Gee (2.5.3) note that game players are learning a range of social skills through this vicarious participation that assist them in coping with lived-world challenges. Because players are often working together online as members of a group, they are learning to engage in collaborative problem-solving; each of them applies their own expertise and tools to engage in mutual problem-solving.

These problem-solving literacies transfer over to students' academic work. In studying a group of "struggling reader" students, we noted that those students who were active game players drew on their knowledge of prototypical narrative patterns and characters derived from video games in constructing and responding to stories (Beach & O'Brien, in press; O'Brien, Beach, & Scharber, in press). For one comic book writing assignment using Comic Life™ (software for creating comics), students who were active gamers drew upon not only these patterns and character types, but also upon their game-playing strategies to develop their comics. One 8th-grade student, David, created a comic book entitled "Die," derived from his experience playing the Mortal Combat™ and Dragon Ball Z™ games. A key strategy in playing these games involves one player teaming up with another player to acquire additional power to beat an opponent. In his comic book, David draws on this strategy to have his two "good guy" heroes join forces to oppose the monster, "Gore." He also drew on another game strategy–creating a clone to deceive one's opponents–so that his "good guy" heroes believe that they have killed the monster, Gore, when actually they have just killed Gore's clone. Similarly, when the heroes are fighting the actual monster, the monster uses "Real Form" to transform himself into an even more powerful monster by draining everyone else's power.

David's use of these strategies in constructing his story suggests that students acquire more than simply knowledge of prototypical narrative patterns and character types from video games. He is also acquiring conditional problem-solving strategies that allow him to create a narrative sequence and dialogue exchanges to dramatize problems facing the hero, and the hero's skill in overcoming these problems.

In assuming different identities or avatars in game worlds, students are learning to adopt alternative perspectives of characters in the game world who move through a series of steps or challenges in order to succeed in the game (Shaffer, Squire, & Gee, 2005). This kind of perspective-taking, or trying on of identities, can lead to an exploration of alternative aspects of gender identity (2.5.4) or even racial identity (2.5.5). And in participating in fan chat rooms linked to games (2.5.6), students are learning to participate in the shared communities of practice associated with different games (2.5.7).

The ability to work collaboratively with others is taken further when students participate in MMORPG (Massively Multiplayer Online Role-Playing Games) such as Everquest (2.5.7a), Lineage II (2.5.7b), Civilization III (2.5.7c), or Second Life (2.5.7d–7h). For example, in playing the game eELECTIONS (2.5.7i), students learn to work together on a political campaign. In doing so, players are acquiring problem-solving strategies unique to being, for example, a historian or anthropologist.

Creating Problem-Solving Simulations in the Classroom

What does all of this mean for you as a teacher? Rather than bringing games to play in class, you can draw on some of the social learning principles driving game design (Gee, 2003) to create gamelike simulations or drama activities (Squire, 2005; for discussions of learning from gamelike simulations, see 2.5.8–10).

Drawing on your students' experiences with these games, you can involve them in creating a simulation based on some issue or conflict they are facing in their school or community.

To take a hypothetical example, let's say students in a small rural town are facing the prospect of their school closing down as a result of declining town revenues, meaning that they would need to be bused to another school 20 miles away. As a class, they decide to craft a letter to their school board arguing that they need to keep their school open through initiating a tax-increase referendum. Students could construct a gamelike simulation in which they construct a setting and roles aligned to different groups or agendas associated with the challenges and conflicts they are facing. To anticipate the kinds of issues the school board is addressing, the students create the roles of school board members, local taxpayers for and against a tax increase, students, parents, school administrators, the town mayor, local businesspeople, Chamber of Commerce members, and local town newspaper reporters covering the issue.

Students adopt different roles for participating in an online discussion bulletin board or listserv. They then write memos to school board members expressing their support or opposition to a tax increase referendum, as well as memos to one another. After the role-play is complete, the school board members vote, citing reasons for their vote.

Students could then publish transcripts of the online exchanges and reflect on the effectiveness of different arguments formulated in their role-play, noting, for example, the value of having a school as the social center of the town. You might have the students use this material to draft a wiki document–the letter to the school board–with different groups of students editing different parts of the document.

Helping Students Reflect on Their Gaming Experience

You can also have students reflect on the specific problem-solving strategies they are learning in playing some of the many games listed on the Website (2.5.11–21). As part of our study of middle school students previously mentioned, we set up an after-school video games club for students to play games on an XBox, surf the Net, work on email, and dabble in PC games such as Civilization, Age of Mythology, and SimCity (O'Brien, Beach, & Scharber, in press). One of the students, an avid gamer who is not active in sports, has assumed a teacher role in the group, demonstrating his problem-solving skills to other students. Because many of the students establish their identities through sports, helping others learn to play the games helps him establish a sense of agency with his peer group. Having students share and reflect on their gaming experiences in this social setting helps students learn to collaboratively acquire the problem-solving literacies involved in playing games. (For further resources, information, and articles on the relationships of gaming and schooling, see 2.5.22–35b.)

CREATING AND BUILDING SOCIAL RELATIONSHIPS IN DIGITAL SPACES

Various organizations associated with what is known as "new media studies" (2.5.36–43) posit that the web has become a central social gathering place in society in which people create and build social relationships through participation in IM-ing, online chat rooms, and sites such as MySpace (2.5.44), FaceBook (2.5.45), or Friendster (2.5.46), as well as numerous online dating sites (2.5.47–52). While there are certain ethical issues associated with the authenticity of online identity construction on these sites (Turkle, 1995, 2.5.56–57), students recognize the important of learning the literacies involved in participating in these sites. For example, in IM-ing, students acquire ways of switching their messages and language use as they address the different audiences who may be simultaneously listed on their screens (Lewis & Fabos, 2005). This requires them to attend to certain cues or emoticons in their peers' messages to discern their social agendas.

In larger, more impersonal sites such as MySpace and FaceBook, students learn to construct their online profiles in ways that will attract others, what Lankshear and Knobel (2003) define as "attention transacting" literacies (Goldhaber, 1997). In a 2-year study of adolescents' use of the popular personals site MySpace, Danah Boyd (2006) found that users were particularly concerned about garnering attention and comments from others as part of establishing their social status in a public digital space of adolescents and young adults who perceive their space as distinct from a controlled adult space.

Digital publics are fundamentally different from physical ones. First, they introduce a much broader group of peers. While radio and mass media did this decades ago, MySpace allows youth to interact directly with this broader peer group rather than simply being fed information about them from the media. This is highly beneficial for marginalized youth, but its effect on mainstream youth is unknown.

As part of your class, you can have students discuss the effectiveness of the strategies employed by participants on MySpace in terms of language, images, intertextual links, and topics employed. For example, some students may note that being overly judgmental or opinionated about a topic on which a person knows little does not convey a positive impression.

You can also have them participate in online class discussions using free online course management systems such as Tappedin.org™ (2.5.58), Moodle.org™ (2.5.59), and Nicenet.org™ (2.5.60). For example, Tappedin.org™ can be used for real-time synchronous individual or small-group chat in one's virtual "office" or in other rooms on the tappedin.org campus. Students can be assigned to small group synchronous discussions at specific times in various rooms. Transcripts of all student discussions can be emailed to the teacher and/or students for use in writing papers, further reflection, or evaluation of student discussions. You could then share these transcripts with students to reflect on the use of specific instances of discussion strategies.

In using these sites for online small-group discussions of media texts, it is essential that you provide plenty of social support and scaffolding so that students can conduct productive discussions (Reinartz, 2004). You need to provide specific directions for discussions and tasks with defined outcomes, for example, produce an idea for a parody of film genre. You may also need to intervene in instances in which students are having difficulty working together in an online context.

In the following teaching vignette, Sara Williams discusses her study of the use of Tappedin.org™ to foster literature discussions in her high school literature class.

A TEACHING IDEA

USING A CHAT ROOM TO FOSTER DISCUSSION IN THE LITERATURE CLASSROOM

Effective classroom discussions about assigned readings where students actively initiate, engage, and interact with one another (instead of giving short answers to discrete questions), encourage students to connect and reflect on texts, thus maximizing their learning. These discussions, however, are often difficult to achieve because of the differences that exist between the rules of classroom dialogue versus conversations between social equals. Feelings of shyness, intimidation, or apathy on the students' part may have a detrimental impact, thus limiting the potential benefit of these conversations.

The participants in this study were 19 students enrolled in the lower-ability-tracked literature class required for juniors at the school where I teach. The purpose of the study was to create an additional environment—a chat room—outside the classroom where students were able, anonymously, to interact and participate in discussions focused on classroom content. I intended this research to see how students would respond to this type of computer-mediated communication, and what effects it would have on their motivation and participation, as well as their enjoyment and awareness of the literature they read in class.

Over the course of the semester, all participants participated in synchronous online discussions as part of in-class work. Those who had the access and inclination also used the medium outside school to foster smaller class discussions. To facilitate these "chat sessions," I used the educational website Tappedin.org™. Tappedin.org™ is a site where educators have the opportunity to dialogue with other educators about curriculum and instruction. In addition, educators may bring their students online to conduct academic discussions. The use of this reputable website ensured that the conversations students would be having would be secure; through a system of identity codes, it gave me the power to "lock" and "unlock" the chat room, thus initiating the conversation. These identity codes also ensured students' anonymity online while allowing me to track their responses. At the conclusion of each conversation, the website would email me the transcript, giving me the opportunity to analyze students' ideas and responses.

In my experience with these students, the use of this computer-mediated communication has a positive impact on overall student participation and engagement in discussion, and thus with the text. The potential impact it has on students' motivation to finish reading assignments is not as clear, but used in conjunction with other pedagogical tools such as consistent reading quizzes and in-class discussion, it is a medium with considerable value when it comes to fostering more democratic participation among students because of the anonymous nature of the discussion. This medium also provides an alternate environment where students can participate in supplemental discussion on the books they read for class.

Reflecting on the experience and the data it produced, there are some changes I would make for future use: these would include limiting the number of participants and addressing the issue of access for certain students who could not connect to the Internet from home. As a pedagogical tool, however, I think the benefits of this form of synchronous online discussion far outweigh the liabilities.

Synchronous online conversations allow students to confidently interact within a technological medium at which so many of them are skilled and experienced. Here they are able to tap into a forum for dialogue where many of them are more apt to get involved, increasing interactivity and thus engagement. As a teacher, I want students to feel they are part of the literature they read, as well as the class for which it is assigned. This medium is a tool that helps to accomplish both these ends. As Dan, a student who participated in the online discussions, remarked, "I think that whenever you talk about the book it's going to get you more interested." If that "talk" is easier online in a chat room, then that may be the best place to have an effective classroom discussion.

Sara Williams, Language Arts Teacher,
Westonka High School, Mound, Minnesota

CRITICAL INQUIRY
LEARNING THROUGH WEBQUESTS

Another important literacy for students to acquire is an ability to engage in critical inquiry-based learning (Beach & Myers, 2001; for a discussion of use of digital tools in fostering inquiry-based learning, see 2.6.1–2). In a critical inquiry approach, students working in teams first define questions of concern to them related to larger issues such as the environment, poverty, schooling, racism, sexism, class bias, and so forth. Next, they identify and critique the institutional forces shaping the issue, as well as media representation of the issues. Finally, they formulate alternative strategies for addressing the issue, with the goal of effective change. This process requires students to move beyond simply accepting the status quo—assuming that problems are intractable and that there is little hope of changing "what is"—to adopting a "what-if" speculative stance that envisions alternatives to the status quo (Lindquist, 2002).

Webquests are designed to foster critical inquiry about some issue, question, or topic by drawing on web-based information and ideas, as well as critiquing websites themselves. For example, the webquest Kyotoquest (www.geocities.com/mteichrob) is based on the question as to whether the province of Alberta should ratify the Kyoto Protocol (Gibson, 2006). Working in teams of four, students select one of four specific roles—that of citizen, environmentalist, Alberta government representative, or Canadian government representative. Based on their analysis of environmental data provided on the web related to the issues of global warming, each student has to formulate their own position. Then, as a team, the students create a collaborative newspaper report and send it to their actual local government representative.

In one of the steps in this process, critiquing media representation requires students learn to critically analyze the information and representations found on the web itself (2.6.3–4). Students need to be on the lookout for misinformation or racist and sexist representations contained on websites. This involves learning to evaluate websites in terms of the sponsoring organization and the perspectives and accuracy of sources of information on a site. For example, the APPLES site at Michigan State University contains activities for analyzing the Accuracy, Player(s), Perspectives, Links, Evidence, and Sources on a site (2.6.5). (For further activities and criteria for evaluating websites, see links 2.6.6–13; for organizations related to uses of the web, 2.6.14–18d; for magazines and journals on issues related to web use, 2.6.29–32).

Employing Webquests in the Classroom

Often, students are not accustomed to engaging in systematic critical inquiry. You can turn to another digital tool—webquests—to scaffold the various problem-solving processes involved in critical inquiry: defining and contextualizing issues, examining and critiquing media representations, and formulating alternative solutions. Webquests may also involve critical analysis of the content of selected websites. (For examples of webquests employed in English classes, see 2.7.1–17).

In designing webquests, it is important that you go beyond the traditional lesson plan format. Webquests typically contain the following components, as suggested by the Bernie Dodge model employed at San Diego State University (2.7.18–33; for other models, see 2.7.34–35):

1. *An introduction:* describes the overall activity, the purpose for the activity, and student's role
2. *Task/outcome:* describes the overall final outcome or product—formulating a solution to a problem or a position, or creating a product—an ad, song, story, final report, etc.
3. *Activities linked to websites:* specific step-by-step activities that are linked to websites that provide relevant material.
4. *Guidance:* help for students in how to organize their material to achieve the final outcome or report.
5. *Assessment:* a specific rubric for assessing their work.
6. *Summary:* a summary of what they learned from completing the webquest.

To create webquests, you can also use a design tool, Filamentality (2.7.36), that provides a template for inserting information and then saving the webquest on a server. You can also use TrackStar™ Track Maker (2.7.37) to organize searches of URLs that are then included in webquests based on a set of related URLs.

A Sample Webquest:
On Gender Equity in Sports Funding

For critical inquiry to be effective, it is essential that students examine some issue about which they have some interest and concern, and that impacts their lives. For example, many high school and college female students express concern about the inequitable funding for female sports teams.

Introduction. I begin a webquest on this issue with a case study description that serves to frame the problem:

Despite the implementation of Title IX some thirty years ago, you discover that while a lot of girls are interested in playing sports, in your school the support for girls' sports is lower than for boys' sports in terms of the quality of practice fields, equal access to the fields, financial support for coaches and equipment, and publicity about games. And while the school should be determining the level of interest in female sports, there is little incentive to do so. Your job is to investigate these differences in your school and then devise a report to be given to the administration and school board. You will also be examining some of the larger forces shaping these gender inequities in sports funding.

Students then access their own and some other area schools' websites to gather information about these sports programs and compare their program to other schools' programs.

Guidance. To help them frame some of the issues, they are asked to search the web for data about sports funding; I also provide them with links to some data from various organizations:

* Women's Sports Foundation (2.7.38)
  Since Title IX was enacted 33 years ago, female high school athletic participation has increased by 875% and female college athletic participation has increased by 437%.

High school female athletes received 1.17 million or 41% fewer participation opportunities than their male counterparts.

* Feminist Majority Foundation: Gender Equity in Athletics and Sports: Analysis of the Commission on Opportunity in Athletics Report (2.7.39)
  Girls comprise 47.3% of the high school population (National Center for Education Statistics, 2004) but only receive 41.5% of all athletic participation opportunities (National Federation of State High School Associations, 2003)

* American Associate of University Women: Equity in School Athletics (2.7.40)
  Young women make up 53% of the student body in Division 1 schools, yet they receive only 41% of the athletic opportunities, 36% of the athletic budgets, and 32% of the recruitment budget.

Activities. Students need to contextualize what they find from their analysis in terms of how larger institutional forces influence their findings—for example, the fact that men's sports often serve as the money-maker in an athletic program, so that more resources are allocated to men's sports despite Title IX rules, or that the U.S. Office of Civil Rights has relaxed enforcement of Title IX compliance. To explore these larger forces, they again search the web and/or go to some other sites related to gender disparities in general in the society:

Womens' Studies links (2.7.41)
Websites for Girls (2.7.42)
Girls at Play (2.7.43)

One key factor shaping larger societal attitudes toward gender differences in sports is the media representation of male and female athletes in ways that perpetuate the dominance of male sports. Students are therefore directed to go to some primary sports sites—ESPN (2.7.44), FoxSports (2.7.45), The SportsNetwork (2.7.46), NBC Sports (2.7.47), CBS Sports (2.7.48), and *Sports Illustrated* (2.7.49)—as well as to view some network television to compare coverage of male versus female athletes. In his analysis, Dave Robson (2006) found that commentators often refer to female athletes by their first name, as "girls" or "young ladies," and note the fact that they are mothers or daughters, while referring to male athletes by a surname, as young men who are tough and strong, and rarely mention the fact that they are fathers or sons. And, as portrayed in the

Media Education Foundation video *Playing Unfair: The Media Image of the Female Athlete* (2.7.50), female athletes are often sexualized by focusing on their physical appearance.

Next, students reflect in writing on how their own beliefs about male versus female sports in their school are influenced by these media representations: for example, the fact that female athletes are not taken as seriously as male athletes.

Students then analyze the findings from their own school as well as comparisons with other schools in terms of the factors that could be influencing those findings. They critique the current funding inequities in their schools.

Outcome. Based on their findings, students, working individually or as a group, write a proposal to their administration and school board on ways to enhance funding for female sports, in which they formulate the benefits in providing for support for female athletic teams. To write their proposal, students consult the web for references to Title IX rules regarding the legal need to provide for equitable funding.

Through engaging in this webquest, students are learning not only to engage in critical inquiry through use of online resources, but also to challenge their status quo system.

FURTHER ONLINE RESOURCES FOR INTEGRATING THE WEB INTO MEDIA STUDIES

There are a range of resources on the web for teaching media literacy that are listed on the book's Website. One useful site is the Webteacher™ site (2.8.1) which contains some useful training modules, as well as the George Lucas Educational Foundation (GLEF) (2.8.2), ALPS site (2.8.3), Apple Learning Exchange (2.8.4), 4teachers (2.8.5), Education World (2.8.6), Western Michigan University's Teaching with Technology site (2.8.7), and the Internet4classrooms site (2.8.8).

There are also a number of sites related to the general use of the Internet in education (2.9.1–10) and to organizations that promote the use of technology in schools (2.10.1–6). For example, the George Lucas Education Foundation, publisher of the magazine *Edutopia*, produces many useful videos on the uses of digital tools in education (2.10.7). And, as noted in Chapter 1, there are many organizations with web-based resources for teaching media literacy (2.11.1–9).

As part of your instruction, you can show streaming video clips to supplement your teaching. Downloadable free clips are available from sources such as the National Geographic Channel: Video (2.11.9a) or Unitedstreaming (2.11.9b), a commercial distributor of some 40,000 clips. (About 1,000 of the unitedstreaming.com videos are royalty-free, which allows teachers to splice and edit them for their own use.) Students can also include Quicktime™ clips or links to online clips in their hypermedia presentations using common plug-ins for viewing online video, Realplayer™ (2.11.10), Quicktime™ Player (2.11.11), or Windows™ Media Player (2.11.12) (for further assistance: 2.11.13–15). The Media Education Foundation website (2.11.16) uses their site to promote their videos related to a range of issues. Many videos available at this site offer at least a 10-minute clip available for free viewing with the Realplayer™ plugin for your browser. Teachers can use clips from this website along with some instruction about what the learners should do when they get there. (For further online video clips/trailers, see 2.11.17–24, for short films, see 2.11.25–32), and for other film clips, see 2.11.33–43).

SUMMARY

Understanding and using digital media are central to teaching media literacy. Students should learn how to use digital tools such as blogs, wikis, video games, and webquests to communicate their ideas to others. And they need to critically reflect on how they are using these tools as well as analyze the influence of these tools on society.

CHAPTER 3

Film Techniques

IN ORDER TO DEVELOP an appreciation for film as an art form, students must learn how to critically analyze the uses of video production techniques. This involves understanding how filmmakers use film techniques to convey certain meanings, as well as how these techniques have evolved in film and television history.

This chapter offers four approaches to analyzing film: 1) studying the elements of film techniques–shots, angles, lenses, lighting, color, sound, editing–in video production; 2) exploring film techniques through engaging in hands-on video production; 3) researching the evolution of film techniques in historical context;

and 4) drawing on this knowledge of film technique to respond to and critically analyze films.

Underlying these four approaches is the basic assumption that students are most likely to learn to understand and critique use of film techniques through engaging in their own digital video productions. In screenwriting, storyboarding, video production, and editing, students have to formulate purposes for the uses of certain techniques: why they use a close-up shot of a woman's face to portray her sense of sorrow, for example, or whether to edit out or leave in certain segments of film. In defining their purposes for uses of techniques, students are going beyond simply being able to identify the uses of techniques in films to thinking about *why* they are using these techniques to convey certain meanings. Through making these decisions, students begin to develop the ability to judge what constitutes effective film production, leading to an appreciation of cinematic quality and how film techniques have changed over time.

VISUAL LITERACY: STARTING WITH THE STILL IMAGE

A good place to begin the study of film technique is with the still image. By having students first learn to analyze the composition of single images, they can then understand how images are used within the larger context of a series of moving images. They can focus simply on the ways in which objects are positioned within the frame of the image.

To study images in my media studies class, students bring in artwork, photos, ads, drawings, and so on, and describe their perceptions of the meanings of these images related to composition, technique, and cultural codes (4.4.10–14). A good source for images is Google Images™, Yahoo Images™, or the many museum and image collections on the web (2.4.10–20).

Studying still images draws on the critical approach of semiotics. As described further in Chapter 4, semiotics focuses on how images or signs acquire cultural meanings based on certain codes audiences apply to those images or signs. For example, the meaning of a red image is based on cultural codes for the meaning of red–as related to danger, power, sexuality, and so forth–depending on the cultural context (4.4.1–9).

Understanding the meaning of images also involves understanding the uses and power of images in the culture (Gitlin, 2001). Images of various products in advertisements are used to define markers of status, power, or popularity in a consumer culture.

Objects Within a Frame

Students then study the compositional elements of images and the photographical techniques employed in creating images. For example, they find instances of placing an object or person at the top of a frame or in the foreground of a picture as implying power associated with being "higher up" or "out in front" in the social hierarchy. They also identify the meaning of placing an object on the left versus right side of the frame. Because the eye initially falls on the left side and then moves to the right side of the frame, they note instances of ads placing appealing objects on the left side and the brand name on the right side. They also note the use of contrast of light and dark images in the frame to attract attention to certain aspects of the image (3.2.1–2).

Digital Editing

Students then study differences in the meaning of images due to variation in color, size, brightness, depth, and illumination (Kress & van Leeuwen, 1996). They contrast older black-and-white images with color images to note how color adds certain meanings. They consider the use of lighting–how lighting the same face in different ways literally and figuratively portrays that person "in a different light." They also use digital editing software to vary these features in a digital photo, recording differences in meaning in a notebook. They first download free editing software or use purchased editing software such as Photoshop™ (3.2.3–5). For example, as they vary a person's face color, students describe their inferences about that person based on differences in their skin color, as well as other aspects of composition (3.2.6–8). They also note the variation in meaning in terms of how the image positions themselves–as close up versus far away from an object or person, or whether the image invites them to adopt the perspective of an outside voyeur or a insider participant (3.2.9). And they infer photographers' underlying purposes for selecting certain images. For example, the Walker Evans photography of scenes of poverty during the Depression was designed to foster empathy for people experiencing poverty (3.2.10–11).

Through these activities, students are developing visual literacy analysis skills that will transfer to their analysis of film techniques (for other resources and activities related to teaching visual literacy: 3.2.12–41), as well as taking their own digital photos. Students take digital photos in which they experiment with different types of shots, angles, use of color, and editing (using editing software). (For information on the use of digital photography, see 3.3.1–14).

Comics and Film Technique

As will be described in Chapter 7 in more detail, another approach to studying still images is to examine the use of images in comics (7.7.n1–43), graphic novels (7.7m.1–20), and films that are based on comics such as *Spider-Man* (Raimi, 2002) and *Spider-Man 2* (Raimi, 2004) (3.4.1) and *American Splendor* (Berman & Pulcin, 2003) (3.4.2), comparing the use of techniques in comics and in films based on those comics (3.4.3–4). One advantage of using comics is that they provide a storyboardlike portrayal of both individual shots and relationships between shots. Students analyze how comic book artists vary their images to position the reader in relationship to the unfolding story through changes in focus–moving closer to an object or person (close-up shot) versus further back (long shot), or positioning readers as looking down on an object or person or up at an object or person.

Students also study the uses of newspaper comic strips to convey social or political messages. For example, Lalo Alcaraz's strip *La Cucaracha* reflects the satirical perspective of an artist who grew up on the U.S./Mexico border, providing him with a outsider "Mexican" perspective on American culture and an "American" perspective on Mexican culture (3.4.5). Gary Trudeau's *Doonesbury* also satirizes various aspects of political and social life in America (3.4.6).

Students can then create their own comics using the Apple™ software program Comic Life™ (3.4.6a), which provides templates, images, balloons, and other features for creating comics; student can also import digital photos into their comics. For other links to comics book/graphic novel sites, see 3.4.7–22.

TEACHING FILM TECHNIQUES

Once they can analyze the meaning of still images, students in my class then study the relationships between separate shots through analysis of various film techniques employed in cinematography. For teaching analysis of film techniques, consult any number of the following books: Bordwell & Thompson, 2003; Costanzo, 2004; Giannetti, 2004; Golden, 2001; or Monaco, 2000. The IFC Film School units contain lessons and activities related to film, video production, and literature (3.5.3a).

In studying different types of techniques, what's essential is that students understand the underlying purposes for why filmmakers are using these different techniques. Simply having students memorize a lot of definitions for different techniques will do little good unless they are able to understand the ways in which these techniques are used to develop the storyline, setting, or characters.

Table 3.1 summarizes a number of different types of film techniques that students can identify in analyzing films.

The Website contains illustrative examples of different types of shots (3.5.4–6), glossaries of film terms

Table 3.1. Different Types of Film Techniques

Frames	The frame is what is included as well as left out of a shot related to what is known as "off-frame" action–the fact that an audience may be aware of someone or something that is outside of the frame.
Establishing/ extreme long shot	A shot that serves to initially set the scene is an establishing shot often framed by a shot of a landscape or locale in which characters are only specks in the scene.
Long shot	In contrast to the extreme long shot, people are now shown at the point at which the audience can view their entire body.
Medium shot	A medium shot portrays the people's bodies from the waist up; in some cases, an over-the-shoulder shot with two people portrays one person looking up or down at the other person.
Close-up shot	A close-up shot often fills the screen with only a face or an object for the purpose of dramatizing nonverbal reactions or signaling the symbolic importance of an object.
Wide-angle lens	If filmmakers wants to emphasize the relationships between foreground and background aspects of a face or object, they will use a wide-angle lens that creates an exaggerated look.
Telephoto lens	If filmmakers wants to give the appearance that a person or object is closer to the audience, even though they may be quite far away, they will use a telephoto lens. This can be used in shots in which a person is running toward the audience, in a manner that seems like a long time.
Low-angle shot	If filmmaker wants to place the audience looking up on a person or object, they uses a low-angle shot, often for the purpose of associating power with the person or object.
High-angle shot	In contrast, a shot down on the person or object places the audience in a dominant position over that person or object.
Pan shot	A pan shot is used to scan across a locale.
Tracking shot	A tracking shot is used to following a moving person or object; the camera itself is moving, on a dolly or moving car.
Zoom shot	A zoom shot is used to focus in on or to move back from a person or object.
Point-of-view shot	A point-of-view shot mimics the perspective of a person so that the audience is experiencing the world through the eyes of that person.

(3.5.7–8), and links on different aspects of film production (3.5.9–23).

Audience Positioning

Central to defining the purpose for use of techniques is the concept of audience positioning and perspective–where and how a certain shot positions or places an audience relative to the person or object. For example, if students are creating their own video and want to portray a character as alone and desolate, they may employ a long shot showing a character in the middle of a large, expansive field or area in which the surrounding field or area is highlighted as overwhelming the relatively small, insignificant person. This places the audience at a distance from the person, creating a similar sense of being isolated from that person, just as the person is isolated in the larger frame of the long shot. Or if they want to portray a character as continually suspicious about impeding dangers, they may employ subjective shots in which the person is warily scanning the landscape out of the fear of potential threats. The audience is positioned to identify with the person's perspective of fear, all of which builds up the suspense that something dire will happen.

Lighting

Lighting is a technique used to convey meaning through emphasizing or highlighting certain aspects of people or objects or through uses of different colors, based on the types of lighting described in Table 3.2.

As previously noted, students can use digital editing software to vary the kinds of lighting in shots and then reflect on how shifts in lighting project different meanings. For examples of use of color and light, see 3.5a.1–2.

Shot Sequencing

Another important aspect of film technique is how individual shots are combined in sequence to convey certain meanings. The relationships between shots themselves convey certain meanings. The Russian filmmaker Sergei Eisenstein believed that montage–how images are combined together in dialectical ways–created conflict between image A (thesis) versus image B (antithesis) to create a new meaning (synthesis) (Giannetti, 2004). In his famous sequence of shots of civilians being shot by soldiers on the Odessa Steps in the 1925 film *Potemkin*, he combined shots of the soldiers as they marched down the steps shooting the innocent civilians with shots of the civilians being wounded and a baby in a baby carriage moving precariously down the steps, editing that created a sense of anger at the soldier's cruelty through juxtaposition of helpless victims and soldiers firing shots (3.5b.1–4). In analyzing editing in films, students need to consider how combining images in certain ways serves to convey certain meanings, for example, how juxtaposing the images of the soldiers firing their guns and people falling on the steps serves to dramatize the cruelty of that event.

Manipulating Time

Another function of editing is the portrayal of time. Most often, editing serves to contract lived time in terms of film time so that actual events that would take longer to occur in real time are truncated or reduced to fit into film time, typically about 2 hours. However, time can also be expanded. For example, in shooting a horse race that would normally last about 2 minutes, a filmmaker would include cutaway shots to people reacting to the race, making the race longer than 2 minutes. The Website contains study guides for learning different types of editing techniques (3.5b.5–6).

Table 3.2. Different Types of Lighting

Low-key lighting	Low-key lighting is employed in detective, mystery, gangster, or horror films to emphasize contrasts between light and dark images to emphasize the shadowy, dark worlds of these genres.
High-key lighting	High-key lighting employs a lot of bright lights with little variation of dark and light; often found in traditional comedies.
Backlighting	Backlighting involves placing the light behind the person or object to create an halo effect.
Colored lenses	Different-colored lens are also used to set the mood in a film based on certain semiotic or archetypal meanings for colors. Red or yellow can be used to create a sense of warmth, while a bluish color creates a sense of coldness.

Adding Sound

Another important film technique is the use of sound. A filmmaker may use the same music across different shots to provide continuity across different shots. Sound effects can also be used to create suspense, as with use of an eerie sound in the background to signal impending danger.

The musical score for a film is used to add additional meanings. Students could discuss how specific musical motifs and sounds contribute to a film's meaning. To add to a fast-paced chase scene, a filmmaker may employ a fast-paced score. To add to a slow, romantic scene, a filmmaker may employ romantic violin music. The Website contains resources on for analyzing film sound (3.5c.1–9) and scores available on Film Music Radio (3.5c.10–13).

EXPLORING FILM TECHNIQUE THROUGH VIDEO PRODUCTION

One of the best ways to teach film technique is to have students engage in their own digital video production (Bell, 2005; Kenny, 2004). Students can make documentary videos about a local issue, a commercial for a fictional product, a public relations ad, or a narrative video based on a short story.

In making these videos, it is important that students limit their production to one story or topic with a highly visual focus. It is also important that they carefully plan out their production prior to shooting through the use of a script and storyboard so that they have a clear idea of what they want to communicate to their audiences. From the experience of planning and then shooting their videos, students recognize the ways in which techniques can be used to convey certain meanings, knowledge they can then apply to analyzing films.

In the following teaching activity, Thomas Reinartz describes his approach to teaching film technique.

A TEACHING IDEA

CREATING SHORT MOVIES OR COMMERIALS

My objective in teaching film technique is to have students come to their own understanding of how film technique choices impact the meaning of what is seen. On the first day, we go through some film technique vocabulary and examine one film in particular to see some of the techniques in action. Alfred Hitchcock's films usually contain an ample range and supply of film technique, but any film will work. I ask students to bring in their favorite films.

The next day, each student is assigned one of five film elements to examine: lighting, sound, camera angles, framing, or editing. The class views from one to three clips chosen from the films they have brought in, and each student takes notes on their particular technique. Then students sit in groups of five, with one student representing each film element. Groups must discuss the effectiveness of the clips and then rate the film based on the use of each film technique. Groups also must reach consensus and report to the larger group the choices they made and why they made them.

On the third day, I introduce the notion of storyboarding. If computers are available, I have them choose a word processing program to make six to eight table cells to use for each frame in their film. In the same groups, students begin to make a commercial to sell a product in the school. The commercial should be about 30 seconds in length and include some film technique to attract buyers. Or students create 2- to 4-minute movies about groups represented in the media, for example, women in sports, football fans, television mothers, or Disney characters.

Once students collect at least 10 images from Google Images™ or other sites, they examine each image closely and use a chart to write down separate ideas about what they see. Contents of the charts can vary, but generally include who is in the image, the behaviors and actions associated with each image, common themes among the images, and students' own commentary about the image. For an alternative activity, students create a 2- to 4-minute iMovie™ documentary that shows how a certain side of a news story is told while leaving out the many other sides.

Students make their movies using free movie software. On the Macintosh, iMovie™ is used, and on the PC, Movie Maker™ is used. After viewing their movies, we have an awards ceremony to determine the winners.

Thomas J. Reinartz,
Rosemount High School, Rosemount, Minnesota

Reinartz begins his instruction with analysis of film technique in some Hitchcock films so that students become familiar with purposeful use of film techniques. He then builds on that analysis to have students create storyboards in which they describe how images in their videos communicate certain meanings. They then produce and edit their videos. Note that while these are short 2–4 minute productions, they still require time for careful planning and production. The Website contains information about methods for teaching digital video productions, particularly through use of iMovie™ (3.6.1–17b).

Reinartz ends this activity by having students share and judge each other's videos. In doing so, students are learning to judge how certain techniques enhance or detract from the quality of video productions. Students can also go the Website to view other students' online videos (3.6.18–27); for film festival sites, some of which include online productions, see 3.6.28–44.

Reinartz's activity points to the importance of prior planning, as opposed to simply having students go out and shoot their videos without a plan. Planning includes creating a script that outlines the key events or scenes in film, specifying actions, dialogue, sound effects, and music. In creating a script based on a literary text, students need to consider how they can translate characters' actions, dialogue, or thoughts into a visual form that conveys the ideas they want to convey. Students can go the Website for some computer script-writing resources (3.7.1–7c). The Website contains links to free storyboard-creation software programs: Atomic Learning's StoryBoard Pro™ (3.7.8) or other free storyboard software (3.7.9–12); for methods for creating storyboards (3.7.13–15); and online samples of storyboards (3.7.16–22).

USING ANIMATION

Another option for video production is to have students create animation videos. One advantage of making animation films is that students have total control over the material, as opposed to attempting to shoot actual events or people, which means that they are less likely to encounter difficulties in shooting the material. Students can create an animation by simply moving an object or reshaping a piece of clay and shooting separate stop-motion shots to capture the movement of the object.

One way to introduce students to the idea of animation is to have them create their own flip animation with a small pad of paper in which they vary an object slightly on each page, as illustrated on the random motion sites (3.7.23–28). Students then use their flip charts to discuss the key concept of metamorphosis in animation—the idea that objects or things can be readily transformed into human form and vice versa. Trees turn into people and people into trees. Students can also study uses of figurative language in literature to note similar comparisons of animate and inanimate things.

Computer Animation

A major development in film technique has been the increased use of computer-generated digitized special effects, as employed in films such as *The Lord of the Rings* films (Jackson, 2001, 2002, 2003; 3.7.29) and *The Matrix* and *The Matrix Reloaded* (Wachowski & Wachowski, 1999, 2003; 3.7.30), as well as films such as *Titanic* (Cameron, 1997; 3.7.31). In these films, a central characteristic is that of metamorphosis—how humans can now be transformed into animationlike figures or perform superhuman feats such as seamlessly moving about in space. Students can employ computer software programs such as Macromedia's Flash™ (3.7.32–33) to create digital animations (for further information on computer tools related to animation, see 3.7.34–38; for information about the development of animation, see 3.7.39–44.

Combining and Comparing Traditional and Digital Animation Techniques

To teach her students animation techniques, Ann Ayers of Coral Springs High School in Broward County, Florida, had students working in groups to create characters who would serve as the basis for clay or cutout animations (3.7.45). Some group members then selected objects, worked on the clay figures, or created cutouts to portray their characters. Others worked on the background settings using boxes, poster board, and other art materials. Students used digital cameras to take frame-by-frame shots of their characters as they were being moved. They then imported these digital images into iPhoto™ for sorting, enhancing, cropping, and/or rotating. Based on their storyboards, they integrated the images to iMovie™ and added sound, voice-overs, and music. Their final products were then exported to QuickTime™ to burn CDs.

Students can also study a major recent shift in animation production from the traditional cel animation of earlier Disney films to the more recent digital animation films in terms of differences in quality and engagement (3.7.46). Given the reduction in costs, after 2005, Disney produced only digital animation. Students could compare a traditional Disney cel film with a more recent Disney digital film, noting differences in the level of detail employed in the images as well as the quality of metamorphosis or transformation of figures. The Website contains examples of Disney animation films: 3.7.47–50. Students could also study the use of animation techniques in terms of representations of gender, class, and race on television animation shows such as *The Simpsons* or Saturday morning cartoon shows for children contained on the Website: 3.7.51–55.

MAKING VIDEOS

During video production of either live or animated material, students need to avoid attempting a lot of special effects that can call attention to the overuse of techniques, for example, the excessive use of zoom shots. They also should use a tripod so that they keep the camera steady. And they need to attend to issues of lighting, making sure that they have adequate lighting for whatever they are shooting.

Once they have completed their shooting, they can download their material into a computer and edit that material using iMovie™ (3.7.56) or other editing software programs (3.7.57–60).

Once students have imported material into iMovie™ or another program, they name or rename the different clips using the box below each small picture. They then insert the clips into the horizontal bar on the bottom of the screen so that they rearrange the clips, crop them, and add sound, fades, wipes, or dissolves between shots (3.7.61).

In editing video clips, students are thinking about how to combine parts into a coherent whole, how, for example, separate events serve to build narrative suspense. To help his 11th-grade students think about part-whole relationships in literary texts, 11th graders in Adam Kinory's class conducted an analysis of themes in the film *Inherit the Wind*, about the Scopes trial (Kramer, 1960; 3.7.62). As they viewed the film, students recorded instances of these motifs, as well as making certain textual connections:

1. *Text to Text*–This reminds me of something in another book, film, or media.
2. *Intertext*–This reminds me of something in this book, film, or media.
3. *Text to Self*–This reminds me of something in my own life.
4. *Text to World*–This reminds me of something in the world.

Adam took the students' analysis of patterns and digitized the 30 most noted clips in the film. After viewing each of these clips, the students discussed the significance of the clip related to the film's themes. Adam then had students select three clips that were thematically related, leading up to formulating a thematic interpretation and writing about that theme.

The Website contains some further examples of methods for digital production and some sample student videos (3.7.63–69), as well as a discussion of different digital editing techniques by Walter Murch, a veteran Hollywood editor who did the editing on *Cold Mountain* (Minghella, 2003; 3.7.70–74).

As students are producing their videos, they continue to examine how film techniques are used in Hollywood films. In my media studies class, students select a scene from a film, video, DVD, or television program; in their journals, they describe what happens in the scene; the uses of film techniques and the purposes for use of these techniques. Students then share their analyses of the scene with the class. The Website contains some further resources on analyzing film techniques in the classroom, including the very useful *Annenberg: How Are Hollywood Films Made?* (3.8.1–5).

FILM HISTORY: PUTTING TECHNIQUES IN HISTORICAL CONTEXT

Students also learn about the use of film techniques by studying how those techniques have evolved over time as filmmakers invented new techniques that improved on older techniques. By studying the historical development of filmmaking, students learn to appreciate the ways in each new technical development provided filmmakers with additional tools for conveying meaning, how, for example, the use of the 35mm wide screen allowed filmmakers more space to place their actors in relationship to each other. The Website contains a link to online exhibits on the history of the film camera from the National Museum of Photography, Film, and Television (3.9.1).

One of the central developments in film history was the silent movie era, featuring major figures such as D. W. Griffith (3.9.2), Charlie Chaplin (3.9.3), and Cecil B. DeMille (3.9.4). The fact that the story and character development needed to be conveyed through nonverbal means required high-quality acting and uses of black-and-white images, as evident in the emphasis on the visual in Chaplin's films (3.9.5–7).

One of the most important episodes in film history was the introduction of sound in the 1920s. The addition of sound resulted in a major shift in film that focused more on drama, as well as the use of music to augment the drama. This led to the rise of the Hollywood studio production system in the 1930s in which films could be produced quickly in an assembly-line manner for showing at the increasing number of local movie theaters. The studio system also resulted in the rise of certain directors who established their own unique styles despite the assembly-line process: John

Ford, Frank Capra, Michael Curtiz, and, later, Orson Welles and Alfred Hitchcock. It also resulted in the rise of the movie star, around whom films were often developed.

Another important development in film history was the evolution in editing. One of the early American filmmakers, D. W. Griffith, employed cross-cutting between two different events in different locales or settings to give the impression that the two events are related. During the 1940s and 1950s filmmakers such as Orson Welles employed what is known as deep-focus shots. Rather than using cuts between different shots, he juxtaposed persons or objects within the same scene, creating a tension between foreground and background images. For example, in *Citizen Kane* (1941), the parents are shown in the background signing documents that relinquish their legal rights to their son as he is playing outside in the foreground, unaware of what is happening to him. (For clips and analyses of *Citizen Kane,* see 3.9.8–12).

During the 1950s and 1960s, filmmakers such as Alfred Hitchcock and, later, Martin Scorsese, carefully planned out each shot with elaborate scripts and storyboards that were designed to create dramatic effects. For example, a famous scene of Cary Grant in Hitchcock's *North by Northwest* (1959) being lured to an Illinois cornfield only to be attacked by a low-flying dust-cropper plane demonstrates the deliberate juxtaposition of shots of Grant's face and escape movements with shots of the plane as it makes another turn to swoop down on him (for a storyboard of this scene, see Giannetti, 2004; 3.9.13).

After World War II, the rise of television had a negative impact on the film industry, as audiences no longer went to the movie theaters as much as they did in the 1930s and 1940s. During the 1960s and early 1970s the industry reacted by creating films with innovative, novel, highly realistic material that would not be suitable for network television, leading to what is referred to by some as the "golden age" of American films, epitomized by *The Godfather* and *The Godfather Part II* (Coppola, 1972, 1974a). However, as studio profits began to decline, they were purchased by large conglomerates that were more concerned with profits for their companies. This led to the increasing focus in the 1980s to producing safe, predictable genre blockbuster films that would lead to large profits for the studio's owners.

In the 1960s, filmmakers of the French New Wave such as Jean-Luc Godard, François Truffaut, and Claude Chabrol experimented with different forms of editing. Godard challenged traditional notions of editing through use of jump cuts (3.9.14).

The development of VHS and Beta videotapes in the 1970s resulted in a major shift in viewing habits; films that may not have been successful in theaters or that audiences missed could now be viewed at a later date. Moreover, film teachers could now easily focus on specific clips or review parts of a film in classrooms. The rise of DVDs in the 1990s only further enhanced film study in that additional materials, outtakes, director interviews, historical background, and so on, included on DVDs could be examined.

During the 1990s, a group of Scandinavian filmmakers associated with the "Dogma" school began developing a new style of filmmaking that challenged traditional Hollywood notions of use of film technique (3.9.18–20). As with Godard, these filmmakers challenged what they perceived to be the artificiality of Hollywood films by using natural lighting and sets, minimal editing, and hand-held cameras.

The 1990s also ushered in the increasing use of special effects and digital technology, with feature films increasingly being made using digital cameras. This allows for less expensive use of virtual sets and special effects, as well as instant distribution on the Internet. When the films *Chicken Little* (Dindal, 2005) and *Monster House* (Kenan, 2006) were released in digital 3-D, theater owners began to convert to digital projection systems, systems that produce a higher-quality image and allow for less costly online distribution of films to theaters. And as the quality of home viewing on HDTV improves and becomes more affordable, the distinctions between movie and home theaters will blur. However, since the 1990s, the increased control of media conglomerates over the content, promotion, and distribution of films has led to the creation of an increasingly important independent film industry outside of the Hollywood studio system.

In teaching film history, you can have students compare films from different decades to identify differences in the use of technique between these films. You can also show clips from breakthrough films that employed novel techniques, for example, the use of improvised scenes in Robert Altman's *Nashville* (1975), the editing techniques in Stanley Kubrick's *2001: A Space Odyssey* (1968), or the use of computer special effects in *The Matrix* (Wachowski & Wachowski, 1999). The Website contains links to further resources on film history: 3.9.21–29.

TELEVISION HISTORY

The development of television beginning in the 1940s and 1950s involved changes in not only television production techniques but also in the content of television programming. The whole concept of live television in the 1940s and 1950s often resulted in high-quality productions because performers such as Jack Parr, Milton Berle, Arthur Godfrey, Jack Benny, and others needed to be able to ad-lib their performances to live audiences. With the advent of color television in the 1950s and 1960s, as well as the increasing popularity of television, television posed a major threat to the Hollywood film industry, forcing the film industry to develop new techniques such as wider screens and higher-quality film stock and sound. Filmmakers also portrayed more adult content that could not be found on television, in films such as *The Godfather* and *The Godfather Part II* (Coppola, 1972, 1974a), *Easy Rider* (Hopper, 1969), *Bonnie and Clyde* (Penn, 1967), and *The Conversation* (Coppola, 1974b).

As video cameras became lighter and smaller, news journalists were able to access and capture news events more readily than in the past. This resulted in the portrayals of battle scenes and dying soldiers in the Vietnam War, often referred to the as the first "television war," something that had a strong influence on public opinion about the war. As Marshall McLuhan noted in a famous quote, "Television brought the brutality of war into the comfort of the living room. Vietnam was lost in the living rooms of America—not on the battlefields of Vietnam." The Website contains activities for analyzing the television portrayals of the Vietnam War: 3.10.1–2.

During the 1970s, the success of prime-time soap operas such as *Dallas* (Jacobs, 1978–1991; 3.10.3) established the pattern of the weekly serial format. This led to more stylized, realistic shows such as *Hill Street Blues* (Bochco & Kozoll, 1981–1987) in the 1980s that employed a more documentary approach and treatment of everyday urban issues. Barry Levinson employed a lot of innovative camera techniques and editing in shows such as *Homicide: Life on the Street* (Levinson, 1993–1999; 3.10.4), including the continually moving tracking camera that become commonly used in programs such as *ER* (Crichton, 1994–present), *Chicago Hope* (Kelley, 1994–2000), and *The West Wing* (Ensler & Karoll, 1999–2006).

Television content also started to slowly become more diverse. *The Cosby Show* (Leeson, Weinberger, & Cosby, 1984–1992) in the 1980s portrayed a middle-class African-American family, although some critics charge that it served to only reify anti-welfare attitudes regarding the value of "hard work." Programs such as *Roseanne* (Williams, 1988–1997) and *East Enders* (Holland & Smith, 1985–present) in the 1990s portrayed somewhat more realistic perspectives on the life of low-income families. And in 2002, PBS introduced one of the first Hispanic drama programs, *American Family* (Nava, 2002–2004). However, despite the fact that there are 36.2 million Hispanics in America (U.S. Census Bureau, 2000), there remains little programming with Hispanic actors or actresses, or about themes and experiences of interest to Hispanic audiences (3.10.5).

The 1980s and 1990s witnessed the rise of cable networks that served as a challenge to the control of ABC, NBC, and CBS over both prime-time drama shows and news broadcasts. The Fox Network introduced *The Simpsons* (Groening, 1989–present) and *Beavis & Butthead* (Judge & Kaplan, 1993–1997) geared for an adolescent audience. CNN introduced the 24-hour news format as well as nonstop coverage of events such as Hurricane Katrina. HBO, which was not restricted by censorship control of sponsors, introduced realistic programming such *The Sopranos* (Chase, 1999–present) and *Deadwood* (Milch, 2004–present). Steven Johnson (2005) finds that these more recent programs often contain complex plot and character developments as well as multiple narratives that require more complex cognitive processing than was the case with simpler programs of the 1960s and 1970s. And the use of HDTV digital television has not only improved the visual quality, but has also meant that different programs could be produced for different audiences during the same time slots.

In teaching television history, as with film history, you can have students compare clips from older versus more recent programs to identify changes in the quality of video production and editing in prime-time drama as reflected in, for example, the complexity of storyline development portrayed through editing (Johnson, 2005). Students could also view video interviews of actors, producers, writers, and directors from 75 years of television history on the Academy of Television Arts & Sciences Foundation's Archive of American Television on Google Video (3.10.6). They could discuss the idea of the increasing participation of audiences creating their own digital video in shaping television content, as evident in outlets such as Current TV or YouTube, to which audiences can submit their own video material (3.10.7).

The Website contains links to museums and organizations that provide archive material for analysis of television history for students to use in conducting analyses of the evolution of television over time (3.10.8–23).

VIEWING FILMS IN CLASS

There is considerable debate about the use of limited class time to show films. On the one hand, it is helpful for students be able to view a film in its entirety without interruptions. On the other hand, given the amount of time required to show an entire film, an alternative option is to simply show clips that highlight certain techniques or as a springboard for discussion of film content. You can also view the same clip repeatedly to focus on different techniques with each viewing. For instance, by viewing without sound, students can focus on the camera techniques; by blackening the screen, students can focus just on the sound effects and/or music.

Selecting Films

It is important that you select high-quality films for use in your classroom. To determine the quality of films, as well as provide students with background information about the films you use, an invaluable resource is the Internet Movie Data Base (IMDB) (3.11.1–4). This site consists of a database of 260,000 film and television productions, including information about directors, filming locations, awards, and trailers, as well as the directors, actors, actresses, cinematographers, and producers involved in making films. It also includes a Photo Galleries Section with movie stills and celebrity photos, and more. Films can also be searched in terms of genres.

Another useful site is Rottentomatoes.com (3.11.5), which provides ratings for films based on the percentage of positive reviews based on a cross-section of largely newspaper and journal film reviewers. Yahoo (3.11.6) also provides audience ratings information about current movies.

MovieLens (3.11.7) uses "collaborative filtering" technology to make recommendations of films based on user ratings of preferred films. The more user ratings that are included in their database, the more valid the predictions that a user will or will not enjoy a film.

The Website contains other film review and rating sites for students' use in writing their own reviews

(3.11.8–14a), as well as online short films for showing in class for practicing analysis of films (3.11.15–30).

Having Students Write Reviews

In responding to films, it is important that students learn to describe specific aspects of their viewing, as opposed to global generalizations such as "There was a lot of action." As noted in Chapter 1, students can employ the "image-sound" skim to list specific images or sounds and describe the types of emotions or feelings evoked by these images or sounds. For example, if they list "close-up of raised knife in killer's hand," they may then list "fear about what will happen." Students could then share their lists and discuss some of the reasons for the associations between certain images/sounds and certain emotions.

In formulating their responses to a film, students are also judging the effectiveness of a filmmaker's use of certain film techniques. They should be aware that they need to cite specific evidence from the film related to reasons for their assessments, often entailing multiple viewings of a film. They also need to consider how their judgments of specific techniques add up to create a composite assessment of the film based on their engagement with or enjoyment of the film—while the effectiveness of techniques may vary, they may respond positively to the overall quality of the film. Students could write film reviews for sharing with their peers to post on classroom blogs or websites.

To familiarize students with ways of writing film reviews, they could study film reviews located on previously mentioned film databases such as IMDB, Rottentomatoes.com, the Movie Review Query Engine (3.11.31), Metacritic.com (3.11.32), other film review sites (3.11.33–37), or other databases (3.11.38–51). You can use these reviews to note how reviewers cite specific examples to support their contentions.

In writing their reviews, students could address some of the questions listed in Table 3.3 related to describing and judging different aspects of film production.

To help students recognize the need to provide supporting evidence in their reviews, you can formulate specific criteria for assessing the quality of students' film reviews.

A TEACHING IDEA

EVALUATING FILM CLIPS

In her 11th-grade literature class, Jennifer Larson shows film clips and then asks students to discuss the following

Table 3.3. Responding to Different Aspects of Film Production

Camera shots	How does a filmmaker use different types of shots, angles, or speeds to portray events or people? How would you characterize a filmmaker's consistent style in the use of camera shots and the effectiveness of that style? How effective is this use of shots in portraying people or developing a storyline?
Editing	How does a filmmaker use editing techniques to develop a film's storyline or subject matter? What does a filmmaker include or exclude through this editing? How effective is the use of editing in developing suspense, engagement, or interest?
Sound/music	What specific sounds or kinds of music does a filmmaker use to convey a film's meaning? Does this use of sound or music enhance or detract from conveying these meanings?
Lighting	What are some specific uses of lighting in portraying people or places? What makes this use of lighting effective or not effective?
Casting	Are the actors/actresses cast in the film the most appropriate for the roles in the film?
Acting	What acting techniques do the actors/actresses use to portray their characters' roles? How effective are they in portraying these roles?
Script	How would you judge the quality of the characters' dialogue in the film's script? Does the dialogue effectively portray the characters?
Directing	What are some of the unique features of the film that could be associated with the director's influence or directing style? How does this influence or style contribute to or detract from the film's quality?
Setting	How does the selection of the setting contribute to or detract from the quality of the film?
Special effects	How are the specific effects employed in film, and are they effective in enhancing the story development?

questions requiring them to infer purposes for film techniques:

- How is the character being portrayed?
- What is the mood in this part of the film?
- What's happening with the plot? Why is this plot development important to the overall story?
- Why is this setting important to the overall story?
- How does the film technique communicate any of this—lighting, camera angle, camera movement, camera positioning, framing, color, sound, and so on?

Working together in pairs, students choose a 5-minute clip and present an analysis of the clip to the class in which they give a brief summary of the film, define the context of the clip, describe the message being delivered and how the film technique delivers that message, and then show the clip. She uses the following point system to evaluate the presentations, with 1 point for each item checked off in numbers 1–6.

_____ 1. Summarizes the film
_____ 2. Sets up the context for the clip
_____ 3. Points out the message being delivered
_____ 4. Explains how the film technique delivers that message
_____ 5. Shows the clip
_____ 6. Meets the time limit (10–15 minutes)
_____ 7. Accuracy 2 3 4
_____ 8. Quality insight into how technique delivers message 2 3 4

_____ 9. Clear, accessible delivery 2 3 4
_____ 10. Succinct explanations 2 3 4

Total: _____/22 points

Jennifer Larson,
Maple Grove High School, Maple Grove, Minnesota

Fostering Classroom Discussions

In fostering classroom or online chat discussion of films, it is important to remember that students are responding to a film for the first time, while you may have viewed and interpreted a film many times. You therefore need to suspend your well-formulated interpretations and empathize with your students' perspectives as novice viewers who are working through their initial reactions and attempts to make sense of a film.

Students may have more opportunities to talk in small groups; they can then report back to the large group so that they have some sense of accountability to the larger group; for Harvey Daniels's discussion of the use of small-group discussions, see 3.12.1.

In leading discussions, you may also be a participant by contributing your own responses. In doing so, you're modeling the uses of different critical approaches and response strategies (Langer & Close, 2001; 3.12. 2–4). You also need to be able to employ a wide range of different types of questions. Bill Martin (2000) employs the following questions to foster discussion in his film class: "Whom do we like?"

"What don't we understand?" "What does the title mean? The beginning? The ending?" "What things are repeated?" "What things seem out of place?" "Can we complicate our formulation?" "What values does the film endorse?" "What do we think of the endorsement of these values?" "What foregrounded details did we notice? Can these be integrated into our way of understanding the film?" "What techniques were used?" (p. 36).

Student can also share their responses to viewing of online films through "think-alouds," making explicit their responses as they are viewing (3.13.1–2).

As students are viewing a film, they can take "image-sound skim" notes to share in discussions (for the use of different kinds of notes, see Burke, 2002; 3.14.1–2). Or they can free-write prior to discussions about their reactions and interpretations to films. Or you can give them specific journal assignments to formulate their responses to viewing in their journals (3.14.3–6). Students can use maps or diagrams to chart out and define the relationships between the different aspects of a text.

In formulating writing assignments, students are often more motivated to write for actual audiences, such as when they are sharing film reviews with their peers. For example, in a college course on drama, Russell Hunt (2002) had students study the script, author, and production of a particular play that was being produced at a local theater. The students then wrote their own playbills for actual use in the theater (3.14.7–9). (For resources on writing about literature that also apply to writing about film, see 3.14.10–15).

RESOURCES ON FILM STUDY

There are extensive film study resources available on the Website, including resources provided by organizations such as the Australian Film Commission (3.15.1), the American Film Institute (3.15.2), and the British Film Institute (3.15.3), as well as other related sites (3.15.4–26). There are also numerous film journals that contain articles about film directors, genres, and specific films, many of which provide online access to these articles (3.16.1–38).

SUMMARY

By learning to analyze the use of specific film techniques, students develop the ability to judge the effectiveness of filmmakers' purposeful use of these techniques to convey certain meanings. They also learn to employ these techniques through their own video productions, in which they are making decisions about reasons for the use of certain techniques to achieve certain audience responses. By studying the historical development of film and television, they understand how film and television techniques have evolved over time as filmmakers invented new techniques to engage audiences. This historical and practical knowledge of film techniques enhances their ability to discuss and write about the quality of films and to support their judgments with specific examples. These activities should then enhance their appreciation for the aesthetic quality of film as an art form.

CHAPTER 4

Critical Approaches to Media Texts

Key to Topics

ONE OF THE BASIC GOALS of media literacy is to help students adopt a critical stance in responding to media texts. Taking a critical stance requires that they know how to examine instances of overgeneralization, bias, sensationalized portrayals, and propaganda techniques, in order to identify underlying economic and political agendas. First, students must reach beyond their own initial engagement responses of simple likes or dislikes if they are to critically analyze media texts (Appleman, 2000). In this chapter, you will learn about a number of different critical approaches or lenses that can help students respond critically.

ADOPTING DIFFERENT APPROACHES

In using these different critical approaches with your students, it would be helpful to model your own application of each approach, showing students how you would undertake a narrative analysis, for example, before having them do their own analysis. For certain grade levels, some of these approaches may be too sophisticated, requiring that you clarify or simplify an approach. Middle school students may have difficulty with approaches that require a lot of theoretical analysis.

It is important that you avoid implying that there are certain "correct" interpretations consistent with your own analyses or biases; otherwise students will perceive the analysis as simply a game and will mimic what they assume to be the correct interpretation.

Finally, as suggested by critical pedagogy and cultural studies advocates (Giroux, 2004), it is important to go beyond critique to engage students in some proactive activity challenging status-quo practices. If they discover biased reporting in their local television news, they could then write a letter to the television news director. If they discern racist overtones in a product's ads, they might make a formal complaint to the company making that product.

For more in-depth discussion of these different approaches see Appleman (2000), Berger (2004), Bertens (2004), Carey-Webb (2001), McRobbie (2005), and Stokes (2003). For introductions to concepts employed in critical analysis of the media, see Bennett, Grossberg, and Morris (2005), Hartley (2002), and Nealon & Giroux (2003). The Website contains links to different critical theories and approaches relevant to media studies, for example, the theory.org.uk (4.1.2) and Popcultures.org (4.1.4) sites, which summarize different critical approaches to analyzing the media, including definitions by Rhonda Hammer of critical media literacies she teaches through having her students create their own media productions (4.1.1–14).

APPLYING CRITICAL PERSPECTIVES

For the rest of this chapter, I will be talking about applying and teaching different critical approaches, using as a focus for much of the discussion a series of magazine and television ads for Coors Light™ beer housed on the Center on Alcohol Marketing and Youth Website (4.2.1). These ads for Coors™ beer, the third-best selling beer in America, are geared to a youth audience. Research indicated that adolescent alcohol use in the United States continues at a relatively high rate, with the average adolescent female taking her first drink at age 13 (Talan, 2004). Much of this alcohol consumption is linked to exposure to advertising in magazines popular with adolescents such as *Rolling Stone* and *Sports Illustrated* (Garfield, Chung, & Rathouz, 2003). These magazine ads typically combine images of alcohol consumption with depictions of females as sex objects and men as sports-lovers and athletes. The Coors Light™ website (4.2.2) contains promotional contests to vote on the "next Coors Light™ Maxim™ Girl Search" as well as contests that equate watching NFL professional football with drinking beer.

Audience Analysis

A rhetorical or audience analysis of media texts involves examining how media texts use language, signs, and images to position audiences to adopt certain desired responses, beliefs, or practices (Abercrombie & Longhurst, 1998). Doing such an analysis can also touch upon the research referred to in Chapter 1, regarding whether media texts themselves actually *cause* change in audiences' attitudes or behaviors, or whether there are other factors influencing those attitudes and behaviors. As a springboard for discussing whether the positioning in, for example, the Coors beer ads actually causes audiences to perceive women in sexist ways, students could read some of the research reports cited in Chapter 1, as well as discussions about cause/effect models in this research (4.3.1–15). While younger, more impressionable audiences may

be influenced by media, a key question remains as to whether (or to what degree) they change their attitudes and beliefs due to exposure to this media. For younger students especially, undertaking an analysis of this kind can provide a window into their responses to advertising messages, as well as an increased awareness of the ways in which ads are constructed to manipulate audiences.

Identification. In considering how texts position audiences, students might address the questions: "Who is this text being written for?" and "How am I being positioned by this text?" (Ellsworth, 1997; 4.3.11). A key concept here for critical analysis is the idea of "identification." Ads are doing more than simply persuading audiences to buy a product. They are seeking to gain an audience's identification with a certain set of activities or beliefs that can be equated with a product. An L. L. Bean Subaru Outback™ ad that pictures the car driving through a forest equates the car with the image of nature associated with the L. L. Bean™ brand, and thus associates the idea of owning this car with valuing nature. Audiences who identify with the idea of valuing nature may then be attracted to the car, if they associate this positive attribute to use of the product. In the Coors Light™ ad series, drinking Coors Light™ is associated with meeting women in bars and with other popular male activities such as watching NFL football. Adolescent male audiences who identify with these activities then associate engaging in these activities with Coors Light™ beer. Critical analysis of these ads involves challenging these associations: e.g., that alcohol use can be equated with meeting women or having more sex.

Media texts also position audiences to adopt certain stances or attitudes. Students can identify these ideological assumptions by asking: What beliefs or attitudes is this text asking me to accept? For example, the sexist portrayals of females in the Coors Light™ ads implicitly ask audiences to accept the belief that females are sex objects whose primary role is to appeal to males' "male-gaze" stance (Mulvey, 1975). Once they have identified these underlying assumptions and the stances implied by them, students can consider whether or not they accept those assumptions.

The Website contains links to glossaries of certain key concepts related to audience positioning, such as "copycat effect," "cultural dope," "interpellation," "preferred reading," and "propaganda model" (4.3.16–16a).

Active Participation. In analyzing audience response to media texts, students may need to be reminded that audiences are more than simply passive targets or dupes of media texts. They need to consider how audiences assume roles as active consumers, performers, or producers in mediascape spectacles or as participants in internet chat rooms, blogs, computer games, interactive television, sports/music events, entertainment retail/shopping, and theme parks (Abercrombie & Longhurst, 1998). As discussed in Chapter 6, in these mediated "youthscapes" (Maira & Soep, 2005) or "scenes" (Bennett & Kahn-Harris, 2004), audiences become members of symbolic, imagined communities: participants in talk-shows, consumers, sports-fans, or television program fans (Harris & Alexander, 1998; Nightingale, 1996). As some of the reports and articles on the Website indicate (4.3.17–19), some audience members actively respond to and construct their own versions of the media, for example, through blogging about their responses online; in the process of responding, they become aware of how they are being positioned.

In my class, students describe their participation on reality TV blogs in which they speculate about whether participants on the show will or will not be successful. They note that they can be influenced by others' interpretations, and that they can be positioned in the group as central or peripheral depending on whether they agree or disagree with the majority opinion emerging in the discussion. They also note that they need to discern the norms for appropriate participation in a discussion site: for example, the degree to which one shares information about one's personal life or whether one criticizes characters in a show. It might be interesting to have students study some of the online fan clubs and program blogs listed on the Website (4.3.19–27), noting ways in which certain group norms influence how individuals respond.

Socialization as Consumers. Students in my class also study how audiences are socialized by the media to think of consumption as a route to status or popularity. The documentary *Merchants of Cool* (4.3.33) portrays how commercials equate drinking Sprite™ with "being cool," a "coolness" with which audiences want to identify. After viewing the documentary in class, my students discuss how they have been socialized to equate consumption of certain brand-name clothes, music, and other products with "coolness" as consumers (4.3.34).

As part of this socialization, audiences may learn to prefer media that are predictable, safe, and familiar: a "McDonaldization" of the culture. Or, as Douglas Kellner (2000) argues, they experience media as mesmerizing spectacles designed simply to entertain rather than inform mass audiences about current issues; hence, the popularity of nonstop cable news and sensationalized network coverage of disasters, wars, or scandals (4.3.35–39).

The effects of socialization are potentially far-reaching: audiences may grow more concerned as consumers about their own personal well-being rather that about the good of the larger community. They may also become less inclined to critically examine the complicit role of the media in supporting as opposed to challenging governments, as was the case in media's support for the Iraq War or the "war on terror" (Borjesson, 2005; Schechter, 2006).

One primary aspect of media as spectacle is an emphasis on visual display of televised events at the expense of thoughtful analysis of events, as evident in media coverage of the invasion of Iraq that provided little information about civilian casualties. The links on the Website discuss methods for analyzing the visual rhetoric in the media, particularly the ways in which focusing primarily on visual coverage detracts from analysis of events (4.3.40–47).

A TEACHING IDEA

INTERRUPTING CONSUMER "FEED"

To foster her students' awareness of operating in a consumer culture, Becca Dalrymple, a student teacher in our English Education program at the University of Minnesota, created a unit based on the fantasy young adult novel *Feed* (Anderson, 2002), in which adolescents are continually being fed consumer messages through computer chips in their brains. Becca began the unit by having students identify their consumer habits: what they buy, and what influences what they buy. The students then read popular teen magazines, identified teen consumer norms; and went to a shopping mall and interviewed store employees about their teen patrons. Students also reflected on their feelings about being in the mall: whether they found it stressful, rejuvenating, exciting, boring, and so on.

Students then responded to the first section of *Feed*, entitled "Eden," which portrays a world dominated by large corporations. Students discussed their attitudes about large corporations that control much of the media—particularly Clear Channel, Fox News, Disney/ABC, Time Warner, and News Corporation—and identified examples of alternative media texts such as *Utne Reader* and *Mother*

Jones magazines that portray perspectives outside of the media conglomerates' texts.

Becca's students then speculated about the types of ads they might receive in the world of *Feed,* given their own possible consumer "types" and debated positive versus negative aspects of constant advertising or "feeds." They also discussed the way the school in the novel ("School™") is run by corporations to teach students how to consume, and the ways in which adolescents' spending can result in financial debt and depression, as portrayed by the death of one of the characters in the novel, Violet.

For a final writing assignment, students could 1) compare Anderson's novel to Orwell's *1984,* 2) create a futuristic society that is similar or different to the society in *Feed,* 3) survey their peers' consumer habits and create a "handbook" for responsible teenage consumerism, or 4) address an issue associated with media conglomerate control in which they assume an active role in challenging a corporation's control.

Through participating in this unit, students learned to reflect on how they are being positioned to adopt certain values within a consumer culture.

Becca Dalrymple,
graduate student, University of Minnesota

Semiotic Analysis: Cultural Codes

Semiotic theory focuses on the social and cultural meaning of signs and codes (Scholes, Comley, & Ulmer, 2001; Thwaites, Davis, & Mules, 2002). Signs consist of an image, a word, an object, or even a certain type of practice. The meaning of signs depends on the relationships between the signifier (the image, word, object, or practice), the signified (the implied meaning), and the referent (what the image, word, object, or practice refers to) (Barthes, 1968). For instance, people learn that the colors red and green as signifiers have certain signified meanings—stop and go—with the referent being stopping and starting a car on the street based on a set of cultural codes and conventions. Roland Barthes (1968), a key figure in semiotic theory (4.4.1–3), argues that these meanings are cultural: thus, members of some cultures may not associate the meaning of red with "stop." Semiotic theory can therefore be used to analyze how the meaning of images in media texts is constituted by cultural or ideological codes (see links 4.4.3–9).

In my class, students discuss the meanings they attribute to images from the Coors Light™ ads, or images from some of the many online image data banks (4.4.10–14). One of the Coors Light™ ads (4.2.1) shows mountains in the background, along with the image of a clenched fist emerging from a crowd. Another (4.2.1) employs a 1960s-style psychedelic image of a rock singer. Students note that these images associate Coors Light™ with rock music as an expression of youthful resistance and protest but also with images of mountains and nature associated with freshness.

Codes define the conventions that define meaning of images or signs. An image or sign can have multiple meanings depending upon the different codes used to interpret the sign. The meaning of images of beauty as portrayed in romance novels, soap operas, romantic comedies, or song lyrics is constituted by what Linda Christian-Smith (1990) describes as "codes of beautification"–that a woman's physical attractiveness contributes to building relationships. In S. E. Hinton's novel *The Outsiders,* "the word Cool, the cars that the Socs drive, the imagery of sunsets, and the way that Ponyboy Curtis slouches, his body language, are signs with which these two gangs socially construct themselves" (Moore, 1998, p. 212).

Audiences draw on their knowledge of these codes to interpret the meaning of images and signs; the articles on the Website describe how these cultural codes constitute the meaning of images (4.4.15–19). Students in my class discuss the codes related to masculinity, sports, rock music, and sexuality they use in interpreting the images in the Coors Light™ ads.

Audiences also draw on cultural codes in interpreting the meaning of images in film genres. The codes of the traditional Western genre constituted the meaning of "good" (heroes dressed in white) versus "evil" (the "bad men" dress in black), or the open vistas as defining the West as reflecting the American dream of an "open," endless development.

Narrative Analysis

Another approach to analyzing media texts involves analysis of the narrative structures or patterns employed in genres such as mystery/detective, comedy, quest/journey, or action/adventure (Huisman, Murphet, Dunn, & Fulton, 2005). The specific events or episodes in stories are defined in terms of how they function to develop the story structure. For example, the meaning of the "road" imagery in *Lord of the Rings: The Fellowship of the Ring* (Jackson, 2001) reflects the code of the open-ended journey in which the heroes confront multiple challenges within what archetypal critics define as the "romance" quest narrative.

I have my students reflect on how they draw on their knowledge of narrative structures in interpreting texts or predicting story outcomes: how, for example, they use their mystery genre knowledge to note instances of red herrings in the plot. David Bordwell (1991) argues that audiences are continually applying these learned prototypical schema to organize story events around certain narrative patterns, engage in gap-filling, or predict story outcomes. The Website contains discussions of Bordwell's analysis of narrative structures in films (4.4.21–23) and an analysis of the typical narrative structure of a James Bond movie (4.4.24).

Narrative analysis can be used to identify archetypal story patterns in films: the initiation of adolescents into adulthood in *American Graffiti* (Lucas, 1973) or *Stand by Me* (Reiner, 1986), or the journey/quest in the *Lord of the Rings* trilogy (Jackson, 2001, 2002, 2003), or ironic quests such as *Thelma and Louise* (Scott, 1991), and so on. The Website contains analyses of typical narrative patterns defined by Northrop Frye: comedy, tragedy, romance quest, and irony, and character types in films (4.4.24–26).

Students can also analyze how narratives reflect certain cultural values. For example, prime-time television dramas often revolve around the portrayal of a particular kind of problem or villain who challenges the status quo; then, at the end, the status quo is restored (Green, 2005). The fact that certain problems are framed as problems in these shows reflects a society's cultural values. For example, the persistent problem of crime in American cities is reflected in the predominance of urban crime-show narratives in prime-time drama, where it is consistently dealt with by police work. This reflects an ideological stance, in that the problem is depicted but the roots of the problem are not. For Green, "we must be *shown* violence even at the risk of highlighting it or even, occasionally, seeming to glorify it, in order to show the *suppression* of violence" (p. 90). He notes that these narratives avoid portrayals of causes of crime related to reduction in government support for housing, education, employment, and health care.

To study the ideological assumptions underlying narrative development, my students identify 1) the nature of the problem portrayed in a media text, 2) who solves the problem, and 3) how the problem is solved. They then infer the underlying value assumptions for each of these three components. I also ask them to reflect on the narratives they draw on to interpret texts, and to brainstorm ways of using their own students' knowledge of prototypical narratives found in the media as a basis for story-writing. For example,

one high school English teacher, Andrew Huddleston, constructed story–writing activities based on his students' knowledge of professional wrestling as a form of narrative melodrama (Alvermann, Huddleston, & Hagood, 2004). Students graphed the plot lines associated with particular matches related to rising action, climax, and moment of high suspense, as well as comparison of these plots to literary texts. From this activity, students recognize how they used narratives to structure their perceptions of both texts and lived-world events.

From engaging in either semiotic or narrative analysis, students learn how images and narrative structures reflect cultural values. The Website contains further readings on semiotic analysis as well as examples of analyses of magazine advertising images that reflect gender values (4.4.27–32).

Poststructuralist Analysis: Language Categories

A poststructuralist approach examines how language categories in media texts themselves influence characters and audiences' perceptions (Mellor & Patterson, 2001). To take an obvious example, many fantasy and science fiction films revolve around the categories of "good" versus "evil." A poststructuralist analysis examines the limitations of these binary oppositions as reflecting an overly simplistic categorization of characters' actions. The categories "male" versus "female" also represent a binary based on gender stereotypes, for example, that males value physical actions, violence, and operating in public worlds, while females value emotions, relationships, and operating in private worlds (Lacey, 2000; Martino & Mellor, 2000).

In analyzing media texts in my class, students first identify the oppositions operating in the text, for example, "good/evil," "right/wrong," "male/female," "black/white," "high/low," "real/artificial," "love/hate," and so on. In analyzing the Coors Light™ beer ads, they note that being male is equated with professional football, stock car racing, rock music, and drinking with other males, while being female is equated with being sexual appealing to males. They then note counterexamples that contradict these stereotypical gender categories.

The Website contains further resources for analyzing language categories in media and literary texts, for example, the NCTE Chalkface series of high school textbooks applying poststructualist analysis of language in literary and media texts, and a lesson plan for analyzing stereotypical gender categories that serve to essentialize gender differences (4.5.1–6).

Critical Discourse Analysis

Another approach for analyzing media texts is known as critical discourse analysis or CDA (Fairclough, 2003; Gee, 1996). Discourses consist of more than just language uses. They have to do with larger ideological perspectives that shape how people perceive the world and their own identities. The discourses of law, medicine, religion, business, and education define the social and power relationships within a certain culture or community. People adopting a legal discourse think about the world in a different manner than those adopting a religious discourse. Discourses also serve as "identity toolkits" (Gee, 1996, p. 82) to define one's identities; for example, the discourse of the law serves to define one's identity as a lawyer. As ways of knowing and thinking, discourses shape how people define their perceptions of the world and themselves. A lawyer adopting a legal discourse thinks about the world in a very different way than a spiritual leader adopting a religious discourse.

Discourses define what is considered to be "normal" in a social world (Fairclough, 2003), reflecting hegemonic, dominant modes of thinking that permeate a world portrayed in a media text. For example, the film *The Downfall* (Hirschbiegel, 2004), which depicts the final months of Hitler's reign, portrays Hitler and his supporters' continued belief in the notion that the Nazis are a superior race who should rule the world.

The Website contains examples of applying discourse analysis to identify these consistent patterns in media texts, particularly in terms of discourses of class and race in media texts (4.6.4–11); see also Dine & Humez (2002) and Lind (2003).

Discourses of Class. Neo-Marxist criticism examines how discourses of class serve to define the meaning of social practices or artifacts as class markers and to maintain or challenge power structures (Wilson, Gutierrez, & Chao, 2003). In his study of the WWE wrestling programs, Henry Jenkins (1997) argues that wrestling represents "working-class melodrama" in that it portrays the revenge of "good" against "evil"—the "bad" wrestler who employs devious means is overcome at the end by the "good" wrestler.

Audiences who resent the power and wealth of the elite identify with the "good" wrestler, who represents the "little guys" asserting themselves against the "unfair" power structure.

Neo-Marxists are also interested in how characters in a film or television program possess "cultural capital"—the social practices, dispositions, dress, or language use associated with class or social status in society (Bourdieu, 1977). For example, certain "marked" ways of speaking based on cultural assumptions about dialects, register, pitch, topic elaboration, intonation, or hedging, serve to define one as having or not having "cultural capital," a theme of the film *Educating Rita* (Gilbert, 1983).

In my class, we view streaming online clips from the PBS documentary program *People Like Us* (4.6.12–13), which examines people's notions of what it means to be "middle-class" or "working-class." In one clip, a woman is receiving a set of lessons on appropriate gestures and language use associated with being upper-middle class. After receiving her lessons, the woman then attends a party at an art exhibit to demonstrate what she has learned in her interactions with the wealthy guests. My students note that she does not make a positive impression because it is difficult if not impossible to acquire culture capital in a series of lessons.

My students then analyze magazine ads and store catalogues to identify how certain items are advertised or marketed according to class markers (4.6.14–17). For example, they note that ads in *The New Yorker* magazine appeal to images of wealth and power associated with international travel, expensive cars, and financial advising. The Website contains further examples of analysis of class differences in the media, particularly in terms of applying a Marxist analysis of class–structure differences (4.6.18–27).

Discourses of Race. My students also identify discourses of race operating in media texts (Cortes, 2000). In some cases, race is portrayed as simply a matter of individual prejudices or feelings groups adopt about each other—as when characters note that they need to get along better with others or care about others regardless of skin color. This "color-blind" discourse of race fails to acknowledge the institutional racism associated with discriminatory agendas and policies related to housing, employment, schooling, health care, and law enforcement, as well as the deficit notions applied to people of color (4.6.28–30; Bonilla-Silva, 2001). My students examine the portrayal of institutional racism by noting how non-Whites, particularly African-American males, are demonized as dangerous and suspect, an argument Michael Moore makes in *Bowling for Columbine* (2002). They also analyze how racial difference and conflicts are portrayed as a function of individual feelings and attitudes or as a manifestation of institutional racism. For example, in viewing clips of the film *Malcolm* (Tass, 1986), students discuss how Malcolm X was articulating the problems of race in terms of institutional forces limiting African Americans' opportunities.

Underlying institutional discourses of racism is a discourse of whiteness that functions as the invisible norm against which non-Whites are judged, a norm that serves to maintain Whites in positions of power (Feagin & O'Brien, 2003). In viewing Hollywood films, students perceive portrayals of whiteness evident in White characters' obliviousness and insensitivity related to diversity given their sense of White privilege (Bernadi, 2001; Vera & Gordon, 2003). They also note that racism is typically represented in popular media as simply a problem of black oppression and poverty that can be alleviated through adopting a neoliberal political agenda. Giroux (2001) cites the example of the film *Dangerous Minds* (Smith, 1995), in which whiteness is equated with "rationality, 'tough' authority, cultural literacy, and high academic standards in the midst of the changing demographics of urban sprawl and the emergence of a resurgent racism in the highly charged politics of the 1990s" (p. 145). In this film, a White ex-Marine teacher asserts her moral authority to inspire her poor urban students caught in a bureaucratic school. The value of her teaching practices is mediated by a discourse of whiteness that promotes the idea that "character, merit, and self-help are the basis on which people take their place in society" (p. 152), reflecting discourses of individual self-control and achievement as opposed to discourses of institutional racism.

My students noted instances of racism in a Coors Light™ beer ad that appeared in the September 2003 issue of *Vibe* magazine that features four young adult black males (4.2.1) looking out from underneath a door with a sign on it stating BOARD OF DIRECTORS and holding bottles of beer. The caption reads, "Here's to the other 9-to-5." While they note that this ad is clearly designed to appeal to African Americans in terms of its placement in *Vibe* magazine, it reifies a discourse of White privilege by assuming that young black males in business may be more interested in partying after work than in their work.

Discourses of class and race are also reflected in news coverage. In the following teaching vignette, Martha Cosgrove had her students analyze media analysis of the Hurricane Katrina disaster. One of the interesting aspects of that disaster was that while the media was showing scenes of largely poor African Americans who had no means of escaping New Orleans struggling to stay alive, but receiving little or no assistance from the government, spokespersons for government agencies kept claiming that they were assisting the victims. This points to the critical role the media can play in portraying realities that conflict with political rhetoric.

A TEACHING IDEA

THE OPPORTUNITY DISASTER PROVIDES: FROM NON-FICTION TO LITERARY THEORY TO POETRY

Disasters may be appealing to adolescents because of their inherent qualities: chaos; the anxiety produced by a life-and-death situation; or maybe even the heightened recognition of life held in the balance. For us as teachers, disasters may be appealing for a different reason: because such a self-contained story provides a teachable moment—an opportunity for us to maximize our students' critical thinking by looking at a single story from a variety of critical perspectives. Reports of the Hurricane Katrina disaster present us with such an opportunity and offer us some great nonfiction reading as well.

For my 12th-grade English class I chose a *New York Times* September 5, 2005, article, "Texas Way Station Offers a First Serving of Hope" (4.6.34), written a week after the hurricane hit. I asked students to 1) choose three short passages they found particularly effective and underline them, 2) explain the *reasons* for the passages effectiveness, and 3) name the *techniques* the writer used in the passages—metaphors, vivid imagery, or use of connotations.

The students then met in small groups and each group chose two lenses from among the different literary theories they had previously studied: archetypal, feminist, Marxist, psychoanalytic, reader-response, historical, and perhaps deconstruction and structuralism (Appleman, 2000). They then chose two passages they believed would be particularly helpful in examining the article from one of those critical perspectives, explained their reasons for their choice, and wrote a statement synthesizing their understanding of the article from the perspective they chose.

I then asked them to suggest other perspectives they thought would be helpful in understanding the situation described in the *New York Times* article. I returned to an allusion from the third paragraph: "Gov. Rick Perry—who delivered an Emma Lazarus–like vow last week to take in the huddled masses of Hurricane Katrina . . ." No one knew the reference was a poem engraved on the pedestal of the Statue of Liberty, so I provided them with a copy (see Website). After reading aloud and looking at the poem on an overhead transparency, we talked about two things. First, our country has prided itself for taking in the tired, poor, huddled masses, the wretched refuse. Second, we talked about what that commitment would mean as we face the aftermath of this disaster. What did they think the implications of Hurricane Katrina mght be for other disasters that we may face as a nation (natural and otherwise)? Last, we talked about how the meaning of this article, and the key to how the writers are looking at our handling of this disaster, is contained in large measure in the writer's careful choice to include Governor Perry's allusion to the poem written on the Statue of Liberty.

This lesson helped them cross the bridge from real life to literature by ending the lesson with the analysis of a poem that has both historical and literary significance.

Martha Cosgrove,
Edina High School, Edina, Minnesota

PSYCHOANALYTIC THEORIES: SUBJECTIVE DESIRE

While audience stances are influenced by ideological forces, the meaning of media texts is also shaped by subconscious desires, needs, and fears defining one's identity (Alcorn, 2002; Holland, 1998; 3.12.23). During the 1970s and 1980s, film theorists were heavily influenced by Freud's and Jacques Lacan's (1977) psychoanalytic theories of how subconscious forces shape subjective experiences with film, work published in the journal *Screen* (4.7.1–2). More recently, Judith Butler (1999) criticizes the heterosexual biases of this work, noting the need to study repressed desires for members of the same sex. Because these desires must be repressed in the culture, the result is what Butler describes as "gender melancholia" and the need to move toward more acceptable, official femininity or masculinity (Butler, 1999, p. 87). Angela McRobbie (2005) notes that this "full endorsed femininity" is evident in fashion models' "self-absorption, aloof disdain" associated with "gender melancholia" related to the loss of repressed same-sex relationships.

Audiences also respond to film actors or actresses as desirable. Laura Mulvey (1975) describes this desire using the concept of the "male gaze" in which the passive female image becomes the object of male desire (4.7.3). In many films, the threatening, "strong" woman is often punished at the end, serving to remove this threat for the presumed male audience adopting the "male gaze." (4.7.4–5). The Coors Light™ beer ads

obviously appeal to the "male gaze" stance through their use of female sex objects. Mulvey's notion of the "male gaze" has been criticized by others who posit that females can also adopt a "gaze" stance for both males and females (Kaplan, 2000; Modleski, 1988; 4.12.6). And queer theory perspectives related to aspects of perspectives and desire in film posit the need to explore alternative forms of sexuality in media texts and films (4.7.7–9).

Much of the focus of psychoanalytic analysis has to do with how audiences' subconscious forces influence the subjective meanings of images. For example, a prominent psychoanalytic theorist, Gilles Deleuze (1989), describes how audiences assign subjective meanings to moving images in film. The links on the Website describe his analysis of the meanings of three types of moving images: the perception-image, the action-image, and the affection-image (4.7.10–16)

Students can apply psychoanalytic analysis to films by discussing the functions of desire and fantasy shaping their responses to film characters. They can note how their identification with certain characters or actors/actresses reflects their desires to be or become those characters or actors/actresses as part of the vicarious fantasy experience with film that represents what Norman Holland describes as their identity-style (4.7.17). And they can note how characters' actions and perceptions are shaped by their desires and fantasies (4.7.18); for an example of analysis of characters in *Sex and the City* (Star, 1998–2004), see Thomas (under review).

Feminist Analysis

Feminist media criticism has undergone a number of shifts as applied to media texts (Brunsdon, D'Acci, & Spigel, 1997; Gallagher, 2001; Mazzarella, 2005). One focus of feminist criticism has been on the sexist portrayals of females and males. For example, Jean Kilbourne, in her *Killing Us Softly, 3* (2000) series and in *Slim Hopes: Advertising & the Obsession with Thinness* (1995), demonstrates how advertising creates gender images that sexualize adolescent females and define norms for body weight associated with the beauty industry (4.8.1–2). In his documentary *Dreamworlds II*, Sut Jhally (1995) demonstrates how MTV music videos portray women as sex objects within the context of an adolescent male fantasy world (4.8.3).

Judith Butler (1999) challenges this focus simply on sexist portrayals, arguing that gender should be perceived as a historical or cultural set of performances constituted by competing discourses of gender, for example, what it means to be a "girl," that are continually changing to adopt to different cultural contexts (4.8.4–8). Butler (1999) refers to the Aretha Franklin lyric, "'You make me feel like a natural woman'" (p. 98), to note that a woman does not necessarily "feel" feminine all the time, any more than a man feels masculine. Butler suggests that we should think of gender as free-floating and fluid rather than fixed, but also constrained and limited by discourses of desire that position people to adopt different versions of the self.

To apply a feminist approach, students could study how media representations of gender differences are often based on cultural constructions of myths regarding gender differences, for example, that females are more caring than males or that they differ in moral reasoning. An analysis of research on gender differences finds that males and females are far more alike than different (Hyde, 2005)

Butler's argument that gender performances are continually changing given historical and cultural forces is evident in men's magazines that exclude the emotional side of males by emphasizing the assertive masculine side of males as reflected in magazines such as *Maxim* (4.8.8–10), as well as the Coors Light™ beer ads.

The Website includes links to three Media Education Foundation videos related to media representations of masculinity: on the need for males to convey an image of power/control (Tough Guise, 4.8.11); on violence in video games (Game Over, 4.8.12); and on professional wrestling (Wrestling with Manhood, 4.8.13).

In my class, based on feminist media analyses contained on the Website (4.8.14–31), we identify the different gendered versions of identities portrayed in magazines geared exclusively for males and females, as well as the kinds of activities in which males and females are depicted. We then create poster boards with these images from magazines to note patterns in gender portrayals: for example, that contrary to the stereotype that only women are concerned with appearance and fashion, males are also portrayed as having an interest in their appearance or fashion (for a sample production, see 4.8.32). Similarly, in her media literacy class at UCLA, Rhonda Hammer has students create videos critiquing gender representations (4.8.33)–for sample student productions, see 4.8.34. In addition, my students examine critical stances in feminist zines on the Website (4.8.35–37) and portrayals of woman leaders on television, as reflected in the webquest on the television program *Commander in Chief* (Lurie, 2005–2006) (4.8.38).

Students can also go to the My Pop Studio site (www.mypopstudio.com/)–designed by Sherri Hope Culver and Renee Hobbs at the Temple University's Media Education Lab to foster girls' critical analysis of media directed at females. On the site, students create their own versions of a teen magazine, TV show, or music pop star, as well as reflect on their participation in online social networking sites.

Postmodern Analysis

Postmodern theory challenges the modernist's beliefs or "master narratives" associated with "progress," "truth," "human improvement," "high art," "science," and "technology"–the assumption that these narratives will lead humans to a greater sense of happiness and fulfillment (Bignell, 2000; Jameson, 1991; Malpas, 2005). Postmodern perspectives are evident in much of contemporary art, film, architecture, fiction, and music, which challenges and even parodies traditional forms.

A leading theorist of postmodernism, Jean Baudrillard (1998), posits that we are living in a word of "hyperreality" constructed largely of surface media images that challenge and undermine modernist notions of reality and truth. Rather than assuming that the media represents reality, he argues that the media itself is its own reality in which it is difficult to distinguish what is "real" from what is "false" (for a summary of Baudrillard by Douglas Kellner, see 4.9.1). For example, Disney World is an artificial construction of reality that could be said to function as its own reality in which everything is commodified or commercialized (4.9.2). Postmodernism resists critique by both celebrating and parodying consumer products, as evident in Target™ Corportation ads portraying multiple images of consumer products. For more on Baudrillard's theories, see 4.9.3.

Postmodern films such as *Blue Velvet* (Lynch, 1986), *Pulp Fiction* (Tarantino, 1994), *Mulholland Drive* (Lynch, 2001), *Run Lola Run* (Tykwer, 1988), and *Memento* (Nolan, 2000) play with alternative narrative versions of events to call attention to the arbitrary nature of narrative structuring of events. *Mulholland Drive* portrays one version of events in the film's first part based on the traditional story of the innocent female who arrives in Hollywood to become a successful movie star, only to juxtapose this movie celebrity magazine narrative version against a darker version of the same events in the last part in which the star is now involved in a murder of a friend. And *Memento* shows events occurring in reverse, dealing with issues of memory and time.

In my class, drawing on some introductory readings from the Website about postmodern theories (4.9.4–9), we compare clips from the three different plots/outcomes in *Run Lola Run* to discuss how different kinds of narrative structures result in different meanings or versions of reality. We also discuss how the use of alternative forms–animation, still photos, and music–serve to mediate the meaning of the different versions. We also debate the larger issue of the value of postmodern media texts. Some students argue that if these texts are simply designed to parody or mimic other texts, they then rarely move beyond critique to promote a set of alternative values. The Website contains further examinations of postmodern analyses of media, including *The Simpsons* (Groening, 1989–present; 4.9.10), science fiction films (4.9.11), and contemporary media (4.9.12–13).

Postcolonial Analysis

Postcolonial theory examines ways in which colonial or imperialist conceptions of the world are portrayed in literature and media texts (Bhabha, 1994; Gilroy, 2004). It focuses on the fact that much of the media represents the Third World or previously colonialized parts of the world as the "other"–that is, as "non-Western", "backward," "uncivilized" "mysterious," "undeveloped," "primitive," or "dangerous." These perceptions stem from 19th- and early-20th-century conceptions of the world in which Western powers still controlled much of the world–for example, in 1914, European countries controlled 85% of world, while today none of the European colonial powers hold colonies. In his study of "Orientalism," Edward Said (1978) demonstrated how "Orientalism" in popular culture was a racist and sexist discourse for a superior European perception of the Orient as exotic, mysterious, erotic, different, and non-White or "other" (4.10.1–2).

Postcolonial critics posit that Asian, Middle Eastern, African, and/or Muslin characters in Hollywood films continue to be portrayed in ways that reflect European/American stereotypes of these regions and their cultural practices (Gilroy, 2004). In considering reasons for these stereotypes, Homi Bhabha (1994) argues that rather than a simplistic expression of certainty about the colonialized, stereotypes reflect the colonial power's uncertainty, ambivalence, and

insecurity about the colonialized (McRobbie, 2005). The fact that these stereotypes are continually repeated and exaggerated reflects the colonizer's desire for those aspects of the colonialized that they lack (McRobbie, 2005). For example, a black athlete's physical skills are exaggerated out of a sense of envy of those skills. The stereotype portrays the colonialized as consistently degenerate and incapable of self-rule, serving as a self-serving justification for the colonizer's need to control the colonialized out of a manufactured fear of their degeneracy (McRobbie, 2005).

We also examine stereotypical media representations of the Mideast and Muslims that reflect a colonial notion that Muslins are incapable of dealing with their own political problems and therefore require Western intervention, as illustrated by the Iraq invasion (for related postcolonial analyses, including a Webquest on British colonialism, see 4.10.4–9). This leads to a discussion of the alternative perspectives to Western coverage of the Mideast on Al Jazeera, the Arab-based news network (4.10.10), perspectives analyzed in the documentary *The Control Room* (White, 2005; 4.10.11).

This postcolonial approach is reflected in an activity by Elisa Johnson in which students explored alternative perspectives for thinking about their role in the world.

A TEACHING IDEA

DEFINING "WORLD"
IN A WORLD LITERATURE CLASS

Our 11th- and 12th-grade World Literature course began with an investigation of how the world is defined through images, and how these images in turn affect our understanding of the world. To preface a discussion about the constructed nature of our ideas, the students were given journal prompts and created field notes in response to a world maps display.

The students responded in their journals to one or more of the following questions:

1. Do you think everyone's idea of "world" is the same? If so, how did we all get to that same idea of what "world" is? If not, what factors might influence different ideas of "world"?
2. What do you think is essential in a study of World Literature? Do you think that people in other countries view World Literature in the same way? In what ways might the study of World Literature change depending on your location?
3. Define the world in your own words. What is necessary/essential for something to be considered a world?

Three large maps were posted on the wall of the class-room: a typical world map, a Peters Projection (also known as the "upside-down map"), and a Hobo-Dyer Equal Area Map. In small groups, students took two-column field notes based on their observations of these maps. Students were instructed to write only facts that they noticed in the left-hand column, and only their responses to, or ideas about, these facts in the right-hand column. Students then shared their observations with the whole class. Throughout the discussion, the overwhelming response was one of curiosity about why the creators of the Peters Projection and the Hobo-Dyer map made the world look "weird." The observations helped the students formulate possible answers to their own questions. Several students noticed that the focus in the Peters and Hobo-Dyer maps was not the United States, as it is in the traditional map. Instead, Africa appeared much larger. As the conversation continued, students began to challenge the images that they saw in the world display. One student noticed that China was colored yellow in each of the maps, and she found this disturbing. To encourage the students to extend their critical analysis about the ways in which the world is a constructed notion, students were asked to bring in an image that should be included in our visual displays of the world based on what they thought was missing from the maps. Additionally, the students wrote about why their images should be included in the maps.

The response to this assignment was diverse and generally positive. Students' responses included ideas about diverse people living together; the power of money over people's concepts of the world; social worlds as a mode of defining the world, the natural world and its interconnectivity; and the diversity of human attitudes about abstract ideas such as good and evil. An unexpected outcome of the assignment was that many students created their own images out of magazine and Internet pictures artistically combined to illustrate complex views of the world. The students noticed that many of the images they found from various media sources did not illustrate multifaceted views of our world, but were generally one-sided. Combining these images allowed the students to reconstruct views of the world that they wanted to include in the definition.

Elisa Johnson,
Lakeville North High School, Minnesota

SUMMARY

In this chapter, I argue that it is important that students learn to critically analyze media texts such as Coors Light™ beer commercials that promote alcohol consumption by appealing to common conceptions of masculinity and sexuality. I describe the application of different critical lenses (Appleman, 2000) to media texts: audience analysis of the ways in which media texts position audiences to gain their identification; semiotic analysis of the cultural meanings of images in media texts; poststructuralist analysis of the binary language categories operating in media texts; narrative analysis of the prototypical storylines in media texts; critical discourse analysis of the ideological discourses that define ways of knowing and identities in media texts; psychoanalytic analysis of the subconscious desires that shape audiences' experiences; feminist analysis of the cultural constructions of gendered practices in media texts; postmodern analysis of how contemporary media texts challenge the artificiality of modernist narratives; and postcolonial analysis of how white, Western media texts often construct non-Western cultures in negative ways. From learning to apply these different critical lenses to media texts, students begin to challenge the ideological and political assumptions operating in media texts, leading them to examine their own beliefs and attitudes about themselves and the world.

CHAPTER 5

Media Representations

Key to Topics

WHAT ARE MEDIA representations? They are the ways in which the media portrays particular groups, communities, worlds, topics, or issues from a particular ideological or value perspective. It cannot be simply determined that these media representations are true or false, as in "misrepresentations," because that approach assumes a true or fixed meaning associated with some external reality (5.2.1–3; 5.3.2).

An alternative approach is to assume instead that media representations "re-present" or actually create a new reality, which in turn mediates or shapes the ways in which people perceive themselves and the world (Hall, 1997). Studying media representations therefore involves understanding how our perceptions of the world are mediated by popular culture texts (de Zengotita, 2005). For example, the Holocaust has been represented by texts in many different ways over the past 60 years, requiring a focus on differences among these representations themselves and the difficulties of ever capturing the horrific nature of the Holocaust (Hirsch & Kacandes, 2005). Our experience of the Holocaust is mediated by films such as *Schindler's List* (Spielberg, 1993), *Life is Beautiful* (Benigni, 1997), *Night and Fog* (Resnais, 1955), or *The Shop on Main Street* (Kadar & Klos, 1965), as well as graphic novels such as *The Complete Maus: A Survivor's Tale* (Spiegelman, 1996). Each representation affords a different perspective on the Holocaust. As Stuart Hall notes in the link to a Media Education Foundation video clip, media representation goes beyond simply mirroring reality to actually constructing and shaping reality (5.4.1).

Studying media representations involves identifying how groups or institutions represent groups or ideas to achieve their ideological agendas. White politicians may appeal to White voters in their media ads by framing issues according to race, by labeling and scapegoating the "other," like, for example, blaming affirmative action for the cause of loss of jobs. Representing the "other" in a negative light reflects a discourse of racism driven by an ideological political agenda (5.4.2). Similarly, during the 19th and early 20th century, European and American museums often portrayed "other" cultures as inferior, primitive, or exotic (Lidchi, 1997).

TEACHING ANALYSIS OF MEDIA REPRESENTATIONS

Teaching students to critically analyze media representations involves collecting media texts related to a certain phenomenon and then identifying consistent patterns in how these texts construct particular versions of reality. The following are some steps for teaching analysis of media representations:

1. Select certain groups, social worlds, topics, issues, or phenomena to study. Students collect a range of different texts about a particular phenomenon portrayed in multiple media: magazines, TV, newspapers, literature, websites. They can search for certain topics using search engines or search Google Images™ or Yahoo Images™ to find images associated with certain topics.

2. Note patterns or similar images in these representations. In my class, I have small groups of students create poster exhibits based on magazine ads to share with others in the class. Students select certain topics, find illustrative examples of magazine ads, tack up the ads on their poster boards, and, based on perceived patterns in the ads, define the overall theme of their poster board. For example, one group noted certain patterns in the representations of suburbia in magazine ads—images of open spaces, two-car garages, rows of similar houses, traffic jams, and strip malls. Half of

the class shares their displays with the other half, and then the groups are reversed. The Website contains links to discussions of how understanding the meaning of images, for example on t-shirts, as representations requires making intertextual links (5.5.1–3).

3. Analyze how concepts and language are used to represent topics or issues. Students then identify how people typically think about these groups, social worlds, topics, issues, or phenomena as shaped by media representations. For example, suburban students may note that they typically think of urban areas as dangerous or crime-ridden, thoughts that they trace to representations of crime in urban areas on local television news. Students may also reflect on their notions of "success," "beauty," "romance," "masculinity," "femininity," or "the ideal family," and consider how media representations shape those notions. For example, their notion of feminine beauty may be shaped by idealized images of females that objectify women in ways that deny their unique qualities (Wysocki, 2004).

Students can study how language is used to represent or construct worlds by studying language use in cartoons. In cartoons, language is often used to mimic or parody the use of certain discourses discussed in Chapter 4 in which the discourse of one world is used in the context of a totally different world. For example, in a *New Yorker* cartoon, a father is telling a child a bedtime story: "The little pig with the portfolio of straw and the little pig with the portfolio of sticks were swallowed up, but the little pig with the portfolio of bricks withstood the dip in the market," a discourse of accounting that is set against the original *Three Little Pigs* children's world. Students can find cartoons by going to *The New Yorker* collection of cartoons (5.5.4) and under "search" typing in a certain discourse, such as "business," and study the consistent patterns in the language employed in cartoons related to business.

Students can search for cartoons on any number of different websites (5.5.5–6). They can also study the use of language in parody in *The Onion* (5.5.7), a mock newspaper that ridicules current political coverage, as well as other parody sites (5.5.6–9). The Website contains discussions of methods for analyzing parody as a form of representation in cartoons (5.5.10–11).

4. Conduct content analyses of representations. Students can create a set of categories or a coding system for analyzing the types of phenomena in media texts, for example, categories related to types of character roles or traits ("male," "female," "rich," "poor," "powerful," "weak," "aggressive," "passive"), settings ("realistic," "fantasy," "urban," "suburban," "rural"), or story resolutions ("happy," "sad," "resolved," "unresolved"). Creating categories allows students to determine the percentages of certain phenomena in media texts. For example, to determine the representations of diversity in prime-time television drama shows, students could analyze the number of non-White versus White characters and the roles in which those characters are portrayed and the percentages for each of these categories. Or they could analyze the ways in which cartoon characters interact with one another: through physical/violent interaction versus language or through a combination of physical and language interaction. The Website contains discussions of specific techniques for conducting content analysis (5.5.12–15) and examples of studies employing content analysis, for example, analysis of gender differences in children's advertising (5.5.16–19).

Representation and Censorship

Students can also examine how certain phenomena are represented in ways that threaten or challenge certain beliefs or ideas, leading to censorship. When the rock group the Dixie Chicks objected to George W. Bush's arguments for the war on Iraq, there were numerous calls to stop playing their songs on radio stations because people objected to their criticism of that war. There has been considerable controversy about the often sexist, violent messages in gangsta rap songs/videos, in which females often are represented in sexist ways, leading some to call for censorship of these songs/videos.

Students could study censorship cases to examine how particular media representations are perceived to be threatening or challenging to particular beliefs or values. One useful site is The File Room, an interactive archive of censorship cases from throughout history (5.6.1).

Students could also go to the Website to study certain organizations' challenges of censorship based on the need for people's right to know about the world (5.6.2–9b) and ways of developing rationales for controversial texts (5.6.9c–9d), as well as arguments of organizations that recommend some forms of censorship (5.6.10–14).

Representation and Idealization

Students could also examine how media representations are used in public relations or promotional campaigns to idealize certain phenomena. For example, casino gambling has been promoted as not simply an experience involving gambling, but also as an enjoyable, exciting, even romantic experience. In my class, we examine websites for casinos in terms of how the use of images and language serves to idealize the gambling experience. For example, the Treasure Island Resort and Casino™ in Minnesota represents gambling as a visit to a "fun-filled" tropical paradise. We discuss the impact of the idealization of gambling on people. Teachers in the class report that, despite age restrictions, many of their students are engaged in gambling. One study conducted in 2003 found that 50% to 90% of adolescents ages 12 to 17 reported gambling within the past year, even though it is illegal (Lynch, Maciejewski, & Potenza, 2004). They also found that adolescent gamblers were more likely to report gambling for social reasons rather than to win money. (For casino ads, see 5.7.1–3).

REPRESENTATIONS OF SOCIAL GROUPS OR CATEGORIES

In studying various representations of social groups or types, students are examining how people construct generalizations about categories of people: that scientists are nerds, for instance, or Native Americans are alcoholics. This analysis involves more than simply noting the stereotyping of these groups. It also involves examining reasons for these representations as constructions of beliefs about people based on fixed, essentialist perceptions of groups. For example, media representations of black men affect how the society perceives black men in the real world (Hall, 1997; 5.8.1). Or people make generalizations about class—that "all working-class people are like X and all upper-middle-class people are like Y" (5.8.2–3). Discerning the underlying agendas behind these representations leads to questions such as "Where do these representations come from?" "Who produces these representations?" "Why are they producing these representations?" "How is complexity limited by these representations?" "What is missing or silenced in these representations?" (Hall, 1997).

Femininity

Representations of femininity in the media are constructed by a multibillion-dollar beauty industry that frames achieving an ideal, beautiful appearance as central to defining one's identity as a female. Media representations of females often focus on body weight and slimness, a relatively current cultural phenomenon. In the late 1800s, women who were not slim were viewed in a positive light because it was assumed that they were well-fed: a status feature associated with class. Since that time, in media representations of female adolescent body weight, slimness is assumed to be the ideal "look." As noted on the PBS program *Girls in America* (Cassidy, 2004), 50% of White girls ages 12–16 consider themselves overweight and only 15% consider their bodies normal, six times the rate for boys (5.8a.1). These representations have resulted in adolescent females engaging in unhealthy eating habits, anorexia, and bulimia, with long-term negative effects on their bodies (5.8a.2–9). As documented in the video *Playing Unfair: The Media Image of the Female Athlete* (Kane, Griffin, & Messner, 2002), coverage of women's sports also frequently represents female athletes in ways that emphasize their femininity and sexuality: as married, or as mothers, or even as sex objects. In contrast, male athletes are represented more in terms of their physical strength and skills (5.8a.10–12).

Femininity is also represented in the media as fulfilled almost exclusively through heterosexual relationships. For example, traditional Hollywood comedy or romance films, as well as the romance novel, portray females as nurturers who transform the impersonal, distanced male into a more loving character (Radway, 1991). Adolescent females in films such as *She's All That* (Iscove, 1999) convey the message that popularity is achieved primarily by adopting feminine social practices (5.8a.13).

Similarly, females in women's magazines or soap operas are often represented as primarily concerned about relationships, family, personal matters, home, and talk, while males are more concerned with business, institutions, sports, technology, and competition outside the home, which, from a poststructuralist perspective, is a false binary. Female audiences are positioned to be engaged as part of being "in the home," focusing on domestic, interpersonal conflicts or relationships (5.8a.14–17). Female teen magazines contain "quizzes" that position readers to adopt certain stances

and beliefs about femininity through these magazines. The questions employed often presuppose certain attitudes associated with adopting an identity defined by being outgoing, appealing to males, using certain products, or adopting practices associated with the idealized role models portrayed in the magazine. By answering questions in a certain manner, females are then scored on the degree to which they adopt the desired beliefs. (For quizzes in *Seventeen* magazine, see 5.8a.18, and for those from advice books, 5.8a.19.) Adopting a rhetorical/audience critical approach, students may survey their peers' reactions to an article critical of gender representations in *Seventeen* magazine (5.8a.19).

Females are also represented in television commercials and magazine ads as consumers, particularly in terms of assuming the domestic family roles of homemaker, cook, mom, cleaner, laundry person, and as finding satisfaction through shopping. Teachers are typically portrayed as middle-class White females. Students could draw pictures of how they envision "homemakers" or "teachers" and then discuss how and why they portrayed these roles as they did (5.8a.20–24).

It is also important to study counterexamples that challenge or interrogate these traditional roles of femininity, including representations of females in nontraditional magazines (5.8a.28–32). However, as Lisa Featherstone argues, some of these are not terribly different from the more traditional magazines (5.8a.33).

The Website contains sites devoted to examining women's issues in more nontraditional ways (5.8a.34–36), films about and by women (5.8a.37–40), and critiques of gendered media representations, including a study that found that in the top 101 G-rated films from 1990–2004, males are in 65% of all roles and 75% of starring roles (5.8a.40–58).

A TEACHING IDEA

Interrogating Gender Stereotypes

I teach a course, Topics in Literature, in which students explore how the forces of history and community shape what they read, hear, and view, and also influence their individual responses. For each unit, I have them define their specific cultural context and interrogate their assumptions and beliefs about themselves and others.

In a unit on gender roles, I begin with a small group activity based on a Massachusetts Gender Equity Center lesson plan. Each group chooses one gender and creates a chart on a large sheet of paper divided into three columns. In the center column, the students list what it means to act like a man or a woman (defining attributes such as feminine, manly, protective, nurturing). In the left column, they describe the response to someone who doesn't act like a man or woman (types of verbal and physical abuse). Typical occupations for a man or woman are listed in the right column. Coed groups have to negotiate a consensus that confronts their preconceptions of the opposite gender. A representative from each group presents his/her list to the class, and the large group discussion addresses issues of behavior expectations, stereotypes, and career aspirations for both genders. I compile a list for each gender that I leave displayed in the classroom.

The students then investigate how gender, grouped by age and race, is portrayed in the media. They identify a media stereotype (middle-aged White women or young White males) and create a collage from media images (magazines). The collage depicts a lifestyle of their chosen stereotype: what they wear, where they live, what they do for work and fun, what they eat and drink, and what they buy and own. Using popular magazines, students have difficulty finding representations of anyone other than White people. One student, in his search for pictures of black men of any age, went from group to group. He only found pictures of younger black men portrayed as either rap stars or athletes. The creation of the collage makes students aware of how their perceptions of themselves and others are formed. They also make comparisons between the class lists of gender expectations and the media representations to discover how stereotypes are reinforced.

The presentations of the collages to the class reveal how the media define people in our society by race, gender, and class. The students are surprised by what they discover: the uniform representations of White males that vary only by economic status; the sexualized images of young White women; the racist portrayals of Black men and women. This investigation informs their reading of "The Glass Half Empty" by Anna Quindlen (1996), a personal narrative of her experience of workplace discrimination. However, students could also apply their understanding of gender roles and social status to any fictional portrayal of character.

Risa Cohen,
Irondale High School, New Brighton, Minnesota

Masculinity

Masculinity is often represented in ads, sports programs, detective/action-adventure films and television programs, and stories in men's magazines as performances of physical aggression, toughness, competitiveness, and domination (5.8b.1–2). These performances of masculinity evolved out of the rise of the middle class in the late 1700s and early 1800s, in which there was a separation of work and "home" as distinct gendered realms (Nixon, 1997). Men began to become active in men's clubs as well as religious organizations, activity constituted in terms of a discourse of moral commitment to service. And with the rise of a business or industrial economy, men devoted more time to their work outside the home, creating a division previously noted in which men constructed their identities around work and women around the home. Men also began to adopt more austere, "nonfeminine" dress. Lace, which was associated with masculinity in the 1500s and 1600s, was now considered to be a marker of femininity (Hall, 1997).

More recent representations of masculinity emphasize the fixed nature of male identities in which complexity, doubt, or alternative identities are portrayed as negatives (5.8b.3). This is most evident in cross-gender/dressing films such as *Some Like It Hot* (Wilder, 1959), *Tootsie* (Pollack, 1982), *Mrs. Doubtfire* (Columbus, 1993), and others, which not only represent females in limited ways, but also assume that adopting a feminine role is a violation of one's basic, traditional male role (5.8b.4).

Another aspect of the representation of masculinity is how it is associated with physical violence and toughness as an expression of "male outrage." The video *Tough Guise* explores representations of violence as constituted by the need to assert one's masculine identity through bullying or violence against women when challenged by others or the system (5.8b.5). Students could also analyze portrayals of male violence in advertisements (5.8b.6–7).

An analysis of sports programming sponsored by Children Now in 1999 (5.8c.1) found that male adolescents are five times more likely to view sports programs on a regular basis than female adolescents. Analysis of the representations of sports found that aggression and violence among men is depicted as exciting and rewarding behavior, and that violence is often expected. This emphasis on physical display of male prowess is evident in the popularity of professional wrestling with adolescent males (5.8c.2). The highly gendered world of professional football is evident in the representation of female cheerleaders in terms of images of passive femininity and sexuality (5.8c.3). The Website contains sites examining alternative representations of masculinity, including the Media Education Foundation video series, Media, Gender & Violence Series (5.8c.4–5).

Gays/Lesbians

In examining gender representations, it is also important to consider the ways in which gays and lesbians are represented in the media (5.8d.1). Only recently have gays and lesbians even appeared in films, television programs, and commercials; when they did appear in the past, they were stigmatized in negative ways as highly effeminate or deviant. This began to change in the 1990s with the film *Philadelphia* (Demme, 1993), with Tom Hanks portraying a gay man fighting AIDS, and Ellen DeGeneres on her prime-time television comedy, *The Ellen Show* (Ackerman, 2001–2003).

More recently, programs such as *Will & Grace* (Kohan & Mutchnick, 1998–2006) and *Queer as Folk* (Davies, 1990–2005) and films such as *The Birdcage* (Nichols, 1996) have resulted in a shift in representations toward less stereotypical portrayals (Wilke, 2002; 5.8d.2). An analysis of *Will & Grace* indicated that the gay characters are portrayed as operating in realistic social contexts, while at the same time they are having to still deal with stereotypical perceptions that persist in these contexts (5.8d.3). However, the 10th annual Gay & Lesbian Alliance Against Defamation (GLAAD) study found that only 14 out of 110 network broadcast programs portrayed gays and lesbians (5.8d.3a). The GLAAD site also provides a complete list of the lesbian and gay characters appearing on television (5.8d.4).

From a rhetorical/audience perspective, it is often the case that audiences' homophobic attitudes shape their responses to representations of gays and lesbians (5.8d.5). The Website contains some further background readings on media representations of gays and lesbians (5.8d.6–8).

Racial and Ethnic Groups

Students could also study the ways in which different racial or ethnic groups are represented both in terms of the images portrayed and the discourses of race constituting those representations (Gerster & Zlogar, 2005; Larson, 2005; 5.6.5). Much of network television portrays a largely White world in which non-Whites appear primarily as athletes or musicians (Nadel, 2005; Roediger, 2002). Only 1% of network news stories from 1995–2004 were about Latinos, and most of those stories dealt with illegal immigration and crime (Subervi, 2005). One study found that programs aired during the 8-o'clock "family hour" were far less diverse than those aired at 10-o'clock (5.8e.1).

Another study of representations of different groups on prime-time television in Fall 2002 found that the Latino population was represented only 3% of the time on prime-time television, even though they make up 13% of the population (5.8e.2). Thus, when children watch prime-time TV, they are watching programs with little diversity (5.8e.3).

To critique representations of race, students need to examine how portrayals of race vary across and within various cultures (5.8e.4). Central to the cultural construction of race is Gramsci's theory of White hegemony (5.8e.5), by which media representations serve to maintain and perpetuate a discourse of whiteness as the desired norm, against which people of color are defined as "other" (5.8e.5–6). In her critique of how white/capitalistic institutional forces shape representations of race in a video clip (5.8e.7), bell hooks notes, "The issue is not freeing ourselves from representations. It's really about being enlightened witnesses when we watch representations."

Based on their research on the representations of Blacks in television and films, Robert Entman and Andrew Rejecki (2000) find that local news broadcasts frequently portray urban Blacks as more likely to engage in criminal behavior than Whites. They also find that Blacks are represented as either highly talented or as dangerous, with few portrayals of Blacks' ordinary, everyday lives. And, as noted in Chapter 4, Edward Said (1978) found that media representations of Middle Eastern and Muslim worlds reflect White, Western discourses positioning those worlds as an exotic, unfathomable "other" (5.8e.8; Kramer, Vittinghoff, & Gentz, 2006).

Tim Klobuchar's teaching vignette focuses students' attention on how film style is employed to represent alternative perspectives on different racial groups.

A TEACHING IDEA

Film Styles and Social Critiques

This unit began as a social critique of my own against the quarantining of non-American films as a separate genre, denying film's ability to universalize human experience. For example, issues such as terrorism and the death penalty are obviously relevant in America today, but anyone looking for *The Battle of Algiers* (Pontecorvo, 1966) and *M* (Lang, 1931) would not find them in the Drama section of the video store, where weighty social conflicts like these are usually dealt with, but would instead have to search for them in the Foreign Films section. I incorporate these films along with Spike Lee's *Do The Right Thing* (1989) into a unit for 12th-grade English. All of these films employ a distinct (mostly visual) style that helps emphasize their protest or commentary, but none of them are polemics; they present both sides fairly before taking one. For each film, the students must 1) analyze how the director presented both sides, 2) identify which side (if any) was ultimately chosen, and 3) explain how they reached their conclusions.

We start with Gillo Pontecorvo's 1966 film, *The Battle of Algiers*, which depicts the Algerian battle for independence from France. Similarities to recent events are eerie, such as scenes in which Algerian insurgents bomb French civilians and the French military responds by torturing suspects. Before starting the film, I show a few minutes of a documentary on the Criterion Collection DVD of the film, which briefly summarizes the history of French colonialism in Algeria. For all films, I construct viewing guides (Teasley & Wilder, 1997), one for each 30- to 35-minute section of the film, that allows students room to write a summary of that section; literary, theatrical, and cinematic elements they think are significant; and answers to questions that help focus their viewing. For this film, students discuss the importance of Pontecorvo's decision to film in black and white, primarily with hand-held cameras. Hopefully, they talk about how these cinematic elements help make the film seem like newsreel footage—as if Pontecorvo's depiction of events is the absolute truth. That leads us into discussion about who Pontecorvo ultimately sides with. Students talk about his use of close-ups, point of view, and music in reaching their decision.

Lee employs a much more expressionistic style in *Do the Right Thing* (1989), which students see in his use of bright colors, oblique angles, and a montage in which characters hurl racial slurs into the camera lens. Just as Pontecorvo's style suits his critique of colonialism by depicting real-life events matter-of-factly, Lee's style helps illustrate how racial tensions among fictional characters swing out of control on the hottest day of the year through more flamboyant methods. This film provokes more reaction than any film I show because of its climactic race riot scene. Students debate the admirable and not-so-admirable traits of the White and Black characters, trying to determine what and who instigated the riot, and what Lee's ultimate message is. After the film, they read essays by film critics David Denby and Roger Ebert, who had opposite reactions to the film; Denby thought it was irresponsible filmmaking that promoted racial violence, while Ebert thought it "empathized with all participants." Students discuss their reaction to the essays and talk about who made the more valid points.

Finally, we view Fritz Lang's masterpiece *M* (1931), which I save for last because its social critiques are more subtle. It is more difficult to see how Lang's style exposes a decaying German society and mob mentality, though the discussion gets much livelier after the famous scene of the "trial" of the child murderer played by Peter Lorre, which debates the merits of the death penalty. Again,

students try to figure out if Lang takes a position in the debate, and if so, how they reached that conclusion.

For a final assessment, students watch a film outside of class and prepare to write an in-class analytical essay that must answer two questions: 1) What part of society is the film commenting on or protesting; 2) How does the film accomplish this? They must include one piece of evidence that has to do with style, such as types of shots, angles, editing, music, etc. I give them a list of 20 suggested films (both American and non-American), though they are welcome to go off the list if they can explain how their film fits the criteria.

Tim Klobuchar, Edina High School, Edina, Minnesota

The Website contains many sites focusing on analysis of representations of race as well as bibliographies and lesson plans (5.8e.9–32), for example, how the news media typically reflects a White, middle-class perspective. For an alternative, go to the diversityinc.com site in which the news and current events are presented from a more diverse perspective (5.8e.9; see also lessons 5.8e.10–11).

Class

Given the media's reluctance to address issues of class inequity and poverty, representations of social class differences in the media perpetuate stereotypical notions of working- versus middle- versus upper-middle-class groups (Kendall, 2005; 5.8f.1). As evident in the PBS documentary *People Like Us* (5.8f.2), people adopt class markers of dress, language, and social practices typically associated with being middle class as the assumed norm, in which being working class is portrayed in negative terms. Advertisements therefore represent products positively by associating them with the achievement of middle- or upper-middle-class status (5.8f.3–7).

In analyzing representations of class differences, it is useful to examine media texts organized around class hierarchies: the classic PBS Masterpiece Theater program *Upstairs, Downstairs,* Robert Altman's film *Gosford Park* (2001), *Titanic* (Cameron, 1997), and the PBS Mystery series *The Inspector Lynley Mysteries* (Baumgarten, 2005) (5.8f.8) portray the disparities in social practices and values associated with different classes, often leading to conflicts. Upper-middle-class characters that emerged in prime-time shows in the 1980s such as *Dallas* (Jacobs, 1978–1991) (5.8f.9) reflected an increasing sense of a new wealthy class during the Reagan and Thatcher era, in contrast to portrayals of working-class characters coping with the loss of manufacturing jobs. The Website contains lists of films about working-class characters in the 1990s (5.8f.10), as well as analyses of portrayals of working-class people on television (5.8f.11–16, particularly *The Jerry Springer Show* [Klazura, 1991–present]) (Grindstaff, 2002).

In studying media representations of gender, race, and class, students could identify the institutional and economic forces behind these representations and how these representations influence attitudes and policies. For example, Richard Ohmann (2003) notes that a major shift in economic policy occurred beginning in the 1970s from a stable "Fordism" of stable, well-paying, long-term, full-time jobs with benefits and pensions to the instability of a "casino capitalism" (p. 33) with less security and a reduction of benefits and pensions, resulting in working-class people having to work longer hours in several different jobs. (The Website contains film clips of work in the early 20th century, 5.8f.16.) However, media representations of working-class life, on, for example, conservative radio talk shows, often idealize low-income people's salt-of-the-earth authenticity as valued over knowledge-economy workers or government bureaucrats (Frank, 2004). These representations shift attention away from analysis of the effects of fast-track capitalism and corporate power that work against low-income people. The Website contains further reading on how representations of gender, race, and class reflect larger economic forces (5.8f.17–18).

Families and Age Groups

Families. Families have been represented in different ways in the media across different decades since World War II, shifts reflecting changes in gender attitudes (Tincknell, 2005). While television families of the 1950s were portrayed as patriarchal institutions guided by a omniscient, wise father, programs in the 1990s such as *The Simpsons* (Groening, 1989–present) portrayed fathers as bungling and ineffectual. There is also a shift in the role of the mother to someone who is more independent and assertive. More recently, some reality television shows (5.8f.1) portray conflicts and experiences of families in unusual contexts that challenge family unity. The Council on Contemporary Families has found that media representations often fail to recognize the influence of declining economic support and jobs on the family (5.8f.2)

Children and the Elderly. Children are often portrayed in the media or films in negative or stereotypical ways—as mischievous, precocious, and incompetent—as well as in more complex, sympathetic ways (5.9.1; Shary, 2002). One study found that most news stories about children focused on crime and violence, with little attention to child poverty, child care, and welfare (5.9.2). While adolescents are often portrayed as having a lot of consumer options and as engaging in substance abuse, few consequences and strategies for coping with these challenges are portrayed (Stern, 2005; 5.9.3-5). Children are also represented in television commercials in ways that socialize them to become active consumers with defined needs for various consumer products at an early age; advertisers spend billions on encouraging children to nag their parents to buy certain products (Linn, 2004; Schor, 2004; 5.9.6–10).

At the other end of the spectrum, the elderly are often represented in equally limited ways (Featherstone & Wernick, 1995). One study of prime-time television programs in the fall of 2000 found that only 3% of the characters were 70 and older, and only 13% fell between the ages of 50 and 69, in contrast to the reality that 9% of the American population is over 70 and 28% are over 50 (5.9.11). In contrast, as the study found, websites for the AARP (5.9.12) and for the National Council on Aging (5.9.13) present the elderly in a very different, more positive light. Another study found that advertising geared for the elderly also avoids stereotypes, but often because it is attempting to sell them products such as prescription drugs (5.9.14). In analyzing the representations of the elderly in films, one of my students found that they are portrayed in the prototypical roles of "grumpy old men," "feisty old women," "sickly old persons," "mentally deficient," "depressed or lonely," "having unusual wisdom," "busybody," or "having a second childhood" (Landis, 2002).

War

Representations of the complexities of war in films such as *Saving Private Ryan* (Spielberg, 1998), *Full Metal Jacket* (Kubrick, 1987), *Black Hawk Down* (Scott, 2001), *Apocalypse Now* (*Coppola, 1979), Das Boot* (Petersen, 1981), *Cold Mountain* (Minghella, 2003), *Hotel Rwanda* (George, 2004), and *Life Is Beautiful* (Benigni, 1997) focus on individuals' ambiguous experiences of war and how war transforms participants' lives. In contrast to these complex portrayals, governments may use propaganda war films to sway the public to support war, as was the case with anti-Nazi and pro-Nazi propaganda films during World War II that demonized the enemy. However, the realities of war can often challenge official government versions, as was the case in the Vietnam War, in which television pictures of the grim aspects of war influenced public policy about that war (5.10.1). While Mathew Brady's photos of the Civil War portrayed the realities of that war, some of the first motion pictures of a war occurred in the Spanish American War (5.10.2).

During the Gulf War, war was represented as what Garber, Matlock, and Walkowitz (1993) describe as a "media spectacle"–a nonstop, dramatic portrayal of bombs hitting targets and troops moving about in the desert. This more anesthetic portrayal of war without shots of dying soldiers and civilians served to position audiences in a more detached stance than was the case with the Vietnam War. This visual "spectacle" element of the portrayal framed war more in terms of a dramatic conflict between good versus evil (5.10.3). Then, during the Iraq War, to counteract charges of media control and censorship during the Gulf War, the U.S. military employed "embedded reporters." However, these embedded reporters could then themselves be controlled by the unit commanders with whom they served, as opposed to independent reporters who were not controlled by the military (5.10.4).

Thus, a major part of waging contemporary war involves managing the public relations and media representations of a war in ways that serve governments' interests, as opposed to informing the public about interests and perspectives that challenge governments' interests (Thussu & Freedman, 2003; 5.10.5). And different films represent war in different ways, with some glorifying war in terms of "winning great victories," and others portraying more realistic aspects of war in terms of the grim realities of death and destruction (5.10.6–18).

Political Parties and Organizations

Political parties, think tanks, and interest groups use the media to represent their candidates and policies through television ads, press releases, and promotional materials in ways that will appeal to and gain the identification of their targeted constituencies. Students could study how these representations reflect different political beliefs by both conservatives and liberals as portrayed on their websites (5.11.1–4). The Website contains methods for analyzing political representations (5.11.5–13).

As noted in Chapter 4, Noam Chomsky (2002) argues that media representations of political issues often reflect corporate interests. For example, issues of welfare are framed in negative terms of people's unfortunate dependency on the government, reflecting corporations' unwillingness to pay taxes to support such programs, while corporation tax subsidy programs receive little attention (5.11.14).

Journalists who are frustrated by the limitations of mainstream media's representations of political issues often turn to blogs to share alternative representations of the news as contrasted with those found in official new sources. Students could go onto blogs operated by or that include journalists to gain their perspective on the news (5.11.15–22). The Website contains a number of webquests and lessons on media representations of politics (5.11.23–27).

Sample Activity:
Creating Counter-Representations

Once they have critiqued some of the types of representations described in this chapter, students could then create alternative counter-representations to provide more complex, authentic portrayals of a certain phenomenon. Students can create PowerPoint™ presentations, websites, or digital scrapbooks that contain photographic or video representations to present a more complex analysis. For example, as part of a unit on the Website (5.12.1), Sacred Space: Learning About and Creating Meaningful Public Spaces, students presented their own designs for creating public spaces.

Or, having identified negative representations of elderly people, students could then create portraits of elderly people such as their grandparents that portray them in more positive, complex ways.

Students could then write about how their constructions of reality differ from media representations and give reasons for the differences in terms of the forces shaping both representations.

ADDITIONAL WEB RESOURCES
FOR MEDIA REPRESENTATIONS

The Website also contains links to information on media representations of the additional individual topics listed below, which fall within two broad categories of occupations, and geographic regions and communities (places and spaces).

- *Groups*: teachers (5.13.1–4), students (5.13.5), lawyers (5.13.6), criminals (5.13.7), and families (5.13.8–9).
- *Places and spaces*: urban communities (5.13.10–18), suburban communities (5.13.19–24), rural communities (5.13.25–29), geographic regions and neighborhoods (5.13.30–32), and virtual tours and lessons for studying about communities, places, and spaces (5.13.33–45).

SUMMARY

In summary, by examining media representations, students are learning to interrogate the ways in which the media construct versions of reality and to recognize that these constructions influence their lives and identities (5.12.1). In doing so, they are learning to acknowledge the power of media representations to actually create rather than simply mirror cultural practices, just as "reality TV" has created a new, mediated form of "reality." By critiquing the functions of these representations and their underlying economic and ideological agendas, students learn how media representations and institutions themselves shape perceptions of issues and public policy. Finally, by creating their own alternative representations through media productions, students explore alternative, transformative ways of constructing the world.

CHAPTER 6

Media Ethnography Studies

Key to Topics

A GROUP OF 14-year-old adolescents meets every Friday night to watch a horror movie DVD at a group member's house. They enjoy sharing their responses to the DVD, particularly when they can ridicule what they perceive to be fake, ineffective attempts to scare them. Within this miniculture, the meaning of the horror movie is constituted by the participants' purposes, stances, attitudes, and expertise, whose practices reflect certain norms and roles within their culture.

Through this participation with texts, audiences are constructing modes of escape, daydreams, social relationships, and alternative identities (Abercrombie & Longhurst, 1998). All of these activities occur within social and cultural contexts or "fan subcultures" in which fans construct their identities and stances consistent with the culture of, for example, a *Sims* online user club (6.2.1–3).

Media ethnographers study how audiences assume the active role of constructing the meaning of media texts (Beach, 2004; Bennett, Couldry, Herbert, Gillespie, & Livingstone, 2006; Bird, 2003; Brooker, 2002; Buckingham, 1996; Hills, 2002; Moores, 2003; Schrøder, Drotner, Kline, & Murray, 2003; Staiger, 2005). These ethnographers assume that the meaning of media texts is not "in" these texts; nor is the meaning simply "in" audiences. Rather, the meaning of texts evolves out of the activity of audiences' social participation with media texts, as is the case with the 14-year-olds' horror movie viewing group. As Grossberg, Wartella, and Whitney (1998) argue in defense of their model of "mediamaking":

the media are *themselves being made* while they are simultaneously *making something else*. . . . we must see the media and all of the relationships that the media are involved in as active relationships, producing the world at the same time that the world is producing the media. This means that the media *cannot* be studied apart from the active relationships in which they are always involved. (p. 7, emphasis in original)

Elizabeth Bird (2003) argues that media ethnography serves a valuable purpose in providing a complex perspective on audiences' media participation and challenging some of the simplistic claims made about the overpowering effects of media on people:

It is a mistake to conclude that all people, all the time, are in the vice-like grip of all media. The pervasive talk of "media saturation" overlooks the more complex reality, which is that people's attention is variable and selective . . . it is indeed very difficult for most of us to live without *some* media, but other media we can happily take or leave. Similarly, ethnographic research paints a more subtle and optimistic picture, showing people who engage enthusiastically with some messages, while letting much wash over them—and spending much of their time loving, caring, and sparring with each other. (p. 190)

Given the importance of understanding the complexity of audiences' social uses of the media, this chapter describes techniques for engaging students in conducting their own media ethnography studies as well as some research illustrating topics they could study.

WHAT DO MEDIA ETHNOGRAPHERS STUDY?

Media ethnographers study how audiences have become active performers through participation with the media. Audiences engage in fan club chat exchanges about favorite television programs. They burn music CDs and share those CDs with peers. They critique mainstream media coverage of the news on blogs. They organize viewing events around going to films or viewing at home, such as Super Bowl parties. They visit theme parks, attend concerts, or shop in malls, experiences that are highly mediated by media. Or they construct their own versions of media texts. For example, game players create their own video productions of game-playing described as "machinima" in which players add their own voice-over dialogue or commentary to shots of game characters moving through the game world (Thompson, 2005). Games such as *Sims 2* include editing software that allows players to create their own movies to share with other players on the Electronic Arts website (6.2.3a).

Media industry researchers, as well as media ethnographers, study audiences' uses of media and variations in levels of engagement with that media. The use of diaries employed in the Nielsen ratings for television viewing, however, may not provide accurate data about actual television viewing, since they rely upon self-reportage; nor do they allow for the fact that while respondents are watching television, they may also be sending emails, and therefore not really "watching" television. Direct observations of people's media use, in which observers record instances of media use every 15 seconds, find greater levels of media use and multitasking media use than do diary recordings (Center for Media Design, 2000).

Audiences as Consumers

As noted in Chapter 4, audiences are being socialized to respond in certain ways consistent with the values of consumerism (Attallah & Shade, 2002). An ethnographic study of visitors to Disney World found that they were continually being encouraged to take pictures at "Kodak photo stops" as a means of selling Kodak film and cameras (Project on Disney, 1995). The researchers noted that visitors had been socialized to believe that their visit to Disney World was incomplete without taking pictures. In these commercialized virtual worlds, "reality" is often mediated by the producers' own ideological versions of history and community. The Project on Disney (1995) researchers

also found that the history of the world, in the Epcot exhibits at Disney World, was portrayed primarily as a continuous improvement of living conditions through technology and corporate agents (who are also sponsors of the exhibits.) For example, in an exhibit on "The Land" sponsored by Kraft, "no relationship to the land other than commercial use by business is posited as possible or even desirable" (p. 59). In an exhibit on "Universe of Energy," sponsored by Exxon, there is no reference to energy shortages, oil spills, or solar power. Representations of American history emphasize "unity" and "equality" achieved through global capitalism and make no reference to conflicts associated with gender, class, race, or cross-cultural differences between societies. The future is portrayed as a world populated by intact heterosexual families; "in 'Tomorrowland Theater' the chorus tells us that 'Disney World is a wonderland for girls and boys and moms and dads'" (p. 69.) The prevailing narrative in these historical representations is one of "capitalist expansion masquerading as science fiction in which the heroes of the next century are not people but machines, with faith placed not in courage but in technology" (p. 86).

As a result of this commercialization, markers of class, race, and gender become less important in defining one's identity than a lifestyle defined by the use of certain commodities. Audiences adopt the stance of a "possessive gaze" that focuses on surface images and brands associated with "coolness" (Abercrombie & Longhurst, 1998). For example, in the experience of shopping at a mall, adolescents perceive products in terms of how those products will enhance their own image. That shopping experience is mediated by advertising and brand images throughout stores designed to foster a "possessive gaze" stance–for example, with models wearing certain clothes or having shoppers participate in "entertainment retail" uses of products.

As documented on the PBS program *Merchants of Cool* (entire program on-line, see 6.2.4), advertisers and marketers use ethnographic methods to study what adolescents perceive to be "cool" based on teen informants who observe new styles or trends. They then use that information to promote products by connecting them to images and practices associated with "coolness."

Identity Construction and Virtual Communities

Media ethnographers also study how audiences assume certain identities through participation in fan clubs or online chat rooms (Bailey, 2005: Hills, 2002). For example, soap opera fans display pictures of soap opera actors in their bedrooms, write letters to the actors, or attend social events to meet the actors (Harrington & Bielby, 1995).

Increasingly, adolescent audiences are turning away from the "represented" worlds of much of broadcast media, which "created a world awash in events but largely devoid of shared experiences" (Travis, 1998, p. 46), to participate in shared communal experiences of interactive media in virtual communities. In these virtual worlds, adolescents can experiment with different roles and stances without concern for the constraints of gender, class, race, age, or disability markers that inhibit their participation in lived-world, face-to-face interaction.

As Sherry Turkle noted in her study of online participation (1996), "you are who you pretend to be" in these virtual communities, where you are free to experiment with different identities/roles. She quotes one participant:

> You can completely redefine yourself if you want. You can be the opposite sex. You can be more talkative. You can be less talkative. Whatever. You can just be who you want really, whoever you have the capacity to be. You don't have to worry about the slots other people put you in as much. It's easier to change the way people perceive you, because all they've got is what you show them. They don't look at your body and make assumptions. They don't hear your accent and make assumptions. All they see is your words." (p. 158)

Social Connections

Media ethnographers also study how audiences use their responses to media texts to build social relationships. For example, adolescent females often share responses to teen magazine advice columns and quizzes. Currie (1999) studied adolescent females' social uses of teen magazines to define their identities. She quotes one of her participants, 17-year-old Alexandra:

> My friend loves doing the little surveys, like the "Friends" survey and stuff. She always gets me to fill them out with her, or she'll ask me questions and we go through—actually, lately, we've been going through them like crazy because it's graduation. So we've been all going through those magazines you've listed, basically just for style of grad dresses, and stuff like that. (p. 252)

Similarly, Internet games can provide a social connection. Playing Pokémon online, children can play the game outside of the adult world, communicate with peers about playing the game, and use knowledge of the game as a membership marker in peer groups (Vasquez, 2005).

Audiences of children and adults alike may view certain television programs in order to acquire information necessary for participation in conversations with others. Many view television news as part of a nightly ritual celebration that provides a virtual link to "community" constructed by the television news program. The same is true of print news. For example, in a study of reasons for reading *The National Enquirer*, avid female readers often perused the tabloid in order to obtain information about celebrities that they could then share with their friends as a form of gossip (Bird, 2003). Women who could cite the latest celebrity "insider story" from sources such as *The National Enquirer* and dramatize its relevance for their peer group assumed status within the peer group (Bird, 2003). (For Dan Chandler's module, The Active Viewer, and an extensive bibliography, see 6.2.5.)

Understanding the various purposes of participation in virtual worlds may explain their appeal. One purpose may be to engage in a pleasurable, ritual-like experience that connects participants with larger, mythic, collective dramas (Real, 1996). For example, soccer fans viewing World Cup soccer television broadcasts as a social group engage in ritual-like social practices as well as acquiring information about the teams and players (a "learning dimension"), sharing time with friends and family (a "companionship dimension"), and using sports viewing to kill time (a "filler dimension") (Wenner & Gantz, 1998, p. 237). In short, part of the appeal of virtual worlds may lie in participants' need to transcend the everyday through collective rituals.

Class, Gender, and Racial Identities

By adopting certain stances associated with the practices and discourses portrayed in certain texts, audiences align themselves with certain class, gender, and racial identities. In his analysis of professional wrestling on television, Jenkins (1997) posits that the staging of a melodramatic encounter between the "good guy" who ultimately seeks revenge on and overcomes the trickery of the underhanded, villainous "bad guy" is a genre tool that is highly appealing to a working-class male audience. Vicarious participation in this drama allows males to vent "their own frustrations at a world which promises them patriarchal authority but which is experienced through relations of economic subordination" (p. 560).

In her study of female adolescents' responses to the popular television program *Beverly Hills 90210*, McKinley (1997) found that the females rarely challenged the program's predominate narrative of women employing a range of practices to make themselves attractive to males. The girls perceived themselves as experts on these topics, and gained pleasure and status from sharing their expertise. She found that "never did they question the media definition of 'pretty,' or their own unproblematic equating of appearance and identity" (p. 77). They "accepted the show's invitation to foreground appearance, then enthusiastically cycled that way of attending to female identity back toward their own lives" (p. 78).

One ethnography of female audiences' responses to and online discussions of the feminist-oriented content on the Oxygen Cable Network found that female audiences responded positively to programs that address their everyday lives as females (Penley, Parks, & Everett, 2003, 6.2.6–7).

Viewing of television sports often serves as a male bonding experience. One student in my class examined his own family members' responses to a televised baseball game. He recorded and took notes on his father's and brothers' responses to a series of baseball games. He analyzed these data in terms of what aspects of the game the participants focused on, their physical behaviors in responding together as a group, and any ritual-like patterns of response. The student found that his family members, all of whom were or had been baseball players, responded to the game by vicariously experiencing the actions of the players. In some cases, the actual physical act of responding—of standing up and swinging as if they were a hitter or giving high fives to one another as if they were on the field—was part of a shared drama of mutual engagement in the game. Through mimicking the ballplayers on the field, they were vicariously playing out their own enjoyment of the game as a form of male bonding. The participants also frequently adopted the "sports talk" lingo of the television commentators to formulate their own descriptions of the game.

Aspects of racial identities also influence response. In a study of African-American females' responses to the film version of *The Color Purple* (Spielberg, 1985), Jacqueline Bobo (2003) found that the participants empathized strongly with what they perceived to be the positive aspects of the film related to portrayals of strong female identities consistent with the daily lives of black females. The findings were surprising in light of director Steven Spielberg's uses of black stereotypes and widespread criticisms of the film by reviewers, particularly male reviewers.

But Bobo notes that, given black females' experiences and their own ideological discourses, the film evoked positive responses that may have led them to bracket out what may have been critical responses to some of the stereotyping in the film (p. 312).

Media ethnographers also study cross-cultural differences, particularly between Western and non-Western audiences' responses (Askew & Wilk, 2002; Ginsburg, Abu-Lughod, & Larkin, 2002). For example, when television first became available to Australian Aborigines, they were mystified by the cultural content of the programs, the focus of a major tension between their own and the White, commercial cultural content of television. There are also interesting within-culture differences. For instance, the Al Jazeera (subject of the documentary *The Control Room* [White, 2005]) and the Al Arabiya cable television networks, which broadcast throughout the Arabic world, walk a fine line between appealing to Arabic viewers' cultural attitudes while also challenging some of the traditional policies of certain Arab countries (Shapiro, 2005).

In a study of viewers' responses to the evening soap opera *Dallas*, Liebes and Katz (1994) found that viewers in American, Russia, Israel, and Saudi Arabia generated quite varied responses to the same programs, differences reflecting different discourses or ideological perspectives. The Americans and the Israelis interpreted the characters' actions in terms of various psychological needs and themes. The Russians interpreted the characters' actions in terms of thematic beliefs. The Saudi Arabians interpreted the characters in terms of moral issues associated with family values. These different groups of viewers therefore constructed meanings of *Dallas* consistent with their own ideological orientations. The Website contains other examples of how audiences construct the meaning of media texts (6.2.8–15).

CONDUCTING MEDIA ETHNOGRAPHIES

To help your students learn to reflect on how they and others construct the meaning of media texts, you can have them conduct their own small-scale media ethnographies. In my class, I ask students to choose one type of media involvement to study: 1) television or film viewing, 2) participation in Internet chat rooms or fan club activities, 3) responses to popular music, or 4) participation in media events such as rock concerts. After obtaining written consent from participants and guaranteeing that their confidentiality will be protected, students take notes of or tape-record their responses and social practices in responding to a text. They may also interview participants about their responses. They then analyze those responses in terms of stances, attitudes, engagement, purposes, interpretations, and the influence of social context. To prepare students to conduct these studies, we discuss theories of how audiences construct meaning and look at some sample studies.

The Website contains further information on methods for conducting ethnographic studies (6.3.1–5). It also includes links to folklore studies that examine how local social practices reflect the culture of a particular place or region (6.3.6–12), as well as some illustrative examples of students' use of media ethnography methods (6.3.13–15).

The following journal entry by student Luke Lecheler is a portion of a small-scale media ethnography report:

A Sample Student Ethnography: On Watching a Teen Drama

I interviewed a college-aged friend about her viewing of Fox's hit teen drama, *The OC*. She was watching episodes on DVD in her apartment late Friday night. I was interested in why a show that takes place in a rich California high school is so appealing to college students, especially women.

What she did say was that she liked having something to talk about with friends who also watch the show. I guess it is gossip without the negative real-world consequences. We can talk about how Ryan is such a(n) (insert adjective) because he did X, without Ryan being too concerned with what we think about him. I'm not going to pretend I know why humans have this urge to gossip about each other, but it is a pervasive desire within many of our various social groups. For my friend, *The OC* fulfills this desire.

She also watches the show for the trends, especially new music groups. This fulfills her need to feel "with it" in her various peer groups. However, she is careful to note that she does not accept all this passively; no one can tell her what to think.

My friend clearly has certain values. She values being hip and being able to participate in conversations regarding equally hip TV shows. However, she recognizes that *The OC* often wants her to take a passive, consumer stance. She likes to hear the new music the show presents, for example, but she refuses to go out and buy a CD simply because the show tacitly says she should.

She also says she recognizes that the characters in the show present different values that may be accepted by the less critical viewer. For example, the materialistic culture presented by the rich high school students may cause certain people to believe that objects can make them cool, sexy, and happy. She does not share their materialism and therefore feels like her contrary values are somewhat validated when she watches the show; she can simultaneously be entertained by the adventures of the characters while knowing that her own life, while not nearly as eventful, is more meaningful than the lives of the characters she uses for weekly entertainment.

SITES FOR MEDIA ETHNOGRAPHY STUDIES

Students can study audience participation in countless media venues. What follows are a few possibilities.

Computer and Video Games

Students participate in a range of different types of computer and video games (6.3.15). In games such as *Sim City 3000, Populous,* and *Alpha Centauri,* students are involved in constructing different aspects of community—housing, transportation, shopping, business, schooling, waste disposal, day care, and so on (6.3.17–18). In web-based computer games, players participate with other players with varied abilities and expertise, a characteristic that mirrors the reality of lived worlds. Within this social hierarchy, players advance as they learn new practices and strategies. In studying the players of these games, students may examine participants' perceptions of differences and similarities between playing the game as a virtual reality and experiences in similar lived-world realities (6.3.19–27). Students may also study participation in massively multiplayer online games or MMOGs (2.3.28–30m), perhaps looking at how players shape the identities of their avatars to succeed within the game community. Students could observe and interview players about the specific strategies they employ as well as about their social connections with co-players.

Fan Clubs and Fanfiction

Students can also study various types of fans or fan clubs organized around television programs, films, rock groups, *sports* teams, or memorabilia. Being a fan involves active participation and knowledge of a particular media text or event, as displayed through logos, photos, clothes, and so on.

Some television shows actually encourage and foster audience participation through websites linked to shows. These web-based fan clubs are organized around highly interactive audience exchanges, transparent navigational links, and hybridity of texts, images, sounds, links, or references (Hocks, 2003). (6.3.31–34). Studies of fan participation on these sites are themselves becoming increasingly hypertextual, framing reports of their data through web-based links. Mary Hocks (2003) cites the example of an online dissertation research report by Christine Boese (1998), a study of the fan culture of the television series *Xena: Warrior Princess* (6.3.35). This research report contains narrative constructions of program episodes, surveys, photos, 1,100 websites related to the show, data on fan conventions, and an analysis of fan responses. Moreover, visitors' own responses to the dissertation site have been added to her website. Boese uses this web-based tool to demonstrate a primary finding: how female fans developed a sense of agency and social empowerments through sharing responses to the lesbian/feminist themes portrayed on the show and in the chat exchanges. The Website contains other examples of audience response to *Xena* (6.3.36–42).

Television fans, like soap opera fans, display their allegiances to programs by hanging pictures of soap opera actors/actresses in their bedrooms, writing letters to the actors/actresses, or attending conferences to meet them—practices that serve to mark their identities as avid fans (Harrington & Bielby, 1995). *Star Trek* fan club members employ video editing to construct their own versions of *Star Trek* programs through editing clips from programs (6.3.43–44). Students could examine online discussion forums to determine responses to specific films and the to see the reasons audiences cite for liking or not liking certain films. Several sites contain discussions of much-anticipated previews for the *Lord of the Rings* (Jackson, 2001, 2002, 2003) films (6.3.45–47).

Students could also study fan fiction, in which audience members create their own fictional versions of TV, film, or novel characters' lives to address issues they are coping with in their own lives. The Fan Fiction site contains thousands of fan fictions as well as users' favorite authors, stories, bands, video games, anime series, and home page links (6.3.47a). Users also provide feedback or post reviews that can be linked back to reviewers' biographical information (Black, 2005; 6.3.47b). Audiences also use fictional blogs to create fan fiction (6.3.47c–47d).

In studying fan fiction, students could examine how writers combine or fuse their own identities with those of characters to create hybrid identities (Black, 2005; Thomas, 2004; 6.3.47e). They could also study the social interactions and support provided by other veteran writers giving feedback to writers. The Website contains fan club sites and studies of fan clubs (6.3.48–55).

Internet Chat Rooms

Students also study participants' engagement in online chat rooms (6.3.56–58). In these chat rooms, participants employ acronyms or shorthand lingo in order to keep pace with the fast-moving conversation, for example, AYT ("Are you there?"), YIAH ("Yes, I am here"), Pmfji ("Pardon me for jumping in"), BRB ("Be right back"), PG11 ("Parent nearby"), GTG ("Got to go"), CYA ("See ya"), POOF (Gone, left the chat room) (6.3.59). Participants often have no knowledge of others' real-world identities defined by gender, class, race, age, or disability, and assume none of the accountability associated with lived-world relationships (Turkle, 1995, 1996).

One positive aspect of this anonymity is that participants intimidated by nonverbal markers of appearance or physical behaviors in face-to-face conversation no longer need be concerned about these markers. In their study of AOL Instant Message (IM) interactions, Lewis and Fabos (2005) found that adolescents experimented with a range of voices in order to build social ties with peers.

Students could study specific aspects of participants' conversations in these chat rooms related to their construction of identity, varied social roles, and relationships. However, students need to recognize, as Matt Hills (2002) warns in citing the "transparency fallacy" (p. 175), that these responses are mediated by the Internet technology, which itself is shaping the practices of social exchange, including the ease of being a "lurker" on the site. Hills argues that the chat room performance needs to be studied specifically as it is mediated by the conventions and norms operating in chatroom exchanges, as well as the commodification of chat rooms associated with the promotion and marketing of the text. And students need to address the ethical research issue of studying online participants without their permission, a violation of rules on research on human subjects; it is therefore important to request permission from participants in an initial posting (Bird & Barber, 2002). The Website contains more information about online research methods; see 6.4.60–88a; also see Hine (2000).

Talk-Radio Shows

Many call-in morning radio program shows geared for adolescents consist of "shock/jock" talk radio, in which hosts engage listeners in "hot-button," provocative topics only to subject them to ridicule or challenge as a form of entertainment. On sports talk shows, callers share technical expertise about players, rules, and "stats." These radio talk shows serve as a virtual world of conversation in that students could potentially call in and participate in a conversation, but, unlike lived-world conversations, the callers have little or no control over the direction of that conversation. Hosts may marginalize, trivialize, or dismiss guests' comments or create an adversarial stance that reflects what Deborah Tannen has described as a "culture of argument" (Tannen, 1999). For example, many male hosts of these programs demean women in an attempt to maintain a male audience. Students can contrast the topics, conversational modes, and roles on these shows—again, as with chat room talk, comparing it to lived-world talk (6.3.89–90).

Teen Zines and Web Pages

As previously noted, students are also actively engaged in responding to and constructing zines or web pages geared for adolescents (6.3.91–102b). In studying these zines or web pages (described in more detail in chapter 7), students may examine how they appeal to adolescent audiences and capture their interest or engagement, particularly in terms of how female-oriented zines foster feminist perspectives (6.3.103–108). Students could also reflect on reasons for the popularity of websites they frequently visit. In her research on adolescents' popular websites, Jennifer Stone (2005) found that adolescents prefer

highly multimodal, interactive sites that afford them a sense of membership in certain communities or affinity groups.

Music Clubs

Audiences also participate in shared community experiences in music clubs or rock concerts through dancing, singing along, or karaoke singing. In an analysis of adolescents' "clubbing" in rock clubs, Ben Malbon (1998) examined how highly sensuous dancing in the club creates an alternative sense of space, and how the continuous, pervasive sound of the music creates a mesmerizing sense of "'losing it' or 'losing yourself'" (p. 274).

Ethnographers of popular music use have recently focused on audiences' participation in and construction of music "scenes" associated with particular types of music played at a local music club or city such as Nashville, Austin, Memphis, or Chicago (Bennett & Kahn-Harris, 2004; Bennett & Peterson, 2004). Audiences participate in the construction of these scenes by going to clubs or participating in online music group fan sites.

Students could observe performances in their local music scene and what aspects of that music appeal to audiences. After reading some musicians' autobiographies (Swiss, 2005; 6.3.108a), students could also write their own autobiographical recollections of enjoying music that served to define their identities as fans of certain kinds of music or musicians (6.3.108b–c). The Website contains sites on music ethnography and studies of music fans (6.3.109–110h).

Sports Events and Rock Concerts

The contemporary sports event or rock concert is highly mediated through a range of multimedia stimuli designed to continually "entertain" audiences with music, commercial messages/images, lights, sounds, color, digital productions, video screens/reruns, and games. Students could study how audiences at football/baseball/basketball games, wrestling shows, NASCAR races, and rock concerts are continually positioned by the multimedia stimuli and promotions of events and how they react to this positioning. To some degree, audiences may have simply grown accustomed to continually being "entertained" throughout a sports event or concert. Fans are actually socialized through various cues, prompts, and messages to become active, experienced fans who participate with the crowd in joint cheers and events as a form of performance (Beeman, 1997; Schechner, 2003).

Fan identity is also related to adopting discourses of race, class, and gender. For example, NASCAR racetrack fans adopt practices that reify their identities as White, often working-class Southerners (Emmons, 2002; 6.3.111–116).

Theme or Amusement Parks and Shopping Malls

As previously noted, theme or amusement parks such as Disney World, Disneyland, the Six Flags chain, and Universal Studios Orlando (6.3.117–123) attempt to simulate realities, but often in highly controlled, artificial ways. As visitors to Disney World, a group of academics (Project on Disney, 1995) noted that while they were being told that they were entering into a "magic" set of virtual worlds, their experiences were continually being positioned or mediated by a highly controlled environment. And shopping malls provide "entertainment retail"—entertaining shoppers through participation in and with products in order to encourage them to buy those products (6.3.124).

Students could observe their peers and/or their own visits to amusement parks or malls, noting their perceptions of shopping practices or social interactions, as well as how adolescents are often monitored in shopping malls based on certain norms for appropriate behavior in a mall. The Website contains a course syllabus (6.3.125) and Webquests (6.3.126–127) on studying shopping malls. Students could also study how media representations of parks, malls, or other spaces shapes their perceptions of their experiences and attitudes (6.3.128–130).

RESEARCH METHODS FOR CONDUCTING MEDIA ETHNOGRAPHIES

When assigning media ethnographies, you will need to demonstrate the use of certain research methods.

Recording and Interviewing Techniques

Students can use written field notes and tape recordings of audience responses. Instead of vague, evaluative comments, they should be required to write specific descriptions of observed practices and to record aspects of the setting (mapping who sits with whom and where, for instance) and specific instances of talk/conversations, noting certain words or phrases (6.4.1). Students can also collect documents or writings, for example, letters to or photos of a movie star.

Another technique involves having participants themselves create hypermedia texts related to their experiences, using images, texts, music, or video clips (6.4.2). Participants could also retell, rewrite, or create their own version of a particular television show, genre, or film script or narrative. Students could then study how these different versions reflect attitudes and discourses through their choices of certain types of character actions, story development, types of conflicts, or resolution of conflicts (Bird, 2003).

Students can also use photography or digital storytelling for capturing and displaying audience participation (Sink, 2001). In her study of events surrounding a Super Bowl game, Dona Schwartz (1998) employed photos of, for example, Native American protests of the Washington Redskins logo and the pervasive use of alcohol ads. The Website contains a number of links on the use of photography as a research tool: (6.4.3–15).

A primary method for conducting ethnographies involves interviewing group members about their responses or practices, either as individuals or in focus groups (6.4.16). In interviewing participants, it is important that students pose open-ended questions that do not imply certain answers. The following are a spouse's responses to interview questions employed by a student, Joel Rogness, who was studying his wife's television viewing with her mother.

STUDENT INTERVIEW: TV VIEWING WITH OTHERS

1. Talk about watching TV with your mom and I: Did our presence do anything for you?

> When I watch TV with you, I get nervous that we are going to miss the program I really want to watch because you are channel-surfing. I also feel like I cannot watch the truly cheesy programs when other people are around (like the WB [Warner Brothers] programs). It was fun to watch TV with my mom because she liked the program so much.

2. Do you ever watch TV in a group of people? Do you watch programs with people that you might not choose to watch on your own?

> Well, I sort of answered this above. I also like to watch *Gilmore Girls* with Ellie [a friend] as an

event (like when you used to watch *Survivor* with Rachel [a friend]). Back when *Friends* was still on (and not reruns) we used to get together at someone's house to watch it. It is fun to have an excuse to get together with my girlfriends and be able to act girly.

3. Were you affected by anything in the show last night more because of your mother's presence (or my presence) than you otherwise would have been?

I don't think so, but I can see how that would happen to me at other times.

4. Summarize how people affect how you view television.

I think they affect my state of mind and thus I process the same information differently depending on whom I am around. Just like if you have low expectations of a movie, it is much easier to enjoy than if you have high expectations that are not met. Same movie, same person watching it, different outcome depending on state of mind. When I watch TV with you, I want to understand the program fully so that I don't seem dumb. So I suppose if you had a teenager in your class that liked a certain boy, she might pay attention more so that she can appear smarter to him when they have small-group discussions together. Anyway, if I watch the same program with my mom or Ellie or something, I pay less attention, but have more fun. So I probably learn less because I allow my thoughts to float around. Also, you discourage me from asking questions during a program, so I tend to have fewer discussions flowing from the television show. Usually I find value in these tangential conversations. So in that sense, maybe I learn more when I learn with people I am more at ease around. The simple answer is, I think the presence of people affects the way you learn quite a bit.

Analyzing the Results

Once they have collected observations, recordings, and information, your students can then analyze certain patterns evident in their field notes or interview transcripts, focusing on the following aspects:

Norms and Conventions. A central focus of the analysis is to discern certain norms or conventions constituting appropriate practices involved in responding to a media text. In my class, students discuss their participation in various television program or rock band fan sites, noting the norms and conventions operating on those sites. They often note that on these sites, gossiping about the personal lives of actors or actresses, or members of a band, or any form of "flaming" behavior, violates these sites' sense of "netiquette."

Text and Narrative Features. In conducting media ethnographies, students may also describe the particular aspects of texts—character types, plot structures, settings, and so on—that evoke or invite certain responses. In a study of females' responses to romance novels, Janice Radway (1991) found that females' responses to romance novels are shaped by their identification with the nurturing heroine who transforms the impersonal male into a more caring person, a plot that reifies their traditional notions of being a nurturer in the home. In a study of college females' responses to "Christian" romance novels, Timothy Rohde (1996) analyzed the plot development of 110 mail-order evangelical novels. He found that these novels contained few references to sexuality, in marked contrast to recent Harlequin and Silhouette romance novels. For evangelical Christians who objected to the trend toward "steamier" romance novels, these Christian romance novels provided a more "pure" alternative. The typical Heartsong romance novel heroine initially expresses doubt in her faith. She meets a "good man," whom she believes is not a Christian. She experiences a conversion, removing her doubt in her faith. The heroine is then rescued from peril by the man, and she learns of his true nature as a Christian. It is only after they marry that they have sex.

A group of women whom Rohde interviewed responded positively to these novels' "pure" subject matter and plot development. These readers believed that they did not have to be concerned about being "'on guard' when reading these novels." They also responded positively to the novels' didactic messages, noting that "reading these books helped them to grow in their faith as they learned the same spiritual lesson the heroine did."

Final Reports

In writing up results, students could present those results in a multimedia format using PowerPoint™, Hyperstudio™, or a web-based format that allows them to present texts, images, sounds, quotes, and analyses in a hypertext, interactive format. In doing so, students can capture and portray their own experiences of media texts for other audiences. You may then evaluate students' reports based on their ability to:

- gather and analyze specific field notes and observations.
- glean audience perceptions of media use through interviews.
- analyze patterns in the data to infer audience stances, attitudes, identities, tastes, or social connections.
- define reasons for audiences' engagement and practices based on their social participation with media.

SUMMARY

In this chapter, I argue that understanding the meaning of media texts requires an understanding of how audiences construct meanings through shared social participation with those texts, for example as members of fan chat sites. Media ethnographers study audiences' responses to media texts through observing and interviewing audiences about their engagement with these texts, as well as how audiences are positioned by texts or social groups to adopt certain responses. Students can conduct their own small-scale media ethnography studies by analyzing audiences' responses in terms of their engagement, interpretations, application of beliefs and attitudes, or identity constructions as fans.

CHAPTER 7

Genres

Key to Topics

IF YOU OPEN UP THE movie advertisement pages of your newspaper or the television program listing, it is more than likely that many of the programs you will see listed are familiar genre texts. Because the commercial film and television industry produces texts primarily to make money, they generally revert to formulaic, prototypical content. However, this does not necessarily mean that all films or TV programs conform to a simple formula. Many films and TV programs play with genre conventions in new and inventive ways. It is therefore important to help students learn to identify the prototypical features of certain genres, and to recognize how genres are continually evolving and how genre texts reflect certain values (Creeber, 2001). Students can then share their genre analyses and critiques. The Website contains links to different genres of television shows (7.1.1) and film genres (7.1.2–6), and a description of genre approaches to the media (7.1.7).

In addition to studying film and television genres, it is useful for students to learn to identity prototypical features in comics, graphic novels, and popular music: forms of media that have much in common with films and TV shows, and often appeal to an adolescent audience. These features are described at the end of this chapter.

CHOOSING AN APPROACH
TO GENRE STUDY

It is useful to consider the different approaches for studying film/television genres, as you think about how to explore this topic with your students.

Formalist/Structuralist

A formalist/structuralist perspective focuses primarily on identifying the components of a particular genre (roles, settings, imagery, plot, themes/values assumptions) that filmmakers draw up on to construct a genre text (Altman, 1995):

- *roles:* roles of hero, heroine, sidekick, alien, monster, criminal, cowboy, mentor, detective, femme fatale, villain, talk show host, etc.
- *settings:* the prototypical setting or world associated with a genre, for example:

   Western: the wide-open vistas of the Western plains/desert, plus a small town
   gangster: dark, urban, back-street settings
   soap opera: indoor, upper-middle-class setting
   spy-thriller: exotic, often urban, international setting
   science fiction: futuristic worlds
   game shows: large studios with a display of lavish prizes

- *imagery and symbols:* prototypical, archetypal images (black = evil vs. white = good) or symbols (the sheriff's badge, water as initiation) associated with a setting or world.
- *plot/storyline:* predictable narrative sequences of events–for example, in a crime drama, the problem/solution structure:

   What is the typical problem?: crime
   Who solves the problem?: the tough cop

   With what means?: violence
   Toward what end?: to show that crime doesn't pay

- *themes/value assumptions* reflected in the text.

In using this approach, students identify the components of, for example, the open, natural setting; the cowboy/sheriff roles; and the problem of crime (bank robbers, cattle rustling). They may then formulate generalizations about a genre based on analysis of several different texts, that, for example, the sidekick role consistently functions to provide the hero with information about the local terrain or town. At the same time, they may also examine, as Henry Jenkins notes, the importance of inventive shifts in a genre that represent new cultural perspectives (7.2.1).

Audience-Based

An audience-based approach assumes that the meaning of a genre lies in the audiences' application of their own knowledge to the conventions of genre construction. Thus, quite different interpretations of the same text are possible. One audience may perceive a movie as an action/adventure film, while another audience may perceive it as a horror film. Using this approach, students can reflect on the processes of applying genre knowledge conventions: that is, *how* audiences construct the meaning of a genre text. These processes can be studied by looking at several interpretations of some television programs by different fan clubs, for instance (7.3.1), and reflecting on how fans' values influence those interpretations (7.3.2). Students might identify and explore some of these processes of genre text construction that audiences engage in, including:

- *predicting story outcomes* based on applying knowledge of prototypical storylines: for example, predicting that at the end of a romantic comedy, differences plaguing a couple's relationship will be resolved.

- *identifying the symbolic meaning of images, techniques, or characters' practices:* for example, knowing that dark images in film noir or a gangster film represent evil.

- *inferring the function or role of the setting or context to explain characters' actions:* for example, that the eerie noise or music in a horror movie is signaling the potential that something dire will occur.

One way to begin this type of study is to have students write their interpretations of a film or other text in journal entries and then reflect on how they constructed these interpretations.

Critical/Ideological

Given their prototypical nature, genre films and television programs generally reflect status-quo values. For example, the "family film" genre reifies traditional notions of the family (7.4.1). In a critical or ideological analysis, students critically examine the normalizing force of genre texts in defining what is considered to be normal based on the need for order, consistency, control, and regularity versus instances of abnormality or deviancy in society (Schirato & Webb, 2004). In my class, students brainstorm what is considered to be a "normal" male, female, father, mother, family, social relationship, teacher, school, or classroom. We then reflect on how these notions of normalcy are mediated by genre texts: for example, how the comedy *School of Rock* (Linklater, 2003), in which students learn to perform rock music, examines notions of what constitutes a normal elementary school classroom.

Students also examine possible reasons for the popularity of certain genres: for example, that during the Great Depression, audiences may have flocked to Hollywood comedies as a means of escape from the realities of their lives. Students also study how audiences challenge these beliefs and attitudes by creating their own alternative versions of genre texts. For example, members of *Star Trek* fan clubs create their own versions of *Star Trek* programs in the form of edited videos or fanzine stories that parody the seriousness of the programs (Jenkins, 1992; 7.4.2).

Students could also analyze how institutional forces use genres to create idealized versions of how problems are solved, who solves the program, and the types of tools employed to solve the problem. Some films about the Vietnam War (*The Green Berets* [Kellogg & Wayne, 1968], for example) portray the "problem" as a lack of military effort, determination, or patriotism, while others portray a failure to understand Vietnamese culture and politics (*Apocalypse Now* [Coppola, 1979], *Born on the Fourth of July* [Stone, 1989], *Full Metal Jacket* [Kubrick, 1987], *Platoon* [Stone, 1986], and *The Deer Hunter* [Cimino, 1978]. These alternative versions of the same problem reflect not only different ideological positions, but also different institutional agendas (7.4.3).

Historical

Students can also study how genres change over time, reflecting changes in the culture or historical period in which the genre is being produced. Since the mid-1990s, increased human resource efforts to improve the quality of the workplace led to the belief in the workplace as "family," as evident in shows such as *The West Wing* (Ensler & Karoll, 1999–2006), *ER* (Crichton, 1994–present), *CSI (Crime Scene Investigation)* (Zuiker, 2000–present), and *Law & Order* (Wolf, 1990–present), in which workplace relationships serve as a substitute for the family.

APPLYING DIFFERENT APPROACHES

In applying these different approaches, students in my class work in small groups to prepare a PowerPoint™ presentation on one genre in which they identify prototypical genre features, audience experiences, and ideological/historical aspects (see sample presentations on the Website: 7.4.3a).

A TEACHING IDEA

ENGAGING STUDENTS IN ACTIVE VIEWING AND THINKING

I wanted my 9th-grade Media Literacy students to think critically about the media and to understand its powerful influences, both positive and negative. We begin by teaching Teasley and Wilder's (1997) six characteristics for analyzing film genre. These characteristics include "setting, characters, plot (both typical conflicts and typical structures), iconography (visual images that appear throughout the history of a genre), mood, and cinematic style" (p. 74). As a class we analyzed a film looking specifically at these aspects. I have used *The Maltese Falcon* (Huston, 1941) as an illustration of the detective genre and *Daddy Day Care* (Carr, 2003), a family comedy, to introduce students to the concepts, patterns, and formulas of these genres. In order to facilitate this activity, I create a table in which I list the six characteristics in the left column. We define these characteristics together, and in the right column students write observations specific to the film we are viewing.

To give students ownership in their own learning, we brainstorm different types of television and film genres. In this exercise alone students begin to see that classification can be difficult, and that not all films or television shows fit neatly into one specific category. Already they are beginning to think critically about classification and labeling. From this list students write their top three choices.

Working within their small groups, students complete a set of three tasks over the next two classes. The first task is to analyze one of their selected genres using the same characteristics we used for our class analysis. The table helps students identify patterns and formulas within their selected genre, and it also serves as the foundation for their presentation to the class. The second task for students is to create a visual in which they can present the aspects of their genre to the rest of the class. Students may create posters, PowerPoint™ presentations, overhead transparencies, or any other visual medium that conveys their analysis. The final task facilitates students' application of their understanding. Each group selects a 15-minute video clip or two 7-minute clips illustrating some of the key aspects of their genre.

One of the most thought-provoking discussions emerged within a group of students studying the reality television genre. The group noticed that the "reality" was actually a result of careful editing and rearranging, designed to heighten interest and provoke drama. The students began talking about *why* editors would want a scene to look a certain way; they had begun to analyze the psychology behind the "reality."

These students were engaging in the type of critical thinking that inspired me to develop and teach this class. Because of the specific genre study, students learned that patterns and formulas exist, and they began to understand that such patterns and formulas are often manipulated and contrived in order to create drama and lure audiences.

Sheila Koenig,
South View Middle School, Edina, Minnesota

DIFFERENT GENRE TYPES

There are not only hundreds of different genre types, but these types also differ between film and television (Creeber, 2001). Film genres (7.5.1–5f) tend to be more general (for example, the Western, action/adventure, comedy, horror, science fiction, etc.), while television genres (7.5.6–8) are often specialized (for example, cooking shows, sports talk shows, children's animation, etc.). A film that is representative of a certain film genre also tends to be self-enclosed; the conflicts are often resolved within the film, even with film sequels. In contrast, a television genre program tends to be serialized, so that a storyline may continue and develop or characters may evolve across many episodes.

The Website contains resources on film/television genres (7.5.9–10) and a site with clips from different genres (7.6.1). One of the best sites is Tim Dirks's website (7.7.1) which provides extensive information about a wide range of different genres.

Action/Adventure

Action or adventure films typically involve high-budget portrayals of main characters engaged in a series of dramatic, dangerous events involving narrow escapes, fights, or rescues, all filmed in a fast-paced style that keeps audiences wondering if the hero or heroine will make it out alive at the end of the film. In films such as *Twister* (Bont, 1996), *Titanic* (Cameron, 1997), *Jurassic Park* (Spielberg, 1993), *Tomorrow Never Dies* (Spottiswoode, 1997), *Armageddon* (Bay, 1998), the *Die Hard* series (Harlin, 1990; McTiernan, 1988, 1995), the *Lethal Weapon* series (Donner, 1987, 1989, 1992, 1998), *Terminator 2* (Cameron, 1991), hyperbolic, sensationalized violence mirrors the violence found in computer games. During the 1990s, films within this genre such as *Last Action Hero* (McTiernan, 1993), *Face/Off* (Woo, 1997), *Con Air* (West, 1997), and *Snake Eyes* (DePalma, 1998), reflected a more postmodern direction toward interrogating the often mindless action of the genre itself (Welsh, 2000). The Website contains sites on action/adventure films (7.7a.1–8).

One of the most important subgenres within action films is the road movie. Examples of this subgenre encompass a wide variety of settings and styles: *Bonnie & Clyde* (Penn, 1967), *Thieves Like Us* (Altman, 1974), *Easy Rider* (Hopper, 1969), *The Wild Ones* (Benedek, 1954), *Badlands* (Malick, 1973), *Grapes of Wrath* (Ford, 1940), *The Wizard of Oz* (Fleming, 1939), *True Romance* (T. Scott, 1993), *Two Lane Blacktop* (Hellman, 1971), *Convoy* (Perkinpah, 1978), *Wild at Heart* (Lynch, 1990), *Two for the Road* (Donen, 1967), *Kalifornia* (Sena, 1993), *Pow Wow Highway* (Wacks, 1989), *Sugarland Express* (Spielberg, 1974), *Natural Born Killers* (Stone, 1994), *Rain Man* (Levinson, 1998), *Smoke Signals* (Eyre, 1998), and *O Brother, Where Art Thou?* (Coen, 2000) (7.7a.9–11). In these movies, characters attempt to escape what they believe are the constraints and limits of society to discover and experience new forms of freedom on the road. In some cases, they are attempting to escape the law or are on a crime spree. The appeal of the road movie reflects the larger cultural need to explore uncharted, new territories as a way of redefining one's identity: for example, the idea of the West as a place in which one could start over as a new person. *Thelma and Louise* (R. Scott, 1991) was an important film in that it challenged the male-dominated nature of the genre by portraying the road quest of two female heroines. The Website contains sites on the action/adventure genre (7.7a.11–19), as well as sites on the TV genre of the anti-terrorism show (7.7a.20–23).

Western

Western films (7.7b.2–5) such as *High Noon* (Zinneman, 1952), *Stagecoach* (Ford, 1939), *Red River* (Hawks & Rosson, 1948), *The Magnificent Seven* (Sturges, 1960), or *Unforgiven* (Eastwood, 1992)–and television shows such as *Bonanza* (Altman & Katzin, 1959–1973), or *Gunsmoke* (Meston, 1955–1975)–are no longer as popular as they were from the 1940s to the 1960s. However, the Western is perhaps a definitive genre in terms of its consistent adherence to the cowboy hero role and the value assumptions associated with the small Western town setting of the last half of the 19th century. The cowboy hero was typically an outsider without geographical or family ties was brought in to deal with a problem (bank robbery, cattle rustling, murder, etc.) because the local sheriff and/or townspeople were unable to cope. This portrayal of the outsider who is not part of the system reflects an ideology of individualism that Ronald Reagan, himself a former actor in Westerns, evoked in running for President: in this case, as the outsider who would clean up and reduce the "Washington bureaucracy." The settings for the Western were often wide-open vistas and landscapes that conveyed the idea of the American West as "free" and without constraints for individual development and exploitation, again reflecting the ideology of individualism (7.7b.1). This focus on the individual hero contrasts with the Japanese samurai films, in which the hero is made up of a collective group designed to protect society. The American hero was cast as the powerful male who could save the female when faced with difficulties. For a 12-minute example, see *The Cowboy and the Ballerina* (7.7b.6).

During the 1970s, more complex variations on the Western hero occurred in films such as Robert Altman's *McCabe and Mrs. Miller* (1971), in which a seemingly powerful male is challenged by an even stronger and smarter female. More recent Westerns, such as *Unforgiven*, have introduced heroes who are more conflicted about the eye-for-an-eye values of the traditional Western, perhaps reflecting post–Cold War ambiguities. The Website contains a webquest on the Western (7.7b.7) and analyses of Western films (7.7b.8–11).

Gangster/Crime

The gangster/crime film (7.7c.1–4) portraying the rise and (usually) fall of the gangster/criminal became popular during the 1930s and 1940s. Films such as *Little Caesar* (LeRoy, 1931) and *Scarface* (Palma, 1983) reflected audiences' fascination with figures such as Gatsby in *The Great Gatsby* (Clayton, 1974) who achieved financial success consistent with the American dream, but did so through illegal means. Then, from the 1970s to the 1990s, the gangster film portrayed the ways in which the gangster operated through alternative, more institutionalized criminal activities associated with drugs, extortion, prostitution, and gambling operations: for example in *The Godfather Parts I, II, III* (Coppola, 1972, 1974a, 1990), *Goodfellas* (Scorsese, 1990), *Miller's Crossing* (Coen & Coen, 1990), *Billy Bathgate* (Benton, 1991), *Bugsy, Casino* (Levinson, 1991), *Prizzi's Honor* (Huston, 1985), *Donnie Brasco* (Newell, 1997), and *Reservoir Dogs* (Tarantino, 1992). More recently, films such as *Pulp Fiction* (Tarantino, 1994), *The Usual Suspects* (Singer, 1995), *Fargo* (Coen & Coen, 1996), and *Jackie Brown* (Tarantino, 1997), and the television series *The Sopranos* (Chase, 1999–present) reflect a more ironic, postmodern stance, combining comic and psychological elements with a portrayal of crime.

The setting for the gangster film has typically been that of a dark, urban world. The film noir films of the 1940s particularly, such as *The Maltese Falcon* (Huston, 1941) and *The Big Sleep* (Winner, 1978) used images of dark, back-alley, urban worlds to portray the world of crime. The role of darkness as associated with criminal activity was reflected in the opening sequences of both *The Godfather* and *The Godfather, Part II* (Coppola, 1972, 1974a). In the beginning scenes, there are large outdoor parties in which guests are enjoying themselves, scenes bathed in a bright whiteness. These "out-front" party scenes are contrasted with dark back-room dealings of *The Godfather*'s main characters, played by Marlon Brando and Al Pacino, as they grant favors or order executions. The Website contains sites on gangster/crime films (7.7c.5–7), as well as links to discussions of *The Sopranos* series (7.7c.8–11).

Crime

The crime genre (7.7d.1–2) focuses on the problem of the violation of the law, determining reasons for the violation, identifying possible violators, relying on informants and evidence, coping with mishaps and false leads, revealing the actual violator, and restoring a sense of equilibrium (Miller, 2001). The 1940s and 1950s crime genre, based on detective novels by such writers as Dashiell Hammett and Raymond Chandler, portrayed the often corrupt world of institutions of law and order: examples include *The Maltese Falcon* (Huston, 1941), , *Double Indemnity* (Wilder, 1944), *The Killers* (Siodmak, 1946), *Notorious* (Hitchcock, 1946), *Key Largo* (Huston, 1948), *The Lady from Shanghai* (Welles, 1947), *The Third Man* (Reed, 1949), *Sunset Blvd.* (Wilder, 1950), *The Big Heat* (Lang, 1953), and *Lady in the Lake* (Montgomery, 1947). These films, usually made in black and white with low lighting, interior settings, and inventive camera techniques, convey a sense of bleak, cynical pessimism.

The crime genre, then and now, also focuses on the character of the often cynical, worldly detective figure (7.7d.6–8). In general, detectives and police on television (7.7d.3–8)—in shows such as *CSI (Crime Scene Investigation)* (Zuiker, 2000–present), *Homicide: Life on the Street* (Attanasio, 1993–1999), or *Law & Order* (Wolf, 1990–present)—tend to be less cynical, and the tone of the shows is more optimistic. Here, the main character of the detective is developed in more detail across the series, so that audiences establish a relationship with the character. The Website contains sites on the crime genre (7.7d.9–17).

Comedy

There are a number of different comedy subgenres that vary according to differences in the comic techniques employed (7.7e.1–10).

Mime. Early film comedy that emerged in the silent film era focused on nonverbal pantomime, in which exaggeration and physical dexterity functioned as comic elements. Early stars of this genre were Charlie Chaplin, Harold Lloyd, and Buster Keaton. In Charlie Chaplin's films, he typically employed sight gags to ridicule and challenge social norms, particularly the pretentiousness of the powerful. As such, he represented the "little guy" in society who is able to use his skills to assert his own power.

Slapstick. Slapstick involves blatant, overt physical pranks—such as slipping on a banana peel or attempting to carry a piano up steep stairs—as evident in the early films of Abbott and Costello, Laurel and Hardy, and The Three Stooges. In later films such as the *Pink Panther* (Edwards, 1963) series, or those starring Jerry Lewis or Jim Carrey, verbal repartee was added to the mix.

Parody/Satire. Films by Woody Allen, Mel Brooks, and the Marx Brothers engage in parody or ridicule of institutions, traditional social norms, and other genres. In the Woody Allen films—such as *Bananas* (1971), *Sleeper* (1973), *Annie Hall* (1977), *Manhattan* (1979), *Zelig* (1983), *The Purple Rose of Cairo* (1983), *Hannah and Her Sisters* (1985), *Husbands and Wives* (1992), and *Bullets Over Broadway* (1994)—Allen uses witty dialogue to mimic and parody different discourses of therapy, religion, business, sports, and academia. Television shows such as *Monty Python's Flying Circus* (Chapman et al., 1969–1974) and *Saturday Night Live* (Michaels, 1975–present) consist of sketches ridiculing a range of topics, including various television genres. The Website contains links on parody (7.7e.11–12) and Woody Allen (7.7e.12–18), and a webquest on parody (7.7e.19).

Situation Comedy. Television situation comedies have made up a large bulk of prime-time television since the 1950s, with shows such as *I Love Lucy* (Asher, Daniels, & Kern, 1951–1957) or *Cheers* (Burrows, Charles, & Charles, 1982–1993) (Dalton & Linder, 2005).

In the typical comedy storyline, there is a movement from equilibrium to disequilibrium—associated with disruptions and confusions over mixed identities—and then back to equilibrium, leading to a happy ending in which challenges to institutional equilibrium are mitigated and society is restored.

The roles in comedy are typically one-dimensional prototypes, as opposed to tragic characters who are complex and contradictory. There is often a "buffoon" who is oblivious to what's going on, a "straight man" who serves as an audience for the main character's comic lines, a "trickster" who creates pranks, and a "wise elder" who straightens out problems or issues, leading to resolution.

Romantic Comedy. Romantic comedy—including films such as *Groundhog Day* (Ramis, 1993), *My Best Friend's Wedding* (Hogan, 1997), *Four Weddings and a Funeral* (Newell, 1994), *When Harry Met Sally* (Reiner, 1989), *Sixteen Candles* (Hughes, 1984), *Moonstruck* (Jewison, 1987), *Sleepless in Seattle* (Ephron, 1993), *Clueless* (Heckerling, 1995), *Notting Hill* (Michell, 1999), and *While You Were Sleeping* (Turteltaub, 1995)—has remained one of the most popular genres since the heyday of the Hollywood studio system in the 1930s; *Some Like it Hot*, released in 1954, was rated the funniest film on the American Film Institute's list, created in 2004.

In romantic comedy, a couple is coping with challenges to their relationship. One popular storyline: a lover suspects that their beloved has not been faithful in the relationship, but then the two characters discover their true love for each other, leading to a resolution and often marriage. The underlying value assumption is that the traditional family/love relationship is a viable institutional norm.

In another variation on this basic storyline, the female heroine becomes involved with a standoffish, impersonal male who has difficulty knowing how to express his feelings for the heroine (Radway, 1991), as reflected in the film and television adaptations of the Jane Austen novels *Pride and Prejudice* (Wright, 2005), *Sense and Sensibility* (Lee, 1995), and *Emma* (McGrath, 1996), or *Clueless* (Heckerling, 1995), a modern adaptation of *Emma*. (By contrast, in tragic romance films—such as *Love Story* (Hiller, 1970), *Fatal Attraction* (Lyne, 1987), *The House of Mirth* (Davies, 2000), *The Bridges of Madison County* (Eastwood, 1995), *The English Patient* (Minghella, 1996), *The End of the Affair* (Jordan, 1999), *Titanic* (Cameron, 1997), *Romeo & Juliet* (Zeffirelli, 1968), and *Jungle Fever* (Lee, 1991)—the heroine/hero seeks forbidden love, thereby violating social norms associated with class, race, religion, or family ties.

Ironic/Critical Comedy. There are a number of comedy films—including *M*A*S*H* (Altman, 1970), *Dr. Strangelove* (Kubrick, 1964), *Men in Black* (Sonnenfeld, 1997), *Working Girl* (Nichols, 1988), *The Truman Show* (Weir, 1998), *The Full Monty* (Cattaneo, 1997), *The Van* (Frears, 1996), *Lost in America* (A. Brooks, 1985), *Broadcast News* (J. L. Brooks, 1987), *Raising Arizona* (Coen & Coen, 1987), *Fargo* (Coen & Coen, 1996), *Life Is Beautiful* (Benigni, 1997), and *Pleasantville* (Ross, 1998)—that contain comic elements, but also raise larger questions about the breakdown of institutions. For example, films such as *The Truman Show* and *Pleasantville* raise questions about media constructions of reality and the blurred distinction between a media reality and a lived-world reality. The Website contains many links on the comedy genre (7.7e.20–34).

Science Fiction/Fantasy

Science fiction and fantasy (7.7f.1–11) are related in that both involve audiences in the experience of alternative worlds and ways of thinking (Barron, 2004). Through the experience of these alternative perspectives, audiences may return to their lived-world experience with new, alternative, creative insights. In both genres, audiences need to be able to suspend their disbelief and momentarily enter into an alternative world without imposing reality-bound assumptions.

The fantasy genre focuses more on the mythic, magical quest journey in which the "good" heroes confront various challenges associated with "evil," challenges that test their tenacity, particularly in the final challenge (Abanes, 2005). Many of the fantasy heroes are loners or orphans who come out of obscurity to become heroes (Scott, 2002). In *The Lord of the Rings: The Fellowship of the Ring* (Jackson, 2001), Frodo Baggins lives alone in a rural village until he is summoned to lead a group to face a whole series of bizarre, supernatural creatures and worlds, each requiring him and his companions to outwit the enemy in the land of Mordor. In the *Harry Potter* film series (Columbus, 2001, 2002; Cuarón, 2004; Newell, 2005), Harry is an orphan who lives with his abusive aunt and uncle.

A. O. Scott (2002) notes that the appeal of fantasy is based on the nostalgic, conservative desire for the restoration of innocence and goodness in a world perceived as cynical, corrupt, evil, and complex. Fantasy worlds revolve around simplistic binary distinctions between good and evil, in which the good ultimately triumphs. And, Scott notes, the hero triumphs not through greater physical prowess, but through his knowledge of specific details, outwitting the enemy. Again, this focus on insider knowledge appeals to outsider, loner audiences who have acquired detailed, seemingly useless knowledge and fantasy lore. This appeal is socially manifested in audience participation in fan clubs (7.7f.13–14) in which knowledge about a particular fantasy establishes one's identity in fan chat rooms, fanzines, and conventions.

In the science fiction genre, as in the horror genre, there is a fascination with the unknown, alien "other" portrayed as a threat to civilization. There is also an uneasy ambiguity associated with the idea that our own technological advances may serve to be destructive. The types of aliens have shifted in association with different real-life threats in different decades. In the 1950s, fear of the presumed pervasive Communist threat was manifested in the fact that alien invaders were "out there" but invisible. Some films, such as *Invasion of the Body Snatchers* (Kaufman, 1978), challenged the cultural conformity associated with the 1950s, as did *Fahrenheit 451* (Truffaut, 1966) in the 1960s and *A Clockwork Orange* (Kubrick, 1971) in the 1970s. With the rise of technological advances in the 1960s, 1970s, and 1980s, the alien threats took the form of technology gone amok: nuclear disasters, mutant insects, computer breakdowns, skyscraper fires, and so forth.

In the 1990s, the threat of environmental destruction, epidemic diseases, mind control, and genetic manipulation was reflected in films such as *Twelve Monkeys* (Gilliam, 1995), *Contact* (Zemeckis, 1997), *The Matrix* (Wachowski & Wachowski, 1999), and *Gattaca* (Niccol, 1997). Since 2000, films such as *The Day After Tomorrow* (Emmerich, 2004), depicting the apocalyptic flooding of cites, reflect concerns with global warming.

Television series (7.7f.15–17)–such as *Star Trek* (Roddenberry, 1966–1969/1987–1994), *Babylon 5* (Straczynski, 1994–1998), or *Firefly* (Davies & Edlund, 2002–2004)–also focus on characters facing challenges, often mixing elements of science fiction and horror.

The effects of changes in science/technology on society, as well as unexplained paranormal psychological events (time travel, mind control, and alien abduction) are the subject of science fiction films such as *Outbreak* (Petersen, 1995), *12 Monkeys* (Gilliam, 1995), *Men in Black* (Sonnenfeld, 1997), *The Matrix* (Wachowski & Wachowski, 1999), and *Minority Report* (Spielberg, 2002a), and television series such as *The Twilight Zone* (Froug, 1959–1964), *Dr. Who* (Newman, 1963–1989), and *The X-Files* (Amann, 1993–2002). In many cases, the technological advances portrayed in science fiction films portend actual advances that later occur. One interesting site compares the technology portrayed in Stanley Kubrick's *2001: A Space Odyssey*, made in 1968, and the actual technology of 2001 (7.7f.18). The Website contains sites on fantasy computer games (7.7f.19), science fiction (7.7f. 20–23), courses in science fiction (7.7f.24–25), webquests/lesson plans (7.7f.26–35), a bibliography (7.7f.36), and organizations/further resources related to science fiction (7.7f.37–47).

Horror/Monster

The horror/monster genre is very popular among adolescents (7.7g.1–3). Examples include the films *Godzilla* (Emmerich, 1998), *The Night of the Living Dead* (Romero, 1968), *Silence of the Lambs* (Demme, 1991), *Cape Fear* (Scorsese, 1991), *The Texas Chainsaw Massacre* (Hooper, 1974), *Jaws* (Spielberg, 1975), *The Shining* (Kubrick, 1980), *Scream* (Craven, 1996), *Scream 2* (Craven, 1997), *I Know What You Did Last Summer* (Gillespie, 1997), *The Blair Witch Project* (Myrick & Sánchez, 1999), and the television series *Buffy the Vampire Slayer* (Whedon, 1997–2003) (7.7g.5).

These films and television programs revolve around a fear of death, which is manifested in the zombies, vampires such as Count Dracula (7.7g.6–7),

werewolves, devils, witches, mutant insects, and monsters who threaten to take over and destroy a family, community, or world. The horror/monster genre creates an initial sense of stability associated with a realistic portrayal of a familiar, everyday world that an audience associates with their own world, stability that is then disrupted by an attack that implies that we are all mortal and susceptible to destruction. In the classic horror film *The Night of the Living Dead* (Romero, 1968), an innocent couple is out driving in a rural area when suddenly the female is attacked by a group of zombies who have come back from the dead and need to destroy humans to survive. The zombies represent not only potential destruction, but also the loss of identity/humanity associated with death.

One of the most important of the horror directors was Alfred Hitchcock, whose films *Psycho* (1960) and *The Birds* (1963) employed innovative techniques to create a sense of horrific suspense in audiences. More recent horror/monster "slasher" films such as *Halloween* (Carpenter, 1978) and *Friday the 13th* (Cunningham, 1980) employ less subtle graphic portrayals of murder and are marketed to adolescent audiences through sensationalized trailers and ads. See the Webiste for additional sites on horror films (7.7g.9–17).

From an audience analysis perspective, students could discuss whether viewing violent horror films has a negative influence on attitudes and behaviors related to violence, and debate the extent to which adolescents are capable of constructing their own alternative meanings of these texts.

Suspense Thriller/Spy/Heist

A genre related to the action, mystery, detective, and even horror film genre is the suspense thriller/spy/heist film, featuring plots in which the audience is never quite sure if a main character will successfully escape being harmed or will succeed on a dangerous mission, or, in the case of the heist film, pull off the heist (7.7h.1–5). Alfred Hitchcock was the master of the suspense thriller. He placed his characters, as in *North by Northwest* (1959) or *Rear Window* (1954), in situations in which they are continually confronting death as their enemies seek to murder them (7.7h.6–12)

The spy genre involves a similar complication in which the spy is placed in dangerous situations in which his true identity as a spy may be exposed. The spy hero must also employ many of the nefarious techniques of the enemy to survive (7.7h.13–14), as in the James Bond series (7.7h.15–20).

The heist genre (7.7h.21), including films such as *The Thomas Crown Affair* (McTiernan, 1999), *Goodfellas* (Scorsese, 1990), *The Grifters* (Frears, 1990), and *Catch Me If You Can* (Spielberg, 2000b), typically involves imaginative attempts to pull off a highly challenging robbery in which it seems as if things will go awry (7.7h.22–25).

Soap Opera

The television soap opera genre (7.7i.1–3) is best characterized by its ongoing, open-ended serial narrative development that engages audiences with its good and evil characters and melodramatic, emotional conflicts in ways that keeps them tuning in week after week.

In a soap opera, dramatic events are built around talk—arguments, lies, shouting matches, gossip, accusations, false promises—associated with a range of complex relationships within and across families and social networks. Underlying these events are ethical dilemmas, usually revolving around whether certain social norms have been violated: norms that are continually being interrogated as society changes.

One variation of the soap opera popular with Latinos is the Spanish-language *telenovela* series, produced in Latin America and distributed on the Univision and Telemundo networks. In contrast to American soaps, these programs portray issues of poverty and crime, although in an equally melodramatic manner (Navarro, 2005), and they come to some final resolution.

An important component of soap opera is the highly active, loyal audience base, as manifested in the multitude of soap opera fan clubs (7.7i.4–7). These clubs provide information about episodes audiences may have missed, speculate about what may or should happen to characters, and discuss the actors and actresses. See the Website for links on teaching about soap opera (7.7i.8–22)

The Talk Show

The television talk show (7.7j.1–8) consists of four different subgenres:

1. morning talk: shows such as the *Today Show* (Michaels & Monemvassitis, 1952–present), *Good Morning America* (Funk, Goodman, & Monemvassitis, 1975–present), and the *Early Show* (King, 1999–present).

2. day time talk: some of these are characterized as "tabloid" or "confessional" (Shattuc, 2001) talk shows.

3. prime-time/late-night talk: some current examples are *Larry King Live* (Douthit, 1985–present), *The Tonight Show with Jay Leno* (Brown & Price, 1992–present), *The Late Show with David Letterman* (Foley & Grossack, 1993–present), *Late Night with Conan O'Brien* (Calderwood & Kartun, 1993–present), and *Charlie Rose* (Charlie Rose, Inc., 1991–present).

4. political talk: shows such as *Meet the Press* (Russert, 1947–present) and *Face the Nation* (Schieffer, 1954–present).

Students could analyze how talk show hosts vary their ways of addressing multiple audiences—the immediate guest(s), the studio audience, and the larger viewing audience—as well as how guests often use the show to promote films, books, or music. They could study how daytime "tabloid" or "confessional" shows such as *The Jerry Springer Show* (Klazura, 1991–present) are designed to deliberately promote conflicts between participants, often resulting in arguments, taunts, and physical fights (Shattuc, 2001).

Similarly, political talk shows (7.7j.9) often dramatize conflicts in a manner that reflects what Deborah Tannen (1999) characterizes as the "argument culture," in which one-upping one's opponents is valued more than enlightening an audience on an issue.

Radio Talk Shows

Talk shows on public radio (7.7j.10–19) such as National Public Radio programs, *Car Talk,* or *Talk of the Nation* are often more substantive because they are not influenced by a visual format or by commercial forces. At the same time, the majority of commercial talk radio hosts reflect politically conservative perspectives, reflecting these shows' popularity.

Sports

Television coverage of sports, films about sports, and sports talk shows constitutes a major genre in terms of audience size. Particularly large are the audiences for championship sports coverage of the *World Series, Superbowl, Final Four, NBA Championships, Stanley Cup, World Cup, Triple Crown, Indianapolis 500,* and other major competitions. These sports championships—many of which are annual events—can be thought of as media events (Dayan & Katz, 1992), in which the techniques, commentary, and promotion hype the broadcast as a special, unusual event "that we have all been waiting for."

Television sports coverage combines two competing genre forms: journalism, which attempts to provide background information about players, coaches, policies, contract negotiations, and strategies; and promotion, which attempts to dramatize sports around conflicts between teams (Brookes, 2001) and emphasizes the theme of succeeding against all odds. The latter also serves as the basis for many sports films. such as *Raging Bull* (Scorsese, 1980), the *Rocky* films (Avildsen, 1976, 1990; Stallone, 1979, 1982, 1985), *Major League* (Ward, 1989), *White Men Can't Jump* (Shellton, 1992), and *Remember the Titans* (Yakin, 2000). An unusual film in this genre is *Hoop Dreams* (James, 1994; 7.7k.1). This documentary about two African-American high school basketball stars depicts the institutional forces of the media, sports equipment industry, competitive high school/college sports programs, and false beliefs about "making it" in professional sports.

Sports coverage is also highly gendered; incidents of violence in hockey or football are often rationalized by commentators with a "boys will be boys" discourse of masculinity (7.7k.2). Also, while males are usually portrayed in ways that focus upon their physical skills and strength (7.7k.3–10), females are often portrayed in ways that focus upon their appearance and attractiveness, rather than their athletic abilities,

One of the more popular subgenres of television sports is professional wrestling (7.7k.11–15), particularly among adolescent males, who often make their own backyard video versions that mimic the shows. Students could discuss how promotions and commentary about matches define wrestlers' identities or reputations as "good" or "bad" as part of the melodramatic narrative structures of these matches (Jenkins, 1997).

Another subgenre is the "outdoors" television show (7.7k.16–18), related to providing useful information about hunting, fishing, camping, hiking, and gardening, as well as the sports talk show (7.7k.19–20) that promote sports stars and teams (7.7k.21). The Website contains lessons on analyzing sports shows (7.7k.22–24), as well as blogs on audience reaction to them (7.7k.25–29).

Game Shows/Reality Television

Game shows (7.7l.1–3) began in the 1950s with shows such as *The $64,000 Question* (Carlin, 1955–

1958), which ultimately went off the air due to scandals associated with providing contestants with answers (the subject of the movie *Quiz Show* [Redford, 1994]). One of the underlying appeals of this genre is the idea that "anyone can win": that someone can walk in from off the street and win large sums of money. This is consistent with the consumerist, capitalist discourse of "winning" in life through acquiring consumer goods.

The similarly competitive "reality television" shows (7.7l.4–8) of the early 2000s such as *Big Brother* (Hepworth & Downing, 2000–2006) and *Survivor* (Burnett, 2000–present) built on the earlier "trauma TV" quasi-documentary shows such as *America's Most Wanted* (Abascal & Brown, 1988–present), which employ camcorder/"actual footage" portrayal of "real" events, first-person narratives, reconstruction of "actual" events, and commentators' voice-overs (Dovey, 2001). One reason for the popularity of these shows is that they are relatively inexpensive to create and involve a high level of conflict between participants, which producers highlight in their editing of content to heighten the drama. One subgenre of reality television is the historical reality TV show, in which participants agree to live as people lived in the past and to be filmed as they do so: for example, in a London house based on life in the year 1900 in *1900 House* (McCarthy, 2000; 7.7l.9) or in Montana in 1883 as in *Frontier House* (Hoppe & Shaw, 2002; 7.7l.10).

Underlying these shows is a basic assumption that the events portrayed are a depiction of "reality," with people breaking down under stress; in fact, the "reality" portrayed is often highly edited, and even staged, in order to show more dramatic moments of what may be disappointingly uneventful lives. These shows also assume that reality entails a highly competitive set of relationships between people: a social Darwinian survival of the fittest in which there are always winners and losers. Students could discuss some of the ethical aspects of operating in these highly competitive situations (7.7l.10a). At the same time, one of the appeals of these shows is that they portray people talking about their own lives. The Website contains additionnal links on reality TV (7.7k.11–23)

Animation

While animation as a film technique was discussed in Chapter 3, it is also important to examine animated films and television programs as a genre (7.7m.1–3). One primary aspect of animation is the metamorphosis of images in which animals, people, birds, trees, plants, and houses are transformed and personified as humans, and vice versa, as in these classic animation films: *Snow White and the Seven Dwarfs* (Sears & Creedon, 1937), *Beauty and the Beast* (Trousdale & Wise, 1991), *Pinocchio* (Luske & Sharpsteen, 1940), *Bambi* (Hand, 1946), *Aladdin* (Clements & Musker, 1992), *Sleeping Beauty* (Geronimi, 1959), *Cinderella* (Geronimi & Jackson, 1950), *The Many Adventures of Winnie the Pooh* (Lounsberg & Reitherman, 1977), and *Peter Pan* (Geronimi & Jackson, 1953). In studying these films, students could trace the transformation of the original fairy tales, with their dark foreboding nature, into these often highly sanitized and cheerful animations. They could also examine the representations of gender, class, and race in these films. In his analysis of these films, Henry Giroux (2001; 7.7m.4) posits that the female main characters in *The Little Mermaid* (Clements & Musker, 1989), *Beauty and the Beast*, and *Pocahontas* (Gabriel & Goldberg, 1995) all adopt subordinate gender roles consistent with patriarchic values. Giroux also identifies instances of racist portrayals in *Aladdin*, in which the villains have Arabic physical features and accents: an example of what Edward Said (1978) calls "Orientalism"—the Euro-American representation of the Arab world in deficit terms as foreign, bizarre, exotic, mysterious, quasi-barbaric, and deceitful. In *The Lion King* (Allers & Minkoff, 1994), the evil lion Scar is portrayed as both physically and thematically darker than the other lions. While the royal family speaks in British accents, the hyena stormtroopers speak in Black dialect. In all of these examples, being White and male is assumed to be the privileged norm against which "others" are subordinated; presumably, this stance has proved effective in appealing to a traditional White, middle-class conservative American audience.

Students could conduct analyses of Saturday morning cartoon television shows (7.7m.5) in terms of their portrayals of characters' gender and race; many of these shows continue to be sexist and largely White. The shows *The Simpsons* (Groening, 1989–present), *South Park* (Parker, Stone, & Stough, 1997–present), and *King of the Hill* (Daniels & Judge, 1997–present) reflect a more cynical, irreverent stance on contemporary society, as well as a critique of the economic decline of the working-class family, the lack of educational and employment opportunities, and contemporary media culture (Kellner, 2000). The Website contains sites on various aspects of the animation genre (7.7m.6–14), as well as blogs on animation (7.7m.15–18).

COMICS AND GRAPHIC NOVELS

As previously noted, in addition to analyzing prototypical features of film/television genres, students can also analyze prototypical features of comics and graphic novels (Cary, 2004; McCloud, 1994; 7.7n.1–5). Students could examine the rise of some of the major comic books publishers—DC, Marvel, Disney, Archie, Dark Horse, Image Comics—and how they each established their own unique styles; for example, the Marvel comic book style of Spiderman (7.7n.6–11). Students could also examine databases of comics to examine historical trends in the shifting development of comics (7.7n.12–20).

Students could also study the artistic aspects of comic book design by analyzing the use of technical aspects of blocking, shifting between blocks, visual display, lines, dialogue balloons, story summaries, and so forth, related to the development of storylines and characters in online comics (7.7n.21–23). They can then construct their own comic books using online resources, fonts, and images (7.7n.24–32) or the Apple program ComicLife™.

The Website contains a useful online book by Robyn Hill about the appeal of comics to students, and how to help students analyze these appeals (7.7n.33), as well as reviews and journals related to comics (7.7n.34–57).

Related to the comic book is the graphic novel, whose popularity in the past 20 years has increased dramatically (Graff, 2003). Probably the best-known graphic novel is Art Spiegelman's *Maus*, which portrays the world of a Polish-Jewish ghetto during World War II in a comic format (7.7o.1). Graphic novels combine the visual material of comic books with the novel form, and tend to be written for an adolescent audience, although a lot of graphic novels are popular with upper elementary school students. Moreover, readers of all ages have shown an increased interest in *manga*, Japanese comics, particularly manga for adolescent females published by Viz Media, Tokyopop, and Del Rey, including serialization in *CosmoGirl* (Glazer, 2005). The Website contains more information on graphic novels (7.7o.2), online graphic novels (7.7o.3–10), graphic novel lists (7.7o.11–12), reviews (7.7o.13–16A), and teaching about graphic novels (7.7o.17 –22).

POPULAR MUSIC

In my class, we identify the characteristics of particular music genres by sampling 10-second clips from the genre catalogue on iTunes™. Students can analyze features unique to rock, soul, blues, country, Cajun, calypso, gospel, punk, heavy metal, hip-hop, and rap. (The Website contains its own separate modules on music genres with unnumbered links that expand on the summaries of music genres in this text). We also explore the relationships between certain music genres and the historical and cultural forces influencing the development of these genres: for example, how the blues and later rock evolved from African-American experiences with slavery, and how rap became a means of expressing political resistence to institutional racism (Chang, 2005).

We examine how music itself serves to voice political perspectives, as portrayed in the PBS documentary *Get Up, Stand Up* (7.8.1). Based on the PBS documentary *Hearing Between the Lines* (7.8.2), we analyze how song lyrics portray themes of self-esteem, body image, and eating disorders. Students then bring in songs representing specific genres, and as the class listens to these examples, they describe the genre features evident in a song. Consistent with the idea of music autobiographies discussed in Chapter 6, they also share their autobiographical recollections of how certain songs or musicians shaped their attitudes and identities.

SUMMARY

In studying the prototypical features of different film/television genres, as well as those of comics, graphic novels, and popular music, students are learning to understand how these features not only reflect historical and cultural forces, but also shape perceptions of these forces. With this understanding, they are better able to critique the ideological aspects inherent in these features.

CHAPTER 8

Advertising

Key to Topics

ADVERTISING IS UBIQUITOUS. It surrounds us: on billboards, sports arenas, television, clothes, movie theaters, and websites, as well as in magazines, newspapers, video games, and DVDs, and as product placements in films and television. Its profusion is predictable in a consumer culture that transforms objects and experiences into desired commodities.

To help students critically analyze advertising, it is important that they frame advertising within the larger context of a consumer culture. In that culture, advertising can be used as part of larger promotion of ideas, images, values, and beliefs that go beyond just products: a form of propaganda to convince people to act or believe in certain ways.

A BROADER DEFINITION OF ADVERTISING INSTRUCTION

In studying advertising, students are focusing on more than television or magazine ads. They are studying all aspects of marketing, merchandising, promotion, sponsorship, and branding associated with being members of a consumer culture. Moreover, they are examining larger issues of consumption associated with environmental impact as well as construction of values and identities in a consumer society. Sut Jhally, in his video *Advertising and the End of the World* (1997; for a video clip, see 8.2.1) argues that the problem with a reliance on consumption is that creating and using consumer goods continues to not only use up the natural resources of oil, water, wood, iron ore, natural gas, coal, minerals, and the land, but also creates pollution. through their use. For example, advertising creates a perceived need to own a car to the point that everyone believes that they need to have one. The more cars that are built and sold, the more resources are used to build the cars, and the more cars are crowding highways and polluting the air, particularly those that are not energy-efficient. As a growing number of countries become consumer economies, natural resources will be depleted and global warming and ecological devastation will follow. By 2070, Jhally estimates, the depletion of materials and water will reach a crisis point and climate change will render much of the planet unlivable (8.2.2–5).

ADVERTISING IN A CONSUMER CULTURE

Understanding advertising therefore requires an understanding of the larger capitalist economic system. In the past, the economy was built simply on an exchange of goods in which the focus was on production and distribution of goods between individuals based on basic needs for food, housing, and health. Advertising during the 19th and early 20th centuries focused primarily on providing information as to how a product served these basic needs. An ad for Arm & Hammer Baking Soda™ simply described the functional uses for baking soda. After World War II, with the rise of a consumer economy, in which products or goods are consumed for more than just meeting basic needs, the focus shifted to consumption as active work involved in defining one's identity and social relationships, consumption that influences global economies and markets (Miller, 1997). Thus, during the past century, advertising moved from simply providing information about a product to associating uses of that product with social status and identity, as well as the promotion of brand images.

Stuart Ewen (1999, 2001) argues that contemporary consumer culture emphasizes the importance of one's social image—how one appears to others—as related to a perceived lifestyle. Advertisers work by associating the use of certain products with a certain image: as hip, cool, sophisticated, or classy. Wearing the "right" kind of clothes or owning certain "in" products serves to mark an individual as having allegiances to certain social status groups. To guide and socialize consumers in making these choices, businesses spend billions of dollars to equate certain lifestyles or identities with certain brand images: for example, linking images of upper-middle-class life with owning a Cadillac™ or wearing Christian Dior™ clothes. The meaning of being a certain kind of person is therefore equated with a meaning system of signs, images, and cultural codes constructed by the advertising industry.

Students could trace shifts in advertising techniques from direct to more indirect persuasive techniques by going to the Library of Congress exhibit "50 Years of Coke Ads" (8.2.5a) or the history of Pepsi ads (8.2.5b). The Website contains sites related to analyzing the history of advertising (8.2.6–28), a minicourse on advertising (8.2.29), and other resources on advertising analysis (8.2.30–39).

ADVERTISING AS THE SOURCE OF MEDIA CONTENT

Advertising often drives the content of commercial television, radio, and magazines rather than the reverse. The content itself is simply filler designed to sell the ads by attracting certain types of viewers or readers who will also be exposed to ads geared for a certain demographic. As veteran television journalist Ted Koppel (Kurtz, 2005) notes, "We exist to put commercials on the air. The programming that is put on between those commercials is simply the bait we put in the mousetrap" (p. c1).

Much of the content of prime-time television is geared for the 18–49-year-old market, who presumably are all engaged in purchasing the products advertised, although the older market has more disposable income (8.3.1). Because ads create the need for targeted audience content, advertisers and content producers pitch their ads to appeal to certain demographic categories (Ang, 1991). For example, the 18–34-year-old male audience is the target for beer, cars, sports promotion (8.3.1a), and computer games advertising, which usually appears on programs that will attract this audience: sports, wrestling, MTV.

The style of advertising also shapes the *style* of content. Critics such as Mark Miller (1990) argue that Hollywood films have actually become more like commercials in their use of high-speed editing and flashy shots, because of an assumption that audiences used to fast-paced ads will not pay attention to slow-moving, traditional cinematography. Magazines and newspapers contain more short, "catchy" articles that are often difficult to distinguish from the ads. (For a lesson on analyzing *Seventeen* magazine, see 8.3.1b.)

However, some recent research suggests that adolescents are not as influenced by ads that equate using a product with social status because they are less interested than previously thought in using brand names and logos to define their identities (8.3.1c–1f).

SOCIALIZATION OF CHILDREN AS CONSUMERS

From their earliest years, children are barraged with ads and socialized to learn brand names; their desire for material goods is continually nourished (8.4.1; Linn, 2004; Schor, 2004; for a unit on branding, see 8.4.1a). Children's television shows contain numerous ads pitching fast food, toys, dolls, and sports items. Based on research that indicated that children under age eight are not capable of critically responding to advertising and therefore tend to accept their messages, the American Psychological Association recommended that restrictions be placed on advertising geared for children, particularly in terms of fast food marketing (8.4.2).

British children view 20,000 commercials a year, including 1,150 junk food television commercials (8.4.3). While it is difficult to prove a cause-and-effect relationship between advertising and obesity, the obesity rate for children in the U.K. has increased by 25% from 1995 to 2003 and affects 1 in 10 six-year-olds. Under the assumption that advertising may be harmful to their health, the Australian government does not allow advertising in preschool programs, limits advertising to 5 minutes for every 30 minutes of children's television, and places restrictions on the content of that advertising (8.4.4). In his documentary, *Supersize Me* (2000), Morgan Spurlock documents the dangerous effects of eating only at McDonald's™ restaurants for a month. In his book *Don't Eat This Book* (Spurlock, 2005), he notes that the U.S. National Schools Lunch Program (NSLP) serves high-fat school lunches to millions of children by using farmers' surpluses that would normally be spoilage. The Website contains sites on the influence of advertising on increased consumption (8.4.5–11).

SEMIOTIC ANALYSIS

As noted in Chapter 4, semiotic analysis focuses on the meaning of images or signs in advertising based on a code system. A diamond is not simply a rock: it is a commodity sign for love. Robert Goldman (1992) cites the example of perfumes:

> Purchasing the right perfume means that a woman will not only acquire a particular odor at a particular price but "a gorgeous, sexy, young, fragrance." A customer will, in consuming the product, acquire the qualities of being gorgeous, sexy, and young? No, she acquires a sign of being gorgeous, sexy, young. It is the look we have come to desire; and the *look* we desire is the *object of desire*. People thus become a kind of *tabula rasa*, a slate filled with desired attributes by the objects they consume; the object becomes an active agent capable of doing all the things that a gorgeous, sexy and young person can do. (p. 24)

See the website for additional semiotic analyses of magazine ads for men's fragrances by Alexander Clare (8.5.1) and food advertising tricks (8.5.2).

Greg Myers (1999, pp. 19–20) identifies four systems or "p's" of marketing that serve to constitute the meanings associated with these brands: product, placement, promotion, and price.

1. *Product.* The nature of the product, as well as the packaging and presentation of the product—for example, ads may describe the unique ways in which a beer is brewed.
2. *Placement.* How products are placed and displayed in a store in order to make certain brand names prominent in a store.
3. *Promotion.* How brands are promoted through various advertising techniques.
4. *Price.* How brands are promoted in terms of being a "good value," or in terms of customers' willingness to pay a premium price.

Students could describe the meanings they associate with the following popular brand names (or others of your choosing) and how they acquired those meanings in terms of Myers's four "p's": Haagen-Dazs™, Sprite™, iPod™, McDonald's™, Saturn™, Rolex™, Wal-Mart™, Nike™, and Campbell's™. The meanings of these brand names are carefully crafted through public relations campaigns to create positive images for products, companies, industries, or organizations. This includes creating logos that are readily identifiable and that evoke a positive image (8.5.3–5). If a logo is perceived to evoke an outdated, out-of-touch image, that logo will then be revised.

In her book on branding, *No Logo*, Naomi Klein (2000) argues that branding is part of a larger multi-international corporate attempt to assume power and control within the context of economic global-ization. She is critical of the emphasis on public rela-tions campaigns designed to sell positive images for companies that are either selling undesirable prod-ucts or violating worker rights or antipollution laws (8.5.6–7). The PBS documentary *Merchants of Cool* (8.5.8) documents how marketers employ word-of-mouth promotions of certain products (Quart, 2003), as monitored by Commerical Alert (8.5.9). Anoth-er PBS documentary, *The Persuaders,* demonstrates some of the subtle techniques employed in market-ing products (8.5.10).

TECHNIQUES OF PERSUASION

Students can analyze the techniques used in ads. Some of the items to be noted and evaluated might include, the believability and status of actors or other spokespeople in the ad, the validity of reasons or evi-dence–including "scientific evidence"–cited to sup-port the product, or the use of celebrity endorsements (O'Shaughnessy & O'Shaughnessy, 2004). They can also critique the use of logic in claims made for prod-ucts–for example, the claim that a product "gives you more," without indicating what "more" the product provides–or specific comparisons made to other prod-ucts. (For links on analysis of techniques of persuasion, see 8.5.10–23).

Students can also trace shifts in the use of certain persuasion techniques on a timeline of ads from the 1700s to the 1980s from the American Advertising Museum (8.6.1). Earlier ads employed a direct-sell ap-proach by providing a lot of information about the product. More recent ads employ more indirect ap-proaches by seeking audiences' identification with portrayals of certain lifestyles or groups and then equating this lifestyle or group with use of the product. For example, the "Joy of Pepsi" ad campaigns (8.6.2) portray the "Pepsi Generation" as a young, attractive group of people enjoting a party or social event, im-ages that are equated with drinking Pepsi™. Underly-ing these more indirect appeals and lifestyle/group-product equations are certain assumptions: that being a member of the "Pepsi Generation" means that one is also going to be popular.

Students could identify certain value assumptions in ads, and then interrogate those assumptions by ask-ing such questions as:

- Who's the intended or target audience?

- What signs, markers, images, language, or social practices imply that audience?
- How is the audience linked to use of the product?
- What are the underlying value assumptions? (Having white teeth enhances your popularity; casino gambling is enjoyable.)

Subjective Appeal

Ads also employ subjective, subconscious appeals to audiences' emotional desires for popularity, status, power, or sex appeal. In ads, products are associated with an instant, magical transformation of the self. By using a certain shampoo, one becomes beautiful. By taking certain pills, one's headache is cured immedi-ately. By going on a certain diet, one loses weight in days. By owning a certain car, one immediately be-comes the center of attention. The use of these sub-jective, mythic appeals is often more effective than ads providing information; audiences who are skepti-cal about advertising claims are more influenced by emotionally appealing ads than ads with specific in-formation (Obermiller, Spangenberg, & MacLachlan, 2005).

Objects of Desire

Ads also position audiences to adopt gazes that de-fine females or males as the objects of desire–as things to be desired (8.6.3–4). In his classic study of portray-als of women in advertising, Irving Goffman (1988) described the way in which ads portrayed women as childlike, dependent on males, often positioned in un-natural poses, and mindless–images associated with what he described as "the ritualization of subordina-tion" (p. 45).

Students could analyze how ads employ various emotional appeals and images to construct a dream-like fantasy world by listing the images and sounds in the ad and then the emotions or fantasies they associ-ate with those images and sounds.

A TEACHING IDEA

ANALYZING PERSUASION IN ADS

In my English course, we study various analytical tools, such as compare and contrast, cause and effect, prob-lem analysis, persuasion, research skills, and literary analysis. When studying cause and effect and preparing for an essay, the class watches the video *Merchants of Cool*, which evaluates at length the various effects of the media. After watching the video, we discuss the influence of the media and create a breakdown of different examples of media–related causes and effects. What causes people to make certain material decisions? How present is the media in our life? What is the effect? To heighten student awareness, I have them chart for one full day every type of advertising that they encounter throughout that day.

After studying different techniques of persuasion, students find a print or television advertisement that they in fact "talk back" to. I can still recall one magnificent example of analysis from a student many years ago who was beautifully cognizant and analytical in her talk back to a popular perfume advertisement. The concept was simple: there was an endearing picture of a woman and her baby and beneath the photo was the product name immediately followed by the adjective "happy." The student made amazing observations about how the ad suggests that according to societal norms, the way for a woman to be "truly happy" is to have a child.

One resource that has yielded thought-provoking articles and activities is the magazine *AdBusters*, which parodies many familiar advertising concepts and offers various articles: For instance, they have an activity that asks the question: "*Are You Losing the Battle of the Mind*?" Each letter of the question is the letter from a commonly recognized label. For example, the letter "A" from the popular laundry detergent "All". The letter "R" was from the candy "Reese's". The letter "E" was from the "Eggo" label. I test the students to see how many of the letters/labels they are able to identify based on a "score sheet" that playfully mocks how much they know. I then replace the letters with pictures of several prominent historical or political figures and again find out who they recognize and can identify. This activity can generate interesting discussion about media and the way in which we digest so much superfluous information.

Heather Johnson,
North St. Paul High School, Minnesota

CRITICAL DISCOURSE ANALYSIS

From the perspective of critical discourse analysis, Guy Cook (2001) argues that advertising is a discourse itself constituting the meaning of both the text (the ad itself) and the context in which people are responding to the ad. He argues that it is important to examine the meanings of ads based on how audiences construct these meanings based on their semiotic knowledge of images/signs, genre knowledge, needs, desires, and discourses applied to the ad. I've summarized his descriptions of the following components of context (p. 4):

Substance: the physical material that carries or relays text.

Music and pictures: designed to entertain and capture people's attention.

Paralanguage: meaningful behavior accompanying language, such as voice quality, gestures, facial expressions and touch (in speech), and choice of typeface and letter sizes (in writing).

Situation: the properties and relations of objects and people in the vicinity of the texts, as perceived by the participants.

Co-text: text that precedes or follows that under analysis, and that participants judge to belong to the same discourse.

Intertext: texts that the participants perceive as belonging to other discourse, but that they associated with the text under construction, and that affect their interpretation.

Participants: their intentions and interpretations, knowledge and beliefs, attitudes, affiliations, and feelings. Each participant is simultaneously a part of the context and an observer of it. Participants are usually described as senders and receivers. (The sender of a message is not always the same as the addressers, however, the person who relays it. In a television ad, for example, the addresser may be an actor, though the sender is an advertising agency. Neither is the receiver always the addressee, the person for which it is intended. The addressees may be a specific target group, but the receiver is anyone who sees the ad.)

Function: what the text is intended to do by the senders and addressers, or perceived to do by the receivers and addresses.

These various components could be applied to a 30-second Sprite™ television commercial in which a group of Hispanic adolescents are riding down the street on their low-rider bikes. Some younger kids stare at them as the words "Some people don't get it" are heard in the background. At the end, one of the riders is shown drinking a bottle of Sprite™ with the words "Obey your thirst" in the background.

The images of this ad are designed to associate the coolness of the low-rider bike image with the product image. The music and images in this ad are geared for adolescents who are not yet driving, so they are still limited to their bikes, although the appeal may also extend to older adolescents. A critical discourse analysis goes beyond simply these images to suggest that the discourses of masculinity and subcultural resistance constituting the low-rider biking practice are then transferred to the practice of drinking Sprite™ (Cowan, 2004) (8.7.1)

As noted in *Merchants of Cool* (8.5.8), to improve their market share in the late 1990s, Sprite™ launched a major campaign using sports celebrities to parody celebrity endorsement ads in an attempt to equate being ironic, hip, or cool with the product. As a result, Sprite sales jumped among the adolescent group. Sprite also increased its advertising on MTV; the program shows a hip-hop concert event sponsored by Sprite: again, a move designed to link certain cultural phenomena, in this case, hip-hop, with the product. (Their 2005 site includes a "hip-hop video generator" [8.7.1a]).

Paralanguage

The voice, speech, and words that appear in the Sprite™ ad are all consistent with an appeal to a young, male, adolescent audience. The words "some people don't get it" and "obey your thirst" are spoken in a defiant manner associated with the image of assertiveness.

These paralanguage uses serve as markers for certain identities associated with gender, class, or race. For example, audiences bring certain assumptions about the relationships between dialects, register, pitch, topic elaboration, intonation, hedging, asides, types of speech acts, and social class as a set of cultural, social practices.

Myers (1999) also notes the importance of the connotations of words in ads used as brand names, for example, Poison™ for a perfume, a word that connotes death or killing, and might be associated with a femme fatale. Similarly, while the denotation or dictionary definition of Opium™ is that of a narcotic, its connotation is that of Romantic poets, the Orient, dreams, or bohemian practices (pp. 107–108).

Myers also identifies how pronouns are used in ads to build personal relationships with the audience, particularly with the use of "you"—as in "Don't let coughs keep you off duty." Similarly, the use of "we" personalizes the impersonal, as in "At McDonald's™, we do it all for you," or, in the Avis™ ad, "We try harder." The use of "he"/"she" implies a certain shared knowledge between ad and audience, as in the Clairol™ ad: "Does she or doesn't she? Only her hairdresser knows for sure." See the Website for more of Myers's analysis of the uses of language in ads (8.7.2).

Students could also examine the use of "doublespeak" language in George Orwell's *1984* and draw parallels to the language of advertising (8.7.2a–2g).

Situation/Context

The Sprite™ ads appear on programs associated with a male adolescent audience, such as MTV programs and sports shows.

Intertext

There is a strong intertextual link in the Sprite™ ad to the phenomenon of low-rider bikes (8.7.3), something that would appeal to a young adolescent market, particularly in parts of the country in which low-rider cars/bikes are popular. This reflects a larger association with an *Easy Rider* adolescent rebellion against the usual, status-quo car or bike. This rebellion against the "some people [who] don't get it"–the status quo–is then linked with the act of drinking Sprite™.

Participants

The clothes, sunglasses, and terrain of the ad evoke a world in which adolescents dominate the neighborhood streets, and in which younger kids who "don't get it" are at a disadvantage because they have not yet achieved adolescence. The potential audience of participants is assumed to be attracted to this portrayal of hipness.

Function

This ad serves the purpose of equating images of coolness with the product. It is also part of a larger marketing effort to promote soft drinks, given recent criticisms of the soft drink industry by health experts and educators who are alarmed by increasing obesity rates and the lack of nutrition in adolescents' diets.

Propaganda

Another perspective for analyzing advertising is to consider it as propaganda for developing positive attitude toward consumerism (Miller, 1990). Ads can be intended to do more than just promote individual products; they can also promote attitudes, values, and ideologies. From this perspective, advertising itself functions to indoctrinate audiences with a view of consumer products as purveyors of happiness, status, and success. For example, ExxonMobil™ ads extol the value of education or even the environment. These ads and websites are part of a public relations campaign to promote the image of Exxon as a corporation that "cares" about education or the environment, despite the fact that oil is the leading cause of air pollution and global warming. These public relations ads qualify as propaganda in that they distort facts in order to promote their own ideological perspectives and agendas: in the case of ExxonMobil™, to resist efforts to curtail oil exploration or production. However, as in any critical analysis of propaganda, students should ask, who does advertising really benefit? Most will recognize that it is the producers, not the audiences, who are benefiting (8.8.1–3).

Students in my class analyze the different components listed above in ads on the AdFlip site (8.8.4) or other online ad sites (8.2.6–28). The Website also has additional examples of ads analyses (8.8.5–10).

IDEALIZED GENDER IMAGES

Advertisers use ads to promote images of ideal femininity (and now masculinity) to create a sense of inadequacy—that one's body or appearance is imperfect without the use of certain products. The video *What a Girl Wants* (8.9.1) documents the ways in which advertising use celebrity females to promote these idealized images of femininity for females to emulate. As noted in Chapter 4, Jean Kilbourne, a leading critic of these ads, in her *Killing Us Softly 3* video (8.9.2, with an extensive teaching guide) and the video *Slim Hopes* (8.9.3), notes that 1 in 5 young women in America today has an eating disorder, 80% of 4th-grade girls are dieting, the average model weighs 23% less than the average woman, only 5% of women have the body type (tall, genetically thin, broad-shouldered, narrow-hipped, long-legged, and usually small-breasted) seen in almost all advertising, and 4 out of 5 women are dissatisfied with their appearance.

Students could examine how these ads influence their own gender perceptions as to what it means to be "female" or "male" (8.9.4–8). For example, they could brainstorm notions of what it means to be "male," and then create poster presentations or collages using ads geared for males with essentialist images of "male" cultural practices associated with beer, cars, sports, or display of physical prowess (8.9.10–21).

ALCOHOL, TOBACCO, AND ADOLESCENTS

Advertisers also promote alcohol and tobacco in magazines or on billboards in ways that appeal to adolescents, as illustrated by the Coors Light™ beer ads discussed in Chapter 4. A study of alcohol advertising in magazines and adolescent readership published in the *Journal of the American Medical Association* (Garfield, Chung, & Rathouz, 2003) found that from 1997 to 2001, in 35 of 48 major U.S. magazines there were 9,148 alcohol advertisements; 13% were for beer, 5% for wine, and 82% for liquor. Analysis of those magazines more likely to have an adolescent audience found that beer and liquor ads were most likely to be read by adolescents. For every 1 million underage readers ages 12–19 of a magazine, there were 1.6 times more beer advertisements and 1.3 times more liquor advertisements in these magazines than in those not geared for adolescents. Fifty-six percent of students in grades 5 through 12 say that alcohol advertising encourages them to drink (8.10.1).

A study conducted by the Center on Alcohol Marketing and Youth (2002; 8.10.2–click on Marketing Gallery for examples of TV alcohol ads) found that there was an increase of 39% in TV alcohol advertising from 2001 to 2002. Adolescents viewed two beer and liquor ads for every three seen by adults. All of the 15 most popular shows for adolescents had alcohol ads (8.10.3). And a study by the Alcohol and Public Health Research Unit of New Zealand found that the more positive adolescent viewers' reaction to these ads, the more likely they were to consume alcohol and to have higher annual alcohol consumption (8.10.4). The Website contains other sites on alcohol advertising (8.10.5–8).

The alcohol industry claims that it has launched ads designed to discourage underage drinking. However, a study by the Center on Alcohol Marketing and Youth (2002) indicated that in 2001 adolescents were 93 times more likely to see an ad promoting alcohol than an industry ad discouraging underage drinking. The Alcohol Epidemiology Program at the University of Minnesota (8.15.9–10) recommends the following steps to reduce alcohol advertising:

- Ban ads on buses, trains, kiosks, billboards, and supermarket carts, and in bus shelters, schools, and theme parks.
- Ban or limit advertising and sponsorship at community events such as festivals, parties, rodeos, concerts, and sporting events.

- Ban advertising in areas surrounding schools, residential areas, faith organizations, etc.
- Restrict or ban TV and/or radio alcohol commercials. (Beginning in 2006, Fox agreed to not broadcast ads for alcohol during Big-Ten football games.)
- Restrict alcohol advertising in newspapers and/or on the Internet.

While television tobacco ads have been banned, they are still prevalent in magazines, billboards, and at sports events. And tobacco companies pay movie producers to include smoking in films. One study (Polanksy & Glantz, 2004) found that of the 776 movies released between 1999 and 2003, almost 80% of PG-13 rated films and almost half of PG and G-rated films included smoking (8.10.10a–11). The total number of films for young people with smoking actually increased from 1999 to 2003. Another study (Sargent et al., 2004) found that middle school students who view R-rated movies were five times more likely to smoke than students whose parents restrict their access to R-rated films, which contain, on average, eight scenes with smoking, compared to four scenes in PG or PG-13 movies.

Given the prevalence of smoking in films, often in ways that glamorize smoking, the American Legacy Foundation has proposed steps to eliminate smoking in films, for example, giving movies with smoking an R rating (8.10.12–15). The Foundation found that three-quarters of people surveyed oppose the prevalent product placement of tobacco brands in films. In 2000, the Foundation (8.10.16) also launched a series of hard-hitting, documentary-style anti-smoking ads, described as the "Infect truth®" campaign (8.10.15), that challenge the influence of peer pressure to smoke as a social status symbol. One study found that broadcasts of state-sponsored antitobacco ads in the 75 largest media markets in America was associated with more negative perceptions of smoking and less propensity to smoke (Emery et al., 2005). However, cuts in these programs reduce exposure to these ads. Despite the use of antismoking ads, a relatively high percentage of adolescents continue to smoke, particularly impulsive or risk-orientated adolescents, characterized as "novelty-seeking," who are more receptive to or knowledgeable about tobacco advertising (8.10.17–18). After a previous decline, teen smoking has been increasing since 2005, an increase attributed to the marketing of flavored cigarettes (Califano & Sullivan, 2006).

Students could analyze the use of smoking ads in magazines, noting the appeals being employed (8.10.18a–18b), and compare these appeals to those employed in earlier television smoking ads (8.10.18c). The Website contains a number of webquests and lessons on analysis of smoking ads (8.10.19–27).

THE PHARMACEUTICAL INDUSTRY

Another major advertiser is the pharmaceutical industry, which has increased its advertising of drugs since the mid-1990s to appeal to the growing baby boomers' health issues (Angell, 2004; Greider, 2003). One reason for the increased number of television drug ads is that Congress, spurred on by industry lobbying and campaign contributions, forced the Food and Drug Administration to loosen controls on drug advertising. The cost of the subsequent spurt of advertising has resulted in the industry refusing to lower the costs of drugs themselves in the United States—which, unlike other countries such as Canada, does not bargain directly with the industry to set drug prices. The effectiveness of these ads is evident: people are increasingly more likely to ask doctors about these drugs (8.11.1). One doctor, Michael Wilkes of the University of California, Davis, Medical School, noted that these direct-to-consumer ads attempt to work around the doctor by fostering a belief that patients should ask their doctors to prescribe these drugs (8.11.2–3). However, given the power of the pharmaceutical industry, a major contributor to Congressional candidates, it is unlikely that the FDA will impose regulations on these ads. The Website contains sites related to the issue of drug advertising (8.11.4–9).

ADVERTISING ON THE WEB

Advertisers seeking new venues to attract audiences' attention have turned to Internet advertising (8.12.1–1a). Their forays range from direct methods such as email to "spam" or "push" messages, often with animation or flashing signals, through more indirect means, such as pop-up ads that inhabit chat rooms and respond to trigger words. Google™ derives much of its revenue from ads that appear on the right side of the Google sites as well as its ads that appear in blogs. Media conglomerates are also turning to social websites such as MySpace.com (bought by NewsCorp) and NeoPet.com (bought by Viacom) as ways to reach a youth market and to gain information about young people's trends and fads (Potkewitz, 2005).

One advantage of web advertising is that marketers can target certain audiences with email advertising, promoting specific products on specific sites associated with specific audiences who use those sites. However, while there are standards for television advertising, there are none for web advertising, particularly in terms of ads for children that engage children through interactivity not present in television ads (8.12.2). While television ads have obvious start and stop times, web-based ads are more subtle and interwoven into the content.

Students could analyze the types and techniques of Internet advertising, as well as the extent to which they perceive them as effective or an annoyance. The Website contains articles and lessons on web advertising (8.12.3–12).

MARKETING IN SCHOOLS

Another recent phenomenon has been the increase in marketing and advertising in schools. Cynthia Peters (8.13.1) and Joel Spring (2003) document how companies pay cash-starved schools for exclusive rights to market their products; advertising images then appear throughout the school and textbook companies sell ad space in their textbooks (8.13.1a).

One of the primary sources of advertising in schools is Primedia's Channel One™ (8.13.2), which provides morning in-school "news," now in some 40% of all secondary schools, by providing schools with free video equipment. Forty-two percent of the 12-minute "news" broadcasts consists of ads, self-promotions, and filler, thereby using what is assumed to be a pedagogical tool to insert advertising into the curriculum. In one study, middle school students were more likely to recall ads than news stories, although students receiving media literacy instruction were more skeptical about the ads (Austin, Chen, Pinkleton, & Johnson, 2006).

In his critique of Channel One™, Harry Brighouse (2005) goes beyond objecting to the commercialism to argue that in choosing to contract with Channel One™, schools violate what he defines as the "anti-commercial principle." He argues that forcing students to watch 2 minutes of commercials within the Channel One™ "newscast" conflicts with schools' mission to provide students with perspectives outside those mediated by corporate sponsors–perspectives essential for students to develop a sense of autonomy and agency. Brighouse argues that the school needs to provide alternative perspectives to consumerism rather than simply endorsing the corporate sponsorship.

Students who are shown Channel One™ newscasts could analyze the ads and how they are pitched to adolescent audiences, as well as the content of the news on the newscasts.

For other critiques of Channel One™, see 8.13.3–6; for attempts to limit advertising in schools, 8.13.7–9; for resources on commercialism and schooling, 8.13.10–17.

POLITICAL ADVERTISING

Another important topic is political advertising; these ads provide information about candidates, but they often stress slogans, sound bites, and deceptive images (8.14.1–11). In many cases, candidates turn to negative advertising focused on attacking their opponent's record. Moreover, these ads are often highly expensive, with the result that only well-financed or wealthy candidates can run for office. Although a campaign finance law passed in 2002, it did not include a mandated reduction in the costs of television ads, sought by proponents of campaign reform, who argue that the high costs of television ads price many candidates out of the market. Providing free advertising for candidates would reduce the emphasis on candidates having to raise contributions, which, in turn, mean that they are beholden to wealthy campaign contributors in making policy decisions.

Another important form of political advertising is issue ads, designed to shape public opinion and policy. These issue ads on topics such as health care, drug benefits, and education are used by advocacy groups to promote their particular agendas. Many of these issue ads are produced and promoted by think tanks that conduct "research" that is then used in these ads. For example, the Heritage Foundation had a major influence on producing ads on behalf of the insurance industry that challenged the Clinton health care proposals in 1993. One Website link contains a study of how issue advertising influenced Congress in 2001/2002 (8.14.12). Often these issue ads are misleading; the organizations FAIR (8.14.13) and FactCheck.org (8.14.14) provide critiques of the accuracy of claims in political and issue ads. The Website contains many additional sites related to analyzing political ads (8.14.15–29).

PRODUCT PLACEMENTS AND "ADVERTAINMENTS"

As audiences increasingly record television programs and fast-forward through ads when they watch them later, advertisers are turning to alternative approaches such as product placements: the practice of having actors use identifiable products during the programs. While audiences are twice as likely to purchase a product based on an ad than from a product placement (FIND/SVP, 2004), product placements are still effective in boosting brand recognition through exposure to characters using a product (Gough, 2004). Given the need to find alternatives to traditional ads, films and TV programs are now filled with characters using products (8.15.1). On a *Will & Grace* program, a character eats a Subway™ chicken parmigiana sandwich, which Subway had just introduced in its restaurants (Manly, 2005). This practice raises an ethical issue: should the sponsors of these products be explicitly identified so that audiences know who is sponsoring the ads? Students could debate this issue, with some assuming the perspectives of consumer rights advocates and others those of advertisers.

One form of product placement is "advertainments," which use entertaining content to promote products through video clips for cell phones or Ipods™ or public restrooms; links in computer games or DVD films to product sites; interactive online ads; or captive broadcasts of information about a product to customers when they lift up the product in the store (8.15.1a)

One example of an advertainment was a series of thriller-type short films on a low-cost DVD produced by BMW, consisting of Clive Owen, a popular movie star, driving BMWs (8.15.1b–c). While there is no direct pitch for BMWs in these films, they serve to equate images of fast driving, adventure, and sex appeal with the brand name.

In examining the issue of product placements, students could address the overall implications of the commodification of a culture, in which all forms of entertainment or social interactions are mediated by underlying commercial agendas. In such a commercially mediated society, individual needs and desires are valued more than collective community activity designed to address societal issues. Students could also envision societies in which alternative agendas prevail. The Website constains sites on issues of product placements (8.15.2–10).

CREATING OR PARODYING ADS

One of the most effective ways to study ads is to have students produce their own ads or create parodies of ads, as illustrated by Elizabeth Boeser's teaching vignette. Students could either design a new product or use existing products and then create magazine, video, or web-based ads. In devising techniques for selling a product, students can also formulate criteria for assessing the effectiveness of their ads, for example, the level of engagement with an ad. They could then share their ads with peers and garner feedback as to the effectiveness of their ads based on these criteria. Or, as mentioned by Heather Johnson ealier in this chapter, based on parodies/spoofs of ads in *Adbusters* magazine (8.16.13), students could select examples of deceptive ads and construct their own parodies or spoofs of ads. Students could then reflect on some of the larger value assumptions they are parodying in their ads, for example, that driving SUVs allows people more "freedom to go anywhere," as opposed to fostering pollution.

A TEACHING IDEA

Producing Television Ads

In my TV Production class, students complete several portfolio projects, among them the Commercial Analysis Assignment. The commercial unit begins with a day of viewing television commercials, which range from local TV to foreign TV, Super Bowl commercials, and even past student work. We talk about the use of dialogue, sound, lighting, and movement throughout the viewing of current and past commercials. In order to prepare the students for the Commercial Analysis Assignment that they do on their own at home, I model a re-creation of a storyboard for a professionally made, completed, and broadcast commercial.

The directions and questions are as follows:

- Select a commercial from any TV station. Make sure that the commercial is appropriate for the class. Please record your commercial. If you cannot tape a commercial on a VHS tape or save it to a CD, please ask me or someone else you know to help you.
- At what time and on which station did you watch your commercial?
- How many seconds long was the commercial?
- Name the product being advertised and explain what it is, if necessary.
- Explain why you chose this commercial. (Was it short, easy, interesting, detailed, etc.?)

- Describe the use of colors and light in the commercial.
- Was music used in the ad? What kind of music?
- Did the commercial use any famous people? Why or why not?
- What types of emotions did this commercial evoke (happiness, pride, fear, etc.)?
- Would you buy this product? Explain why or why not.
- Who is the target audience for this product (teens, young men, older women, etc.)? Explain how you understand this.
- Briefly tell whether or not you think this is an effective commercial and explain.
- Include a detailed storyboard on the back and/or along with this sheet.

The first response I observe when students return the finished assignment is how frustrated they are with the amount of work it takes to "watch" a 15-second commercial. Even after viewing various commercials as a class and working together on the exercise modeled for them, students are still not prepared for the amount of work they have to do to analyze a commercial. They eventually progress into a state of recognition, admiration, and oftentimes awe for the amount of time, work, and money advertisers put into these messages. It is at this point that someone asks my favorite question: "Why do they do it?" .

Since students bring VHS or QuickTime copies of the commercial, along with their answers to the questions provided, we then watch the commercials and ask the questions as a group. The first question on the worksheet asks what time and on what station they watched the commercial. This provides discussion about the particular show

the students were watching, and gives us insight into the demographic associated with particular stations, shows, and broadcast times. We typically talk about when and where we see certain kinds of commercials. As the discussion continues, students discover why they enjoyed a particular commercial if it was marketed to their own tastes, gender, age group, and demographic. In some ways, this assignment is almost as disturbing as it is revealing to all of them. However, it creates an essential basis for making their own commercials, while instructing them as to how and why advertisers spend millions of dollars on television advertisements.

Elizabeth Boeser, Thomas Jefferson High School, Bloomington, Minnesota

The Website contains examples of ad parodies and webquests on advertising (8.16.1–29).

SUMMARY

Students need to learn not only to adopt critical stances toward ads, but also to interrogate the larger assumptions about consumerism inherent in advertising. By examining the pervasive presence of advertising and promotional campaigns as forms of propaganda, they begin to detect the underlying agendas of the promoters behind the ads. Through creating their own ads, they learn to understand how advertisers employ certain techniques to both appeal to and deceive audiences.

CHAPTER 9

News and Documentaries

Key to Topics

PEOPLE DEPEND ON the news media for their knowledge of local, state, national, and global events and perspectives. In democracies, they make their decisions about candidates and issues based on this knowledge. If citizens of a democracy do not have access to objective information about the issues facing a society, they are not able to make informed decisions associated with voting for candidates or supporting certain political agendas. As America's founders recognized in the Bill of Rights, having a press that provides accurate, objective information about these issues is essential for the survival of a democracy. Unfortunately, many young people do not follow the news (Mindich, 2004), and much of the news they do follow is superficial, inaccurate, and shaped by ideological or economic agendas. As future citizens, it is therefore important to engage students not only in following the news, but also critically analyzing the news.

In adopting a critical stance, it is important to begin by asking what constitutes "news." In my class, we select some current community events and determine whether or not these events should be considered "news" based on the following criteria.

- *Significance.* Does the event have significance for particular audiences? What is significant for some may not be significant for others. An environmentalist may consider the pollution of a river to be highly significant, but not a bank robbery.
- *Relevance.* The relevance of certain events may also depend on audiences' interests, needs, and knowledge. A group of high school students may perceive the passing of a school bond referendum as highly relevant to their educational future, while perceiving the opening of a new business as irrelevant to their lives.
- *Sensational.* In some cases, stories of unusual or sensational events are perceived as news because they attract audiences' attention or are entertaining to audiences.
- *Practicality.* Audiences may also consider something newsworthy if it has practical, utilitarian value for them. This accounts for the increase in the amount of information on medical/health or consumer topics that audiences may find useful for their own personal health or shopping, even though the information provided may not be considered highly significant in terms of political or economic considerations.
- *Community impact.* Audiences and news producers also consider a story's significance relative to their community's needs and interests—does that story contribute to enhancing a community's well-being?

NEWS ANALYSIS

A place to start when teaching analysis of the news is to have students continually reading online news outlets geared for classroom use. Online services are produced by the *New York Times* (9.2a.1), CNN (9.2a.2), *USNews* (9.2a.3), *Scholastic* (9.2a.4), *Newsweek* (9.2a.5), *Time* magazine (9.2a.6), and *Education World* (9.2a.7), as well as state and local news sites, for example, those in Minnesota (9.2a.8–10). (The Website contains a

number of sites on online journalism: 9.2a.11–15). A useful site for analysis of national issues is the C-SPAN Classroom site (9.2a.16) that contains teaching materials and videos about national news stories.

Print newspapers are of course also a source for local and national news coverage. Despite that fact that they view newspapers favorably, audiences are increasingly accessing news from a range of different sources—online news, blogs, television, and radio—leading to declines in readership and revenue (9.2a.17–24).

Newspaper Sections

Students need to understand the functions of different sections of the newspaper, particularly the difference between reports and editorials (9.2b.1). Students could examine aspects of newspaper design and layout by comparing different newspapers, using even online versions. They could identify the uses of certain typeface/type styles, the font size and nature of headlines, and the "grid": the number of columns, the size and number of pictures, and how the news is organized in a paper. (For a unit on analyzing newspapers, see 9.2b.1a.)

Photography and Design

Photography plays a major role in illustrating the content and gist of a story (9.2b.2). Readers process photos 75% of the time and text only 25% of the time (9.2b.3), suggesting that photos need to be effectively integrated into a story (9.2b.4–6e).

Students could also analyze the use of various formats or design features employed in newspapers or news websites on the Newseum site of daily front pages from 193 papers from 27 countries (9.2b.5) as well as photos by award-winning photojournalists on the site (9.2b.6).

Genre Features

News stories employ certain genre features to frame an event in certain ways. For example, while stories typically follow the traditional expository format of the "5 W's" (who, what, where, when, and why), writers may employ narrative to frame their stories in an unfolding narrative sequence in an attempt to engage their audiences. (For a discussion of framing the news, see 9.2b.6; for an activity in which students condense a short story into a newspaper article and expand an article into a short story; see 9.2b.6a.)

Many articles begin with the reporter describing herself in the context of an event or story: "I'm walking down the street of a quiet, suburban neighborhood in which everyone knows everyone else. No one would ever have believed that one of their neighbors would have committed such a horrific crime." This use of what Norman Fairclough (1995) describes as the "narrativization" of the news focuses more on the dramatic aspects of new events and less on analysis of ideas or larger institutional forces. However, newspaper readers often are more engaged with such stories, particularly because they are familiar with this genre format on television news (9.2b.7).

Students could take an event that occurred in their school or community and create a traditional 5 W's report about it, then rewrite that report in narrative form to dramatize the unusual, extraordinary nature of the event. They could then share these two versions with their peers and ask them to indicate which version is more engaging, and why.

Students could also analyze the effectiveness or persuasiveness of an editorial, op-ed essay, or letters to the editor, in terms of the clarity and the quality of the argument (9.2b.8–11). And they could analyze examples of political cartoons in terms of the techniques employed: exaggeration of physical features, visual portrayal of an issue, parodying of language/social practices, and portrayal of a certain attitude or stance (9.2b.12–16d).

Language Use

Students could also study how news writers may use metaphors or hyperbolic language to describe an event in a manner that represents a particular attitude toward that event. For example, in writing about the Palestinian/Israeli conflict, a writer might describe one side's bombing or attack as an "incursion," "deadly destruction," or "massacre": each descriptor reflects an increasingly strong ideological orientation toward the attack (9.2b.17).

Students could study uses of language by creating their own parody of news articles similar to those found in *The Onion*, a parody of current news coverage (9.2b.18)—including how language is used to gain an audience's identification with a certain belief or perspective (9.2b.19–21). Students could also critique the lack of news coverage of critical issues facing the world in favor of more sensationalized, entertaining content (9.2b.22–31).

NEWS ACCESS

Audiences may differ in their perceptions of what constitutes news depending on their preferred means of accessing the news. There has been a decline in the number of local daily newspapers—currently about half the number of those published in 1910 (9.2c.1). Newspaper readership peaked in 1984 with 63.3 million readers subscribing to 1,688 papers; in 2005, there were 45.2 million readers of 1,457 papers (Seelye, 2005). One reason for the decline is that young people under 30 find traditional newspaper coverage of less interest to them. A project by the *Minneapolis Star Tribune* in which topics of interest to young people was featured served to enhance younger readers' interest (9.2c.1a).

Most audiences acquire their news from television and/or radio as opposed to newspapers. However, audiences are now turning away from TV and radio news as well as newspapers to acquire news from the web (Foust, 2005; Gunter, 2003; for a list of web-based news sites, see 9.2c.2–3)

According to a Nielsen/NetRatings study, about 40 million readers or one in four Internet users access newspaper websites (Sharman, 2005). While 22% of readers prefer the online version, 71% prefer the paper version. The NYTimes.com site was the top site, followed by USAToday.com, WashingtonPost.com, the LATimes.com, and SFGate.com. Part of the appeal of these sites is their highly interactive use of streaming video and audio, blogs, podcasts, and continuous updates. At the same time, increased use of these online sites has meant a decline in print newspaper circulation, causing newspapers to turn to their online sites for increasing revenue, including fees for access to stories.

Students could examine how newspapers differ according to the type of town or community they represent (9.2c.4), the country represented (9.2c.5–6), the cultures and groups who create newspapers (9.2c.7), mainstream versus tabloid newspapers (9.2c.8), and their political ideology (9.2c.8). Or they could examine how online news sites (9.2d.1–13) serve local community interests based on who owns or operates the site.

Web-based news has served to "re-mediate" (Bolter & Grusin, 2000) television and newspaper news: note how cable television news provides a constant scrawl of news items on the bottom of the screen, and newspapers continually reference websites. Audiences can participate in an interactive mode with some online news sites in which they engage in a simulation, survey, or game related to an issue or share views with others (9.2d.14–16). Students could contrast news devised specifically for a student audience with news designed for an adult audience on the same site (9.2d.17), determining differences in the depth, quality, nature of information, and understanding gained (9.2d.18–19). They could also analyze how online political lobbying groups influence or frame news policy or ownership issues (9.2e.1–2). (For units with additional student activities for analyzing the news, see 9.2e.3–9).

Students could also study the increased influence of blogs on news reporting—in some cases, newspapers are now printing quotes from blogs (Gosney, 2004; Warlick, 2005). Blog writers are not constrained by commercial or political pressures associated with mainstream media outlets. At the same time, these writers do little of their own research or reporting, relying on mainstream news stories (9.2f.1–10) and political organizations (9.2g.1–8) for their material. Moreover, there is no editorial oversight related to the accuracy and validity of the claims made in these blogs, raising issues about the journalistic quality of blogs. Blog advocates counter this argument by pointing to failures of editorial oversight in mainstream media: for example, the failure of the *New York Times* editors to review the accuracy of stories of weapons of mass destruction in Iraq.

Students could compare "progressive" blog sites (9.2g.9–11) with "conservative" sites (9.2g.12–14) in terms of differences in their ideological perspectives. Connectforkids.org is a useful site for blogs for middle school students (9.2g.15).

Digital tools are therefore transforming the news, as reported in a forecast from The Media Center, George Mason University (9.2g.16).

CORPORATE INFLUENCES

Another key component of news coverage is comprised of editorials and op-ed columns, which provide subjective perspectives on current events (9.2h.1). Students could examine the impact of media conglomerate ownership on the editorial perspectives of newspaper and television news, both in terms of the opinions expressed and the selections of certain stories to cover. The largest owner, The Gannett Company, as of 2006, owns 110 daily newspapers and 21 television stations (9.2i.1). The second-largest owner, McClatchy Company, owns 31 daily newspapers (9.2i.2). In 2002, 10

companies owned newspapers with a distribution of more than half of all readers (Staubhaar & LaRose, 2004). While these companies claim that as owners they do not interfere with news content, there is a difference between the independence and quality of family-owned papers such as the *New York Times* and papers that are owned by large corporations.

One danger in this increased concentration of ownership is the decline of any competition for news within local markets. With the drop in the number of different newspapers in a particular local area, there is less demand on newspapers to have to compete. Moreover, as newspapers and television stations own each other, they may combine their operations, as is the case with the newspaper and television station in Tampa, Florida, with the result that producers avoid controversial subjects that might jeopardize profits (Green, 2005). This increased concentration is a result of the further deregulation of ownership rules passed under the 1996 Communications Act by Congress, as well as efforts by the FCC in 2003 to further relax the number of newspapers and stations owned by the same owner. The Website contains sites related to issues of media ownership (9.2i.3–5).

Noam Chomsky and Edward Herman propose a "propaganda model" of the news related to attempts by corporate and conservative interests to propagate their own ideological perspectives in news content and coverage (9.2i.6–9). According to this model, a swing to the right or the left in the ideological focus of news editorials would reflect the influence of either conservative think tanks (9.2i.10–20) or liberal think tanks (9.2i.21–24). As Trudi Lieberman (2000) documents, think tanks and similar organizations have acquired public relations and promotional skills at framing issues for the media in ways that fit their agenda. They also provide newspapers with op-ed essays, as well as spokespersons and "experts" who can be reached for comments or quotes in news articles (9.2i.25).

Lieberman cites the example of an attack on the Federal Drug Administration, beginning in the early 1990s, that succeeded in loosening FDA regulation of drug advertising and testing of new drugs. Various think tanks began to circulate stories to the media about drugs being "withheld" from the market by FDA delays and "burdensome" regulations, drugs that would save people's lives, but were not available due to "deadly overcaution" (pp. 94–96). They also criticized the FDA for its "bureaucratic delay" in testing drug safety. And they posited the need to cut back on labeling of supplements, an emerging business. They provided newspapers with reports on drugs and health issues that cited their own polls of doctors who complained that the FDA approval process was too slow. Congress then loosened FDA regulations, but after the bill went into effect, the FDA had to recall five different drugs that were prematurely approved and turned out to be dangerous, including two leading anti-pain drugs, Vioxx and Celebrex, which had to be pulled from the market in the fall of 2004. There was also a marked increase in drug advertising, particularly on television: a 150% increase from 1997 to 2001.

Lieberman notes how both think tanks and the media use questionable polling data to shape and construct public opinion (for a video clip on this topic, see 9.2i.26); and analyzes government and political public relations campaigns by The Center for Media and Democracy (9.2i.26) and The Free Press (9.2i.27).

Corporations also influence control over the dissemination of information and ideas through use of copyright law to limit distribution and authors' right to circulate that information—issues discussed in a free online book copy of Lawrence Lessing's book (9.2i.29); see also PBS: Copyrighting in the Digital Age (9.2i.30).

Community Journalism

In reaction to corporate control over news production, "community," "public," or "citizen" nonprofit, local journalism focuses on the idea of having persons who may not be professional journalists create their own local news outlet or contribute reports to existing outlets (Gillmor, 2004; Merrill, Gade, & Blevens, 2001). For example, as reported on a PBS News Hour story, "The Rise of Citizen Journalism" (9.2i.31), residents of Deerfield, New Hampshire, created their own online local newspaper. Citizens of suburban District of Columbia contribute to an online community paper, Backfence.com. People collaboratively write stories on Wikinews (9.2i.32) or send videos to the Current TV news broadcasts (9.2i.33). However, some research indicates that audiences do not respond any more positively to reports created by their peers than to mainstream journalism (Blomquist & Zukin, 1997). Students could reflect on their own level of engagement with examples of community journalism (9.2i.33–53).

Freedom of the Press

Another primary issue has to do with the declining freedom of the press due to government attempts to control, limit, or censor news. A global survey of freedom of the press in 194 countries conducted in 2004 (Freedom House, 2005) found that 75 countries (39%) were rated "Free," while 50 (26%) were rated "Partly Free," and 69 (35%) were rated "Not Free," meaning that a third of the world press experiences government control and/or censorship. Ratings for the United States press declined due to instances in which prosecutors compelled journalists to reveal sources and the Bush administration attempted to give political commentators grants to promote their policies.

Detecting News Bias

Another important focus for analysis of the news is bias: the degree to which a writer does or does not adopt an "objective" stance as a "neutral" journalist, and presents different, alternative perspectives on a topic or issue. According to surveys by the Pew Research Center, 60% of Americans in 2005 believe that news organizations are "politically biased" (Krueger, 2005). Conservatives often charge that the media has a "liberal bias," while liberals charge that certain organizations such as Fox News reflect a "conservative bias." In some cases, writers may present only one perspective, or leave out information related to alternative perspectives. The FAIR (Fairness and Accuracy in Reporting) site provides the following questions for detecting bias in news (9.2j.1):

> Who are the sources?
> Is there a lack of diversity?
> From whose point of view is the news reported?
> Are there double standards?
> Do stereotypes skew coverage?
> Is the language loaded?
> Is there a lack of context?
> Do the headlines and stories match?
> Are stories on important issues featured
>   prominently?

Students could also discuss whether what they perceive as biased presentations influences their attitudes or behavior. One study found that neither Democrat nor Republican viewers of Fox News Channel were influenced in their voting behavior due to their viewing of Fox News (Krueger, 2005). The researchers posited that news simply confirmed what audiences already believed, as opposed to changing their beliefs. The Website contains links on different aspects of news bias (9.2k.2–15).

For students to be able to detect bias, they need to analyze the use of language related to stereotypical perceptions of race, class, and gender. Heather Johnson, whose teaching activity described in Chapter 8 focused on language use in advertising, has her students examine the use of language in news coverage related to racial categories.

A TEACHING IDEA

Monitoring Racial Bias in the News

To teach my 11th-grade students about bias, I have students analyze the news for instances of bias related to race. I ask students to examine common features inherent in news reports related to bias in statements or headlines such as "Police said the suspect was described as a black man in his 20s . . ." "Indian Found Murdered in New Town." "Detectives are investigating the death of an Asian employee of a brokerage firm whose body was found by the company's owner yesterday." I then ask students to consider what these news stories have in common: when race is an appropriate element in a story; whether the racial identifications used in these stories are relevant; and what problems surround unwarranted use of racial identity in crime-related stories.

Over the next month, my students collect newspaper and magazine stories relating to crime. They analyze these stories and sort them under the following categories: 1) no racial identification, 2) relevant racial identification, 3) unnecessary racial identification. When racial identification occurs, students note the use of tools and techniques used in reporting the story, the tone of the story, and the overall effect on the reader. At the end of the month, students will tally and post their total figures and send their results to the magazines and newspapers they surveyed.

Heather Johnson,
North St. Paul High School, Minnesota

PRODUCING
CLASSROOM/SCHOOL NEWSPAPERS

Having studied newspapers, students could then create their own classroom newspaper or contribute to their school newspaper (9.21.1–3). They could analyze and compare these papers in terms of the quality of the design features employed: layout, columns, font size, use of photos, headlines, photo captions, white space, and so on. In helping students design a classroom newspaper, teachers could integrate student production of final projects, reports, or essays into a published classroom paper for peers and parents.

For a classroom newspaper, students could select certain issues facing students in their school: large class sizes, the food service, equity in sports funding, the pressure of college admissions, discipline policies, amount of homework. Groups of students could investigate these issues and then create reports for a classroom newspaper that could be distributed schoolwide. The Website contains further activities related to newspaper production (9.21.4–8).

Students could also discuss issues of school newspaper production with members of the school newspaper staff. One major issue has to do with freedom of the press related to potential censorship of controversial stories by the school administration. In writing for high school newspapers, students are often subject to potential censorship of coverage of stories or issues that the school administration may perceive to be controversial or challenging their school policies. If, for example, a group of students is investigating the school's discipline policies and uncovers widespread concern about those policies, they may face opposition from the school administration for publicly sharing those concerns. Because students are also subject to their disciplinary control, they are highly vulnerable to potential censorship threats. For units/webquests on First Amendment issues, see 9.21.9–12w. The Website contains other units and activities related to analysis of print journalism (9.21.13–31).

TELEVISION NEWS

Most Americans acquire their news from television news, although, as previously noted, they are turning increasingly to web-based news (9.3.1). Because advertisers and therefore producers prefer a younger audience, the content of television news, particularly cable news, has focused more on topics of interest to a younger audience (9.3.2–4).

Television news producers assume that news needs to be highly entertaining and visual in order to maintain audience attention. Much of the news content consists of summaries of events, but those summaries are accompanied by dramatic video clips and bulleted lists of headline summaries. In contrast to the BBC "newsreaders," local anchors are often celebrity stars whose own "happy talk" comments and asides become a part of the broadcast. These anchors' engagement with audiences is maintained rhetorically through direct address—"you'll really enjoy the story about the escaped tiger coming up in our next segment"—as well as direct eye contact with audiences. Anchors also tout the immediacy of their "live, up-to-the-minute" coverage based on the questionable assumption that the immediacy of reporting an event means that audiences will be better informed about that event.

Students could log onto an online news site and analyze which stories are most likely to be featured; it is often the case that those news events that lend themselves best to compelling narratives—unusual crimes, scandals, or natural disasters—are more likely to be given air time, as opposed to topics related to abstract, theoretical issues related to political, social, and cultural issues. (For video clip examples of different types of news stories, go to the NewsLab site, 9.3a.1.)

Moreover, coverage of local events often fails to contextualize events based on different perspectives about an event—unlike the PBS *NewsHour,* for example that generally focuses in depth on three to five topics with background interviews, information, and analysis. However, when a Chicago commercial station, WBBM, adopted a similar format, audience ratings declined (9.3a.2).

In his documentary about gun violence in America, *Bowling for Columbine* (2002; 9.3a.3), Michael Moore argues that the heavy emphasis on crime and violence in American television news has created a sense of fear in the American public to the point that they believe that they need to not only own guns, but use them to protect themselves. He contrasts American attitudes toward fear of crime with Canadians' lack of fear, which he attributes to their low-key television news broadcasts. It should be noted that Moore presents no empirical evidence for his claims, other than the fact that Canadians own just as many guns as Americans but commit far few murders. (For further activities and resources on analyzing television news, see 9.3a.4–8.)

A TEACHING IDEA

ANALYZING TELEVISION NEWS

In my Broadcast Class, we address the following questions: What makes a good newscast? How do news stations decide what is important or headline news? How should a newscast be structured? To answer these questions, students view tapes of ten o'clock newscasts from the four local stations: ABC, CBS, NBC, and FOX. We look at these stations' history, their ratings, their television personalities, the owners of the networks, and the networks' associations with other TV and radio stations and corporations. We discuss bias and how these associations might bring potential bias to a news organization. Students are

intrigued to see how everything from their favorite radio station to their favorite movie company could affect the news and the distribution of it.

Students then view the first 10 minutes of the "meat and potatoes" of the newscasts and write down what each story is about. They understand why the first 10 minutes is important, because research proves that most people change stations or turn the television off after the first 10 minutes. The goal is to pull in viewers immediately with the lead story.

In one class analysis, two broadcasts led with the same headline story: a local shooting. One broadcast led with national news. And the fourth broadcast led with an educational interest story—how are schools failing? Students had never really looked at the news this way. Why would their headline stories be so different? What were the producers/directors thinking? What is good news? What is shock news?

Students determined that the two networks that led with the local shooting were also the two highest-ranked affiliates. So does shock news gain ratings? Ultimately, after watching only the lead story, students determined yes, shock news does increase ratings. One student noted that "If I were watching the news I would want to know if my community was unsafe." Other students agreed. Students do care about what goes on in their own community; however, the educational story on how schools are failing, which directly affected them, did not seem to interest them as much.

Students then discussed the television station that led with the national news story. One boy in the class said, "National news is so boring. I mean, really, how does it affect us?" Ultimately, we had to rank what students felt was important, local or national news. Most agreed that local news was much more relevant to their lives than national news.

Susan Link, Lakeville High School, Minnesota

Story Selection

One of the major challenges facing local news directors is to gauge the relative audience interest and appeal of various news stories. Often the decisions about which stories to run are based less upon journalistic quality and relevancy than upon the need to generate high ratings and please corporate owners. However, high journalistic quality does not necessarily result in lower ratings. Analysis of local television news by the Project for Excellence in Journalism (9.3b.1) examines the content of the highest-rated local news broadcasts in 20 cities. In their 2002 report (9.3b.2), they found that the higher the quality of news, the higher the ratings. Audiences also isolated specific aspects of news broadcasts that were most likely to predict high viewer ratings, including: investigative stories, a focus on the community, longer stories, and the use of multiple sources.

Unfortunately, corporate owners of these stations continue to believe that high Nielsen ratings (9.3b.4), which they use to attract advertising (9.3b.3), derive from a sensationalized, "breaking news" format, even though this format does not necessarily result in increased ratings (9.3b.5).

One reason for producers' focus on bottom-line profits is the increasing influence of corporate ownership. (For example, General Electric owns NBC, MSNBC, and CNBC; Time Warner owns CNN; Disney owns ABC News; Viacom owns CBS News; and News Corp owns FOX News.) Students could go to the PBS *NewsHour* site (9.3b.6) to study ownership information for any one of 50 news markets. They could then compare differences in the local news styles and the quality of news coverage based on differences in ownership of local stations. Students could also view the video clip from the PBS documentary program *Local News* (9.3b.7), about a local Charlotte, North Carolina, news broadcast. In this series, the news director is under a lot of pressure to improve the news broadcast's low ratings. In this clip, he is shown as having to make decisions about a story about a local school bomb threat based on the significance and relevance of the story, as well as its appeal to the viewing audience.

Accuracy and Balance

Another issue for study is the degree to which news reports are accurate and balanced–that is, the extent to which different perspectives or sources are represented (9.3c.1). It may be difficult to achieve such balance when people with different perspectives may not have the right or the power to speak on an issue. It is often the case that in national stories, government officials, think tank spokespersons, or familiar spokespersons (often white males) are far more likely to be quoted than people outside institutions of power. News producers often turn first to those institutional spokespersons because they are more readily available than less well-known people.

News producers also select those stories that have strong visual content. In *Local News*, the station often presented these events over others because of their visual appeal to audiences who prefer such content (9.3c.2). One limitation of these reports of highly visual, dramatic events is that there is often little or no contextual analysis of causes/institutional factors shaping events. Thus, audiences acquire little analysis of the influences of poverty, homelessness, unemployment, and lack of education on crime.

Students could analyze how broadcasts use visual content to portray concepts or ideas, in some cases oversimplifying these concepts or ideas with little contextualizing of issues. The Website contains an analysis of how visuals are used in the news (9.3c.3), as well as the practice of continually alerting audiences to "breaking news" (9.3c.4–5).

Consistent with the question of what constitutes the significance or relevance of these dramatic, visual stories is whether or not they actually contribute to the larger good of the community. One station in Austin, Texas, now considers the extent to which certain events are relevant to the community as opposed to a story's sensational appeal. The Website contains more analysis of TV news (9.3c.6–20).

News Development

National television news has developed over time from only a 15-minute broadcast in the 1950s to the current 30-minute broadcasts. Some local news broadcasts are now 1 to 2 hours in large markets. Cable news networks broadcast 24 hours a day. Cable television news broadcasts, many of which are facing financial difficulties, often dramatize events such as the Gulf War, the O. J. Simpson trial, the Monica Lewinsky scandal, the Iraq War, and other such events in a nonstop, dramatic manner. These portrayals serve to lure viewers away from the more traditional network news by providing continuous coverage–in many cases, about superficial, insignificant matters.

Students can study older versions of the news by going to the Television News Archive at Vanderbilt University (9.3d.1), a site that contains thousands of broadcast clips that can be accessed through a database search. Access is free, but registration is required. The Website contains more on the history of TV news (9.3d.2–3).

Online News

Students could compare the visual emphasis in TV news with radio news, such as that available on *National Public Radio* (9.3e.1), which can provide news without having to be concerned about visual presentation. Students could also compare the headline versions of the 24-hour cable news broadcasts/web pages of different online TV news sites: CNN, Fox, MSNBC, and the PBS *NewsHour* (9.3e.2–5).

Audience Participation

Using the methods described in Chapter 6 on media ethnography, students could analyze viewers' responses to television news. They could examine the nature of their understanding or recall of the news content, as well as the critical stances they adopted in responding to the news. When students in my course keep a log of the stories in a news broadcast and the number of seconds per story, they report that because they are bombarded with so much information, they have difficulty recalling the content of different stories. Students could reflect on how the purposes for viewing or interest in looking for certain topics shaped their recall. One study (9.3e.9) found that viewers were better able to recall information in which they were highly interested. (For some sample student logs of local news, see 9.3e.10.)

Sports Coverage

Students could also examine the ways in which local news sports coverage functions to promote sports broadcasting (9.2f.1–7).

Political Coverage

Consistent with Chomsky's "propaganda model" described in Chapter 8, one of the major criticisms of television news is that it presents only the perspective of those in power, excluding alternative, dissident voices. One study (Howard, 2002; 9.3g.1) found that of the sources used on the big three networks' evening news shows in 2001, three-fourths were affiliated with the Republican Party; only 15% of the sources were women; 92% of the sources were White.

Local television news often provides little or no coverage of political races, in contrast to extensive coverage by newspapers. One study of 122 local evening news broadcasts in 2002 found that there were four times as many political ads as there were stories about candidates (9.3g.2). In each broadcast, there was an average of 39 seconds of political coverage compared to an average of 1 minute of political ads. To some degree, given the lack of coverage, candidates may need to rely on advertising to convey their messages, providing a lucrative revenue source for stations during political campaigns. The study also found that in the little political coverage that did occur, most of the focus was on strategy and the horse race aspects of a campaign, as opposed to coverage of issues. Forty percent of the exposure to candidates consisted of sound bites, which averaged 11.2 seconds, suggesting largely superficial information about a candidate's stand on issues. The Website contains a Newseum interactive site on news coverage of political campaigns (9.3g.3).

Underrepresentation of Women and Minorities

As with print news, critics have examined the underrepresentation of women and minorities in the television news industry. This issue is highlighted during the filming of the *Local News* documentary, when a veteran African-American female reporter loses her job, for reasons that are not made explicit in the documentary (9.3g.4). One analysis of news anchors on the top National Public Radio stations found that 88% were White and 69% were male; only 6 of the hosts were African American, 2 were Asian American, and 2 were Arab American (9.3g.5). The Website contains data on demographics of news people (9.3g.6–8).

Coverage of Wars

In conducting critical analyses of the news, students could examine the role of the press in covering wars, particularly the wars in Afghanistan and Iraq. Students could go on the Newseum site on the war in Iraq (9.3g.9–10) and examine some of the issues associated with the news coverage of that war, for example, the issue of the Pentagon's approved use of embedded reporters. One of the limitations of coverage of the Iraq War, according to Susan Moeller (2004), was that reporters were highly controlled in terms of the sites to which they had access as "embedded" reporters. The Website contains other sites on media coverage of wars (9.3g.11–16a).

Channel One™ Broadcasts

As noted in Chapter 8, many school districts provide students with daily "news" broadcasts on Channel One™ (9.3g.17–18) beamed via satellite to 12,000 schools. In an analysis of the news content of Channel One™, Mark Miller (1997; 9.3g.19) found that the news content is just as superficial as on local television news, consisting of headline summaries of factual information that serve as "content" for commercials aimed at adolescents. Students could then compare the Channel One™ coverage with coverage of the same stories on CNN Student News (9.3g.19a) and MSNBC streaming news (9.3g.19b). One advantage of the streaming video format is that it can be replayed for closer analysis or making comparisons. They could also examine criticisms by a coalition of conservative and progressive groups who object to the intrusion of messages and images into the school (9.3g.20–22).

Creating a Television News Broadcast

As with creating a classroom newspaper, students could also create their own television news broadcast of stories of interest to them and their peers. They could simply videotape their broadcasts or, by creating digital video streaming images, they could put clips onto a web page. In doing so, they are learning about various aspects of television news production, including selecting and writing scripts for stories, using visual content to convey their ideas, and editing material to capture primary content. They could then reflect on their own and others' stories in terms of decisions about the newsworthy nature of their stories–the significance, relevance, or value of the story for their intended audiences. The Website contains information on creating news broadcasts (9.3h.1–10).

RADIO NEWS

There are any number of ways for students to study the quality of radio news, through the sites from National Public Radio, local NPR and commercial radio stations, XM Satellite Radio™ (9.3h.11) and Sirius Satellite™ Radio (9.3h.12), podcast news programs available on iTunes™ (9.3h.13), and sites with podcast directories (9.3h.14–27). Students could also access live streaming audio programs from Youth Radio: Web Radio (9.3h.28) that provides live streaming audio programs from NPR and youth radio news programs on topics of interest to students.

Students could analyze how radio news employs in-depth interviews or monologues that provide context and insights often not available on television news. Radio call-in shows related to news also provide a range of audience perspectives.

Based on their analysis of radio news, students could then create their own podcast news broadcast drawing on their classroom newspaper reports (Gosney, 2004; Richardson, 2006). To do so, they need to first create

a blog site. They then need to obtain a headset with a microphone to plug into the USB port for recording their podcast using Audacity™ (9.3h.29) or Apple's GarageBand™ (9.3h.30). They create an RSS (Really Simple Syndication) feed to a classroom or school site or podcast sites (9.3h.31–33). They could also create a podcast involving dramatic storytelling similar to the famous Orson Welles broadcast *War of the Worlds* (9.3h.34). The Website contains more information on online broadcasting (9.3h.35–38), including some student-run online radio stations (9.3h.39–43).

DOCUMENTARIES

One important component of television news is the use of documentary techniques to portray events and people (Golden, 2006; Nichols, 2001), (The Website under 9.3i contains its own separate module on documentary, along with unnumbered links on different aspects of documentary).

In studying documentary, it is useful to examine the role and function of documentary within the larger context of its relationship to "reality." Documentary does more than simply present or mirror lived-world events. It constructs its own versions of reality. Audiences must then judge the validity, verisimilitude, or success in presenting that version as a social commentary about experience, as well as its motives in doing so.

As illustrated in Jennifer Larson's teaching activity, documentary can used to foster discussions about issues students are studying.

A TEACHING IDEA

ANALYSIS OF A DOCUMENTARY, *HOOP DREAMS*

In my 11th-grade AP Language and Composition class, I use film to instruct students about the choices authors make to create the effect they want and deliver the message they seek; basically, I teach them how to use a formalist critical lens when reading. We start with analyzing film and the choices directors make in film techniques because these are the texts with which students are most familiar. Now that we've moved on to narration and description writing, we've seen how writers use language and structure to deliver their messages about their lives and experiences. Students wrote about an event in their lives; once they produced a first draft, they examined how they presented themselves and their experiences to the readers and whether it was the way they wish to present themselves. To aid them as they think about how to frame their lives for the readers, we watched the documentary *Hoop Dreams* (James, 1994) and discussed how the choices the directors made framed the boys and their lives for the audience to perceive them as the directors wished them to be perceived.

To prepare for viewing the documentary, students read "Hoop Roots," an autobiographical essay by John Edgar Wideman. We then watched the film, considering our responses as viewers: How do we perceive the boys, their lives, their choices, their dreams? How do the choices the directors made in shooting and editing this film lead us to forming those perceptions? After viewing the film, students discussed those questions and then transformed the questions to their own writing. How do *they* want their readers to perceive them and their experiences? What words, descriptions, figures of speech, or structures will lead to the readers forming those perceptions? Ultimately, I use film in my composition class to make accessible for my students the choices writers make when writing in order to achieve their purpose.

Jennifer Larson, Maple Grove Senior High, Minnesota

Documentaries vary in terms of their constructions of reality. Traditional documentary employs techniques in which the filmmaker adopts a clearly defined perspective or agenda as reflected in deliberate selection and editing of material to communicate that perspective or agenda. In his documentaries *Roger and Me* (1989), *Bowling for Columbine* (2002), and *Fahrenheit 9/11* (2004), Michael Moore selects the material that will best convey his perspective on issues of corporate responsibility, gun control, and George W. Bush's presidency.

Traditional documentary also makes extensive use of interviews or quoted material, selecting and editing those interview clips that will most clearly convey the intended message. It also employs voice-over commentary to convey its primary points consistent with its desired message.

In contrast to traditional documentary, cinéma vérité documentary attempts to capture experience in as unobtrusive, unedited a manner as possible. These documentaries consist of long takes with little editing or commentary. There are also far fewer interviews, in favor of having participations converse with one another. Events are portrayed as they unfold, without having the presence of a camera influence those events or any staging or playing for the camera to shape those events. The less obtrusive, lightweight 16mm camera, zoom lens, fast film stocks, and superior recording equipment in the 1960s led to the rise of cinéma vérité documentary at that time (Giannetti, 2004).

Cinéma vérité documentary reflects the anthropological belief in the need to capture social and cultural practices as they occur without imposing one's own interpretive frame. The primary assumption is that the filmmaker should simply portray events or people as they behave in everyday contexts without attempting to manipulate or impose their own perspectives onto such portrayals.

One of the most significant cinéma vérité documentary filmmakers is Frederick Wiseman, whose documentaries (e.g., *High School II* [1994] and *Domestic Violence* [2002]) focus on people's experiences in various institutions or sites–schools, hospitals, towns, government/welfare agency sites, prisons, stores, parks. He shows long segments of people interacting with each other or with the site with minimal editing and no interviews or voice-overs.

Propaganda represents an extreme example of biased selectivity in which a filmmaker uses documentary to promote a distorted or one-sided perspective to achieve certain goals. During wartime, documentaries are constructed in a way that transforms "the enemy" into the object of hatred and anger and the sponsoring country into a heroic, virtuous agent of good. For example, the documentary *Triumph of the Will* (1935), directed by Leni Riefenstahl, was made to glorify the Nazi regime and Hitler as the admired leader who will unify the German people as a master race.

All of this raises questions as to whether it is ever possible to portray reality in an unmediated, unfiltered manner. Wiseman describes his films as "fictions," noting that they are still *his* interpretations of reality, as opposed to a totally unmediated version of reality. In conjunction with studying the reality TV genre, students could discuss the degree to which the editing and selection of sensationalized conflicts between contestants reflects the reality of their relationships (Breton & Cohen, 2003).

Based on their analysis of different documentary techniques, students can create their own documentaries by first selecting a site, person(s), or event about which they would make a documentary, for example, their school or their sports team. Working in small groups, they could then discuss the "truths" they know about this site, person(s), or event that they would attempt to capture, for example, that there is considerable tension between the school administration and the students in their school over issues of dress or free speech. They can then decide which techniques they will employ to portray these truths–which people they would interview, what questions they would ask, what events or images they would employ, and how they would engage their audiences. They can then present their ideas to each other to discern how potential audiences would respond to or understand the truths they were attempting to encourage audiences to explore.

SUMMARY

In studying the news, students are learning to critically examine the accuracy and objectivity of print and TV news. In studying print news, they can analyze the design and layout aspects of the different newspaper sections, as well as relationships between print and online versions and the influence of blogs on content. And they can study issues of objectivity and bias associated with journalists' coverage of certain events, for exam-ple, how issues of racial difference are portrayed. As I have argued throughout this book, they may best understand different features of a newspaper through creating their own classroom newspaper or working on the school newspaper.

Students could also study the depth of analysis of local and national TV news broadcasts, along with the need to entertain audiences. As part of that analysis, they could examine the issue of whether documentaries are able to capture the reality or "truth" of the events they portray, or whether the process of filming an event creates its own set of realities. In creating their own TV news broadcasts, students grapple with issues of objectivity and the portrayal of reality.

For both print and TV news, students can study the influence of corporate ownership on selection of news content, as well as the lack of alternative journalistic perspectives in markets with only one owner.

CHAPTER 10

Integrating Film and Other Media into the Curriculum

Key to Topics

AS NOTED IN CHAPTER 1, film/media is often marginalized in the language arts curriculum as peripheral to teaching "basic skills" of reading and writing. One reason for this marginalization is that the overall curriculum is often defined in terms of separate components of reading, writing, speaking, listening, and viewing, with priority accorded to reading and writing instruction because of the emphasis on high-stakes reading and writing testing. Because "viewing" is assumed to be simply "entertainment," it is therefore perceived as lacking a certain intellectual or cognitive rigor associated with the analysis or production of print texts.

Thus there is a need for an alternative curriculum framework, organized around helping students acquire the interpretive strategies employed in responding to and producing both media and literary/expository texts. Framing the curriculum according to these interpretative strategies serves to integrate the analysis and production of media texts with the analysis and production of literary texts.

Taking such an approach does not negate the value of stand-alone film or media studies classes, which have the value of focusing on specific aspects of film or media. However, there is a need to redefine the English language arts curriculum in terms of the basic processes involved in interpreting and constructing both print and media texts.

Framing the curriculum according to interpretative strategies serves to define the goals and learning objectives related to what students *should learn to do* in understanding and producing texts. As discussed at the end of this chapter, students are then evaluated in terms of criteria specific to each of the interpretive strategies and critical approaches.

This focus on organizing the curriculum around strategies is consistent with current media literacy curriculum development (10.1.1–4). As I argued in Chapter 2, literacy curriculum integration also needs to incorporate the use of digital tools such as blogs, wikis, podcasts, iMovies™, and so on (Jonassen & Stollenwerk, 2000) to help students in analyzing and constructing media texts (10.1.5–7; Hammett & Barrell, 2002). The Website contains extensive curriculum, syllabi, and units available from a range of sites devoted to media literacy instruction (10.1.8–26).

COMPARING AND CONTRASTING DIFFRERENT MEDIA FORMS

One of the basic strategies involved in interpreting and constructing media texts involves the different types of media discussed in this book: film, television, radio, magazines, newspapers, and digital media, as well as literature and theater. By comparing and contrasting the formal aspects and conventions of these different media, students could gain an understanding of their unique characteristics. As we have noted previously, comparing the technical aspects of film versus TV helps students understand the differences between these two meida; for example, the wide screen used in film allows for placement of characters at either end of the screen, while TV characters are usually placed closer to one another.

Understanding these unique characteristics can help students in judging the quality of different media texts based on criteria unique to that specific media. Rather than simply saying that, for example, a film is better than a novel, students can judge the film based on its cinematic qualities, and the novel on its literary qualities. By comparing and contrasting film adaptations with the literary or theater texts on which they are based, students expand their knowledge of the differences between film, literature, and theater.

Differences Between Film and Theater

In his textbook *Understanding Movies*, Louis Giannetti (2004; 10.2.1) describes some of the differences between film and theater. Understanding these differences is useful for an appreciation of the ways in which film adaptations of literature have evolved.

- *Time.* Film can be highly flexible, moving backward (with flashbacks) or forward, as well as compressing or speeding up time; time in the theater is continuous and limited to moving forward in time.
- *Space.* Space in film is two-dimensional and viewers can be positioned relative to the characters through different types of shots—from close-ups to a range of different distances and spaces. Theater by contrast focuses on characters and their relationships within relatively a smaller, limited space.

  Space in theater is three-dimensional and audiences can select where and how to focus their attention. However, a theater is a closed space; once actors leave the stage, for the moment they are no longer receiving our attention, while film often uses "off-frame" action, whereby we are aware of someone outside of the frame, a character who *is* receiving our attention.
- *Audience Positioning.* Film directors position audiences in space in relationship to actors or objects using different shots. In theater space, the audience chooses the perspective to adopt, in focusing on what is happening on the stage. Film directors therefore exert more control over their audiences' placement than do stage directors.
- *Language.* Film employs both cinematography and language to convey meaning, whereas theater employs primarily language, although some theater productions incorporate multimedia/videos as part of the production.
- *Directing.* Film directors can redo a certain scene numerous times until it fits what they want to convey. While theater directors certainly will rework scenes, once the play begins its run, it is generally performed in the same manner night after night.

A TEACHING IDEA

CLASSROOM APPLICATIONS FOR FILM ADAPTATIONS OF LITERATURE

As I began work in my own classrooms 9 years ago on the use of film adaptations of literature, I found that the traditional descriptors applied to adaptations, "literal," "faithful," and "loose" (Giannetti, 2004), belied the range of adaptations that were now available and their versatility in the classroom as texts. I attempted to codify some of the following newer variations I saw emerging in the genre of film adaptations, and began to consider the types of critical thinking questions that each type of adaptation engendered.

- *Displaced.* The film changes the time period, but maintains fidelity to all other major aspects of original text including language, as in the 1996 *Romeo + Juliet* (Luhrmann, 1996) set in a contemporary world of competing gangs and violence, sex, and drugs, an MTV-type visual style, and contemporary soundtrack. *Hamlet* (Almereyda, 2000) is set in New York City, where Hamlet is trying to stop the uncle who has usurped control of his father's Denmark Corporation.

- *Acculturated.* In the acculturated adaptation, while the characters, plot, and theme of the original text are retained, the film shifts its use of language and setting into a new context. *10 Things I Hate About You* (Junger, 1998) is a modern version of *The Taming of the Shrew* set in a suburban high school.

- *Politicized.* The politicized adaptation maintains general fidelity to literary aspects of the original text, but refocuses the theme in order to make a contemporary political statement, as in *Henry V* (Oliver, 1944) and *Portrait of a Lady* (Campion, 1996). *Mansfield Park* (Rozerna, 1999) takes Austen's most silent heroine, Fanny Price, and gives her a voice of her own. In this feminist/Marxist interpretation of the text, Fanny becomes a writer, and uses her literary talent to express her criticism of the hypocrisy she sees around her related to class and race.

- *Hollywoodized.* The Hollywoodized adaptation alters the character, plot, and/or themes in order to appeal to a mass commercial audience, as in *The Most Dangerous Game* (Pichel, 1932) and *Wuthering Heights* (Wyler, 1939). Kenneth Branagh's 1996 version of *Hamlet* includes every line of the text, but neglects to provide any unifying interpretation of the text as a whole. Instead, the interest in the film is supplied by cameo appearances by numerous American and British actors, opulent sets, and scenes replete with special effects, but it has no emotional or critical center, and becomes instead a typical action hero movie.

- *Radical Homage.* A radical homage involves the creation of a highly innovative, unconventional version of the original text through use of allusions to the original text and cinematic techniques. Often, both the original and filmic texts are deconstructed, as in *Prospero's Books* (Greenway, 1991) and *Tempest* (Mazursky, 1982). Al Pacino's *Looking for Richard* (1996) is a fascinating film that blends documentary with a filmed dramatic version of *Richard III*. Pacino roams around New York City asking people on the street and people in show business to comment on their attitudes about Shakespeare. Then he gathers a group of famous actors to create a staging of *Richard III* that will be accessible to the masses. He films rehearsals, location scouting, and arguments over interpretations of passages.

In teaching film adaptations, one of the first aspects to consider is whether or not it is necessary to watch the entire film. In general, if students have read all of an original text, I find it most useful to utilize partial viewings.

With 9th graders, I require a very concrete task during their viewing, such as: "Write down 10 significant changes in character or plot the directors made from the original story." However, the goal is ultimately to push students into more abstract thinking. For instance, I might have them consider how each change in character or plot alters the themes.

I have also concluded these activities with an evaluative writing assignment in which the students have to explain which version of the story is better and why, using textual support. Students actually express a great amount of disagreement over this; some prefer the more clear-cut heroism of the film, while others prefer the ambiguity of the story, which allows them to imagine the ending they wish for the protagonist.

I also use clips from multiple film adaptations whenever they are available. This helps students begin to understand that directors and actors make choices during their performances. Most of the commonly taught Shakespearean plays have multiple film versions, and the more dramatically divergent the adaptations are, the more interesting the class discussion can be. This assignment works well with the two film versions of *Romeo and Juliet* (Zeffirelli, 1968 and Luhrmann, 1996). I usually highlight key scenes from the play and stagger the viewings throughout our reading of the text. Some of the most useful scenes for comparison with the original text are the three fight scenes (1.1, 3.1, and 5.3), and the party scene (1.5).

With older students, I typically teach *Hamlet,* for which there are a wide range of adaptations. My favorite scene for cinematic comparison is scene 3.1, which contains the "To be or not to be" soliloquy and Hamlet's confrontation with Ophelia. I usually use the 1990, 1996, and 2000 films, better known by their lead actors Mel Gibson, Kenneth Branagh, and Ethan Hawke respectively. Once students have read the scene and made their own notes on how they think its main elements should be performed, we watch the three versions. Students take notes on which aspects of each they like and dislike, and decide which one they like best. Then they physically move into different debate teams according to their choice, and debate the merits and weaknesses of each. Such a discussion necessitates that they support their opinions with evidence from both the original play and the films.

Although I typically use clips from films when students have read an entire text, this rule also works in reverse: if my intention is for students to view an entire film version, then we read only selected excerpts. Thus I have frequently taught both Branagh's *Much Ado About Nothing* (1993) and *Henry V* (1989) without reading the entire texts.

Although *Much Ado* can be viewed by students with relatively little foregrounding, *Henry V* is a challenging play because of the specificity of its historical context. However, it is also one of the most rewarding texts to explore with students given our current political context. I set up the background story from the three preceding plays (*Richard II* and *Henry IV Parts I* and *II*) and then we "read" the film. We watch scene by scene, stopping to read excerpts, write, and discuss after almost every scene. I prepare for this type of viewing exactly as I would for teaching the written play; the only difference is that we have the opportunity to hear the language performed by professional actors and staged by an able cinematic director. I supply students with copies of most of the major speeches from the play, which we then analyze in more depth, particularly as examples of war rhetoric. After we have competed our reading of the film, students apply multiple critical perspectives to the film, such as the Marxist, feminist, psychological, and archetypal lenses. I usually conclude this unit with an essay test asking students to consider whether Henry is or is not a hero.

Regardless of the text, film adaptations of literature can engage students in critical interpretations of both literature and media. One of the best ways to begin is to select a scene from the text, and have students watch several different directors' imaginings of it. These different adaptations quickly can become the basis for a spirited debate about the merits of each version, or the basis for a written critical analysis that allows students to delve more deeply into the complex relationship between the mediums of literature and film.

Rachel Malchow Lloyd,
Champlin Park High School, Minnesota

In organizing a curriculum based on film adaptations linked to certain texts, Teasley and Wilder (1997, p. 135) recommend pairing up texts and films in terms of similar settings, themes, or genres. It is important to recognize that not all film adaptations are successful: it may be more productive to pair film and print texts based on similarity of themes, topics, issues, or problems if the book selected for study does not have a suitable film adaptation.

Reading from the Perspective of Film Production

Once students are familiar with film techniques, you can ask them to read a literary text from the perspective of someone producing a film version of the text. In a literature circles activity, Lisa Fink had students assume the roles of casting director, critic, dialogue director, director, manager, production designer, soundtrack designer, storyboard artist, and analyst, and respond to the text according to their role (10.2a.1a). As they are reading, in assuming these different roles, students are then envisioning how they would cast certain characters, employ certain shots, create dialogue, design sets, add music, and so on in creating a film adaptation.

Based on their cinematic envisionments of texts, students could also create storyboard or comic book adaptations that convey their own interpretations of these texts (10.2a.1b–1c). The Website contains extensive sites and books on film adaptations (10.2a.2–61) and approaches to teaching related aspects of literature (10.2a.62–81).

TEACHING STRATEGIES FOR INTERPRETING AND CONSTRUCTING TEXTS

In organizing the English/language arts curriculum around teaching strategies for interpreting and constructing texts, it is useful to employ a "backwards" design (Wiggins & McTighe, 2005; 10.3.1): to first define learning objectives–what you want your students to be able to know and do–followed by defining those strategies designed to achieve those objectives. For example, if your goal is for students to learn to explore their own autobiographical identities, you might consider using a strategy of studying digital texts that portray the past self.

Experiencing Different Types of Media

Students can explore the differences in their experiences of different types of media, and make comparisons that help them define their unique characteristics related to the following aspects:

- *Subjective Experiences.* Audiences experience different subjective experiences with different media. In responding to theater, they become caught up in the live actors' physical performances; in responding to film, they experience a sense of being enveloped by the visual world on the screen; in listening to a baseball game on the radio, they become engaged with their own imagined versions of the game; in playing a video game, they experience a sense of apprehension over the possibility of losing or a sense of exhilaration when winning. By reflecting on these different emotions, students can note how certain media evoke these subjective experiences: How, for example, the use of vivid verbal descriptions on a radio-broadcast baseball game helps them imagine and become part of the game. Or students could compare the emotions they experience when listening to the same song in different media: as a live performance on stage, as a song on a CD or the radio, as a music video, and as a song in a film. Each of these different media involves different kinds of subjective experiences with the song. Their experiences of a song in a music video or film will be shaped by the visual elements of those media, as opposed to only listening to the song and creating their own imagined visual interpretations. (For lesson plans from the Rock and Roll Hall of Fame that involve integrating music with other forms of literacy, see 10.3a.1.)

- *Audience Participation.* Students could also compare differences in the kinds of audience participation that different types of media evoke. In reading a print text, readers construct their own envisionments of characters and events, while in viewing a film adaptation, they are presented with the director's envisionments, which may or may not be consistent with a reader's imagined versions. In watching a TV sports broadcast, their experiences are framed by the use of instant replay and a multitude of different shots of the same play. In contrast, in listening to a sports broadcast on the radio, students must imagine the visual aspects of a game. In playing a video game, students make decisions that shape the direction of narrative development, while reading a story, they have little say about story development.

While comparing differences in their participation across these media, students can also identify the specific aspects of each medium that foster certain kinds of experiences: for example, how the focus on language in radio or podcasts differs from a focus on the visual in film or television. They could then apply those differences in creating their own productions, for example creating radio plays (10.3a.2) using GarageBand™ (10.3a.3) to create sound effects and music.

Interpreting and Producing Narratives

A second strategy involves the ability to interpret narrative or storyline development based on how certain events cause or can be explained by other events. In interpreting narrative development, students are continually predicting subsequent events, predictions that help them determine the nature of the storyline based on their knowledge of prototypical genre types.

If, for example, they predict that the ending will be a happy one, they know that they are operating in the familiar world of a comedy storyline.

Based on interpreting narratives, students can then create multimedia, digital storytelling narratives (10.3b.1a–1w), comics (10.3b.2a–2q), manga or graphic novels (10.3b.2a–2p), or digital multimedia poetry (10.3b.4a–4m). In creating their digital literary texts, students are thinking about how to combine images, clips, music, and text to develop their narratives or poems in ways that engage readers. For example, in writing a time travel story in which they project their hero into the world of 2080, they may consider how to use images of a future world to portray the world of 2080.

Film Narratives. In examining clips of film adaptations of literature, students in my class compare the differences between storyline development in the original text and the film version. They note instances in which certain events were omitted, added, or rearranged, and speculate about the reasons behind these changes in the original text. In many cases, the film version simply cannot include all of the events of the text, due to lack of time. For example, the film version of the nonfiction book *Seabiscuit* (Ross, 2003) was truncated by omitting from the narrative several instances when the horse lost in a race with a hundred-thousand-dollar purse. (Students could compare the storyline variations in the many different versions of *King Lear* [e.g., Brook, 1971], 10.3b.1.)

My students also examine how filmmakers use certain techniques to engage audiences in making predictions for story outcomes. They note how the use of an establishing shot serves to help audiences predict that a particular setting will influence subsequent events, just as writers focus on the influence of setting. Or they note the use of a close-up on a certain object or person, which may suggest that this object or person will play an important role in later shots. They then identify how authors use literary techniques to foster predictions with readers. For example, writers appeal to readers' use of "rules of notice" (Rabinowitz & Smith, 1998) to focus on the importance of titles, key events, images, or endings that foretell story outcomes. And in studying adaptations, they note the use of these film and writing techniques in both films and texts. For example, in both the film and print versions of *Lord of the Flies* (Brook, 1963), changes in the boys' face paint and behavior helped audiences predict changes in the characters' behavior: that the boys are going to become more warlike.

Game Narratives. To help students recognize connections between narrative development in games that might transfer to their reading and writing, Zoeverna Jackson (2003) has her first-year college composition students identify certain games and their experiences in playing those games based on the following questions:

What character did they choose and why?
What was their quest?
How long did they play the game?
How many times did they play the game?
Did they play the game alone or with friends?
Was the narrative in the video game interesting?
    Why or why not?

She then suggests that students create their own video games by writing a narrative and constructing a storyboard for such a game and, if possible, an actual website. Students would then reflect on the following questions:

How does your video game function as a story-
    telling device?
What is the most powerful narrative aspect of
    your video game?
What is the weakest narrative aspect of your
    video game?
How does your video game relate to or interact
    with its intended audience?"

For sites on game research related to players' use of narrative, see 10.3b.5.

Character Interpretations

Another important strategy to develop is students' abilities to interpret characters' traits, beliefs, agendas, and goals from their actions. To do so, students must go beyond the actions or dialogue in a story to infer what characters believe about each other, their agendas or plans, and the goals they are trying to achieve.

In comparing print and film texts, my students examine the extent to which the film portrays their interpretation of a character based on their reading of a text. They note how a filmmaker constructs characters through the choice of a certain actor or actress and their behaviors, appearance, dress, and language use. In his book *Teaching in the Dark*, which describes methods of integrating film into the literature class-

room, John Golden (2001) describes the portrayal of Henry V in the film adaptation of the Shakespeare play (Branagh, 1989) in which Henry delivers the St. Crispin's Day speech to rally his troops to defeat the French:

As he begins, he is in the center, on the men's level, but as he continues he moves to a make-shift platform above the gathered crowd. The nonidegetic music changes radically to a very light, then swelling and rousing, melody. . . .

Throughout his speech, we cut from medium shots of Henry back to shots of the soldiers who are clearly being deeply affected by his words. When Henry says that "We few, we happy few" are the only ones to share in this glorious victory, we the audience see the only close-up in the scene. The music reaches its crescendo just as Henry shouts "upon St. Crispin's day" and we see long shots of the men shouting and pumping their fists in the air. (pp. 65–66)

(For a lesson plan on analyzing fictional characters, see 10.3c.1).

Cultural and Historical Contexts

Another important strategy to develop is students' ability to contextualize film and print texts, by examining the cultural and historical forces shaping characters' actions and beliefs. Understanding, for example, Elizabeth Bennett's social practices as a female in the early-19th-century world of the novel and film *Pride and Prejudice* (Wright, 2005) requires some understanding of how social behaviors were perceived as appropriate for certain social classes: the aristocracy, the landed gentry, the mercantile middle class, the military, and the working class. To take another example, in the novel and film *To Kill a Mockingbird* (Mulligan, 1962; 10.3c.1a), the townspeople are accustomed to a segregated world. Atticus's principled defense of Boo Radley is based on a vision of a new world of integration that challenges the town's familiar segregated world.

This strategy can then be taken a step further. In studying what Machow described as "acculturated" adaptations—in which the film is set in a different setting—students can discuss how the switch in setting influences the characters actions and beliefs. For example, in discussing *Clueless* (Heckerling, 1995), students may note how being in a contemporary setting shaped the females' self-perceptions versus those of females in Austen's 19th-century novel, *Emma*. The

Website contains additional sites on exploring cultural and historical worlds (10.3d.1–4).

Students could also examine how both films and literature reflect the values of different generations. For example, students could examine how films of the late 1960s and early 1970s such as *Easy Rider* (Hopper, 1969), *American Graffiti* (Lucas, 1973), *The Graduate* (Nichols, 1967), and *Alice's Restaurant* (Penn, 1969) represented a shift in films toward a younger audience, both in terms of content and style, and what this trend might indicate about the rise of a new, large group of adolescents who were rebelling against the status-quo institutions of that time. The Website contains sites on historical development of media (10.3d.5–8), film (10.3d.9–10), television (10.3d.11–18a), advertising (10.3d.19–21), digital media (10.3d.22–23), and music (10.3d.24–27).

Students could also envision how the influence of technologies on characters is portrayed in utopian and distopian novels such as *1984* or *Brave New World* (10.3d.28). They could also rewrite classical texts such as *Romeo and Juliet* to place them in a contemporary setting in which characters are using digital technologies (10.3d.29).

Interpreting Point of View and Perspectives

Another strategy involves analyzing the use of point of view or perspective employed in a text and in a film. This includes first person point of view (through the eyes of a narrator or character) as opposed to third-person (through the eyes of an author or director). Golden (2001) uses the concept of "focalization" to work with the differences in point of view with his students. The first type of "focalization" is "subjective"–similar to first-person point of view–in which the audience adopts the perspective or eye-line of a particular character. The audience may perceive everything through the eyes of that character or, alternately, the perspective may switch back and forth from the character's perspective to a third-person perspective of the director. Golden cites the example, of a subjective, first-person perspective, of a lion hunter in the jungle:

> Imagine, for example, that we see a man hunting lions in the middle of a jungle. We hear a sound and we see him looking around then we cut to what he sees: something rushing in the bushes. Then maybe we cut back to his face tensing up, and then we cut back to the lion leaping out. The lion is rushing directly towards the hunter, toward the camera, and thus toward us. We see what he sees and feel what he feels. (p. 73)

The second type of "focalization" is "authorial," in which the director provides an audience with certain information that is not available to a character. Golden cites the example of the same shot of the man in the jungle, but now rather than cutting to the man's point of view, the director shows the lion behind the man, who is unaware of the lion's presence. In this case, the audience acquires information not available to a character, but provided for the audience by the director.

The third type of focalization is "neutral" (p. 73), in which there is no attempt to convey certain information either from a character's or the director's perspective. Thus, the same lion hunter scene would include shots of "the hunt, then cut to the lion, and then cut back to the man as he runs away from the lion and the camera. We might not get an eye-line match, nor might we see some dramatic low angle emphasizing the power of that lion" (p. 74).

Students could compare differences in the portrayal of characters' point of view or perspectives through the use of language in print texts and the use of camera work and language in films. And they could explore differences in perspectives associated with language use in different types of media. For example, in the following activity, students contrast perspectives related to language between a tabloid versus mainstream newspaper, comparisons they then apply to analyzing perspectives in a literary text.

A TEACHING IDEA

USING ANALYSIS OF PRINT JOURNALISM TO EXPLORE LITERATURE

One area that requires particular attention when exploring media is the area of print journalism. In my English classes, I have attempted to examine this genre both as a topic in and of itself but also as a tool with which to explore literature. Most recently, my students have been engaged in the study of the novel *In the Lake of the Woods* by Tim O'Brien (1995), a complex text that is part mystery, part historical fiction, and part nonfiction, and that explores the nature of truth, memory, and historical perspective. Because the reader is left to speculate on often conflicting evidence about the accuracy of the events the novel presents, this text is useful to couple with the study of issues of accuracy in print journalism.

I began the lesson by sharing the following definitions with students from Raynor, Wall, and Kruger (2004):

- *Broadsheet.* A large rectangular newspaper. Broadsheets are generally associated with serious journalism, including information about important events at the local, national, and international levels.

- *Tabloid*. A compact newspaper, half the size of a broadsheet. Tabloids are generally more entertainment-oriented and have a reputation for sensationalizing events rather than providing comprehensive coverage of local, national, and international events.

After a short discussion of these definitions and the examination of several samples, students were divided into groups (3–4 students each). Each group was then provided with copies of a broadsheet newspaper (the *International Herald Tribune*) and a British tabloid (the *Daily Mirror*) and asked to examine each text in terms of featured subject matter, length and depth of coverage, headlines and subheads, layout, images, advertisements, style, typeface, language, style, mode of address, perspectives, ideological stance, and audience.

Each group then reported on their findings, noting the stylistic and ideological differences between the texts, as well as the relative value society places on such publications, the potential for bias and exaggeration, and the general purpose of such texts to entertain and/or inform.

In order to explore the differences between these text types more thoroughly, we then turned our attention to O'Brien's novel. Students were asked to identify one event, character, or situation from *In the Lake of the Woods* that was of interest to them, and could be interpreted from more than one perspective. They then wrote a 750-word article about their chosen aspect, using information from the novel as evidence and quotations as support, in the style of one of the two types of newspapers. (Half of the students were assigned a broadsheet and half a tabloid.)

From this assignment, students gained firsthand experience with each type of publication in terms of alternative perspectives on the novel, and, specifically, differences in tone, audience, and purpose in the writing.

Sandra Landis,
International School of Stavanger, Norway

Intertextual Connections

Another important strategy for studying any media text involves defining connections of language, images, characters, topics, or themes between texts (Shuart-Faris & Bloome, 2005). For example, the film adaptation *Romeo + Juliet* (Luhrmann, 1996) assumes audience knowledge of the family conflicts in the original play (10.3e.1). Students could reflect on how they draw on prior knowledge of other texts to interpret new texts, in terms of images, character types, storylines, settings, or themes.

Students can then use intertextual connections in creating their own multigenre or hypermedia texts,

combining images, video clips, audio, and text to create multimodal texts (10.3e.2–5). In writing a report or story, they may add a photo or video clip to illustrate their ideas. This kind of project requires knowledge of multimodal design related to how images function to augment text (Kress, 2003). And, as noted in Chapter 2, it is important that students learn to use links to critically analyze the meaning of images or texts by shifting or recontextualizing an image or text from one context to a totally different one. For example, McDonald's and other fast food conglomerates advertise their high-fat fast food by portraying it in a positive, enjoyable context. By placing the image of, for example, a Big Mac into a different context–as in the documentary *Super-Size Me* (Spurlock, 2004)–audiences view the image of a Big Mac in a totally different perspective, as related to obesity and numerous health problems, particularly Type 2 diabetes in young people.

You can also used digital tools to make hypertextual connections between texts (10.3e.6–11). Students can use tools such as Quicktime Pro™, VideoPaper Builder 2™, Inspiration™, Noodletools™, or Flash™, which appeal to visual–spatial learners, to create hypermedia texts that connect images, texts, music, and video (10.3e.13–19). Students can also organize collections of digital texts found through search engines based on certain themes, topics, or concepts. For example, Jeff Rice (2003b) asked students to create a "handbook of cool" based on images of dress, behavior, artifacts, and consumer goods, as well as texts from the 1950s to the present, as a way of encouraging them to examine different cultural attitudes toward what was considered "cool" in different decades. And Adrien Miles argues that blogger sites allow for combining different forms of textual links based on Google™ searches and links to previous messages on a site as another way of constructing knowledge, as illustrated by the OzBlog site (20.3e.20). The Website contains other digital media sites (10.3e.21–37) and sites on the analysis of intertextuality in media and digital literature (10.3e.38–53). Students could also reflect on the use of intertextuality in their language use or voices in online chat, blogs, or MOOs (10.3f.1–10).

Evaluation of Literary and Media Texts

A final strategy involves the ability to judge the quality of literary and media texts. This entails going beyond a subjective reaction to assess the specific aspects of a text based on predetermined criteria. To inductively derive some criteria for judging, for example, film quality, students could go online to some of the leading film review sites (10.3g.1–6).

They could compare films that receive high and low ratings and attempt to discern the criteria reviewers are employing. They could also examine different reviews of the same film and note the underlying criteria. In some cases, the criteria may not be articulated, but in other cases, reviewers may refer to the quality of the cinematography or editing, acting, directing, story development, setting authenticity, and portrayals of themes. Students could formulate criteria for judging quality of print texts based on the works of literature they have read to date, criteria that may differ from those used to judge films (10.3g.7).

They could then compare their judgments of a literary text with a film adaptation, recognizing the differences between the two forms. Rather than judging the film as "better" or "worse" than the book, they could then consider reasons why the film succeeds or fails in terms of the use of film techniques. They could also examine the ways in which judgments of quality often reflect institutional biases or attitudes. For example, the Oscars tend to reflect the interests of the Hollywood film industry as opposed to the independent film industry. Students could review those films that have won Oscars and note what aspects of those films may have contributed to them being winners (10.3g.8–11).

Television Programs. In addition to judging film quality, students could formulate those criteria they might apply in judging the quality of television programs, which leads them to contrast film and television production techniques. For example, television is often highly effective in focusing on the "talking head" in on-screen interviews, particularly when using close-ups of people's faces on programs such as *60 Minutes*. As with film reviews, students could examine online television reviews to inductively discern the criteria employed by reviewers (10.3g.12–14).

Webpages and Art. Students could also judge the quality of websites in terms of both design and the objectivity of a site's content, as well as "web art" (10.3g.12–23). They could then use these judgments in thinking about constructing their own websites, particularly in terms of ease of use and appeal. The Website contains further examples of film criticism in newspaper, journal, and blog reviews (10.3g.24–42).

DESIGNING MEDIA LITERARY UNITS

In designing units and classroom activities, you can organize activities around students' development and use of the strategies discussed in this chapter. You can also organize units in terms of some coherent, overall theme, issue, genre, archetype, or historical/literary period.

Organizing Factors

In many cases, units combine different aspects of these alternatives; there is no pure prototypical example for each of these different approaches.

Themes. Organizing your unit around a theme such as power, evil, suburbia, or the family, means that you are finding texts that portray these different topics. For example, you may select a series of texts that portray mother/daughter relationships in film, television, or literature. Students may then compare or contrast the different portrayals of the same topic across different texts (for resources on thematic units, see 10.4.1).

Issues, Questions, Dilemmas. You can also organize your units around issues, for example, the issue of gender and power—the degree to which women may have to assume subordinate roles in a culture. One advantage of an issue is that students may adopt different, competing perspectives about an issue, tensions that may create interest in that issue.

Inquiry-based instruction is based on using the strategies of formulating questions, issues, or dilemmas; contextualizing those questions, issues, or dilemmas; defining how those questions, issues, or dilemmas are represented in a media text; critiquing those representations; and formulating alternative solutions (Beach & Myers, 2001; 10.4.2–3). The Website contains sites on inquiry- and problem-based learning (10.4.4–17).

Genres. You may also organize your unit around studying a particular genre—short story, novel, ballad, rap, drama, memoir, biography, poetry, film noir, or hybrid combinations or mixtures of genres evident in a multigenre approach to writing instruction (Romano, 2000). As was noted in Chapter 7, one advantage of a genre approach is that students learn a larger literacy practice of making generalizations about similarities in different texts based on certain genre features.

Historical Periods or Cultural Movements. Units can also be created based on certain historical periods or cultural movements, for example, the portrayal of World War II in films, the rise of hip-hop culture in music, or the Harlem Renaissance in American literature, music, and art. In studying these periods, you can incorporate background historical events or cultural attitudes shaping texts, as well as similarities between literature, art, music, and popular media.

Other Considerations

Connecting to Students' Backgrounds. In planning a unit, you also need to consider your students' cultural background experiences and perspectives. In doing so, you draw on their background using what Carol Lee (2001) describes as "cultural modeling" of connections between the students' cultural background and what they are learning. In working with urban African-American students from Chicago, Lee builds on their background knowledge of the use of symbolic language in everyday verbal interactions, such as "playing the dozens," to help them interpret symbolic language in literary texts.

Integrating Informal Writing. In your activities, it is important to integrate different types of informal writing activities—free writing, listing, jotting, journal entries, mapping, etc.—to help students formulate their responses to media texts and ideas in a spontaneous, informal manner. Jim Burke's "school tools" (10.4a.1) includes various informal writing tools for fostering student thinking about texts.

Respecting Copyright Laws. In selecting media texts that are copyrighted, you and your students need to follow the guidelines associated with fair use of media texts for educational, noncommercial classroom use, while at the same time examining issues of intellectual property in a digital age (10.4a.2–4h). The Website contains further resources for unit development (10.4a.5–20).

EVALUATION AND ASSESSMENT OF LEARNING

In evaluating student work in units, it is important that you consider the use of performance or "authentic" assessment as a means of evaluating students' written responses, project work, or productions (10.4b.1–4).

Formulating Criteria and Rubrics

To evaluate student performance, you need to formulate specific criteria and rubrics consistent with your goals. For example, if you want to evaluate students' analysis of a literary adaptation, you may want to develop criteria and rubrics associated with their ability to critically examine the film adaptation relative to the original text (Worsnop, 2000; 5.4b.5–15).

Creating E-Portfolios

One way of integrating the assessment of student work in a unit or course is by having students create a portfolio, or collection of work, that showcases their growth, knowledge, and understanding of their work in the unit or course (10.4b.16a–16l). Students could also create digital portfolios based on digital versions of their texts, images, and/or video clips, something that would work well in a media studies course (Wilferth, 2003). As illustrated by the e-portfolios on the Website, students could construct links between their different texts that display their reflections on connections between their work (10.4b.16m).

EXEMPLARY MEDIA LITERACY CURRICULA

There are three media curricula available online that exemplify the use of the strategies described in this chapter

- *The British Film Institute's Moving Images in the Classroom.* The BFI's *Moving Images in the Classroom* (10.4b.17) curriculum, developed for nine different subject matter areas, revolves around analysis of how images are used to demonstrate practices, develop narratives, formulate arguments, and portray places, as well as mislead audiences. In this curriculum, students continually use their analysis of images in texts to create multimodal texts exploiting the power of images.
- *The Maryland State Department of Education Media Literacy Curriculum* developed by Renee Hobbs for high school students (10.4b.18) includes six units on "Asking Critical Questions"; "Who Do You Trust?: Assessing the Authenticity of Media Messages"; "Crime Reporting"; "History, Literature, and the Mass Media"; "The Language of Politics"; and "The Culture of Celebrity." The six units for middle school students (10.4b.19) include

"Asking Critical Questions," "The Art of Slapstick," "What's Real and What's Reel?": analysis of realism in media texts, "History and Media," with a focus on representation of the Civil War, "Entertainment Warriors:" the role of violence in contemporary sports, and "Media Mania!": reflection on students' media use.

- *The IFC Film School curriculum* contains six units analyzing films, video production, and literature, with a particular focus on film adaptations of Shakespeare plays (10.4b.20). Unit 1 includes a review of film techniques and has students write and film their own soliloquies and opening scenes from movies about their lives. Unit 2 has activities on filming Act 3, Scene 2 from different versions of *Hamlet* and a contemporary version of Charlie Chaplin's *Modern Times* (1936). Unit 3 involves writing a film script for Act 4, Scene 2 from *Macbeth,* and in Unit 4 students create a film trailer for a book they are reading. Unit 5 includes creating a film treatment for a literary text and Unit 6 involves producing a short film.

In addition to those referred to throughout the book, there are also other useful curricular materials relevant for the British (10.4b.21–24) and Canadian (10.4b.24) media literature frameworks. And for teaching specific films, there are online film guides (10.4b.25–34), literature guides (10.4b.35–5), literature lessons (10.4b.46–9), and extensive links on my own TeachingLiterature.org Website (10.4b.50).

SUMMARY

In this concluding chapter, I propose integrating media literacy into the curriculum through teaching strategies involved in interpreting and producing print and media texts. Through interpreting the aspects of character and narrative development in texts, students can then produce their own literary texts. At the same time, by contrasting their experiences with print literature, theater, and film, they learn to appreciate the unique characteristics of these different media.

In closing, it is my hope that the activities and resources presented in this book will help to foster your students' critical analysis and production of media, ideally leading them to create their own media texts in which they voice their own critiques. Please share your own activities and resources on my blog at http://teachingliterature.typepad.com/teachingmedia or on the Media Literacy Wikibook at http://teaching-medialiteracy.pbwiki.com/MediaLiteracyWikibook.

Film and Television Series References

FILM REFERENCES

Allen, W. (Director). (1971). *Bananas* [Motion picture]. United States: Jack Rollins & Charles H. Joffe Productions.

Allen, W. (Director). (1973). *Sleeper* [Motion picture]. United States: Jack Rollins & Charles H. Joffe Productions.

Allen, W. (Director). (1977). *Annie Hall* [Motion picture]. United States: Jack Rollins & Charles H. Joffe Productions.

Allen, W. (Director). (1979). *Manhattan* [Motion picture]. United States: Jack Rollins & Charles H. Joffe Productions.

Allen, W. (Director). (1983). *Zelig* [Motion picture]. United States: Orion Pictures.

Allen, W. (Director). (1985). *The purple rose of Cairo* [Motion picture]. United States: Orion Pictures.

Allen, W. (Director). (1986). *Hannah and her sisters* [Motion picture]. United States: Orion Pictures.

Allen, W. (Director). (1992). *Husbands and wives* [Motion picture]. United States: Tristar Pictures.

Allen, W. (Director). (1994). *Bullets over Broadway* [Motion picture]. United States: Magnolia Productions.

Allers, R., & Minkoff, R. (Directors). (1994). *The lion king* [Motion picture]. United States: Walt Disney Pictures.

Almereyda, M. (Director). (2000). *Hamlet* [Motion picture]. United States: Miramax Films.

Altman, R. (Director). (1970). *M*A*S*H* [Motion picture]. United States: Twentieth Century Fox Film Corporation.

Altman, R. (Director). (1971). *McCabe and Mrs. Miller* [Motion picture]. United States: Warner Brothers.

Altman, R. (Director). (1974). *Thieves like us* [Motion picture]. United States: United Artists.

Altman, R. (Director). (1975). *Nashville* [Motion picture]. United States: ABC/Paramount Pictures.

Altman, R. (Director). (2001). *Gosford Park* [Motion picture]. United States: USA Films.

Avildsen, J. G. (Director). (1976). *Rocky* [Motion picture]. United States: United Artists.

Avildsen, J. G. (Director). (1990). *Rocky V* [Motion picture]. United States: United Artists.

Bay, M. (Director). (1998). *Armageddon* [Motion picture]. United States: Buena Vista Pictures.

Benedek, L. (Director). (1954). *The wild one.* [Motion picture]. United States: Columbia Pictures.

Benigni, R. (Director). (1997). *Life is beautiful* [Motion picture]. Italy: Cecchi Gori Distribuzione.

Benton, R. (Director). (1991). *Billy Bathgate* [Motion picture]. United States: Buena Vista Pictures.

Berman, S. S., & Pulcin, R. (Directors). (2003). *American splendor* [Motion picture]. United States: Home Box Office.

Bont, J. D. (Director). (1996). *Twister* [Motion picture]. United States: Warner Brothers.

Branagh, K. (Director). (1989). *Henry V* [Motion picture]. United Kingdom: Curzon Film Distributors.

Branagh, K. (Director). (1993). *Much ado about nothing* [Motion picture]. United Kingdom: Samuel Goldwyn Company.

Branagh, K. (Director). (1996). *Hamlet* [Motion picture]. United Kingdom: Columbia Pictures Corporation.

Brook, P. (Director). (1963). *Lord of the flies* [Motion picture]. United Kingdom: British Lion Film Corporation.

Brook, P. (Director). (1971). *King Lear* [Motion picture]. United Kingdom: Altura Films International.

Brooks, A. (Director). (1985). *Lost in America* [Motion picture]. United States: Warner Brothers.

Brooks, J. L. (Director). (1987). *Broadcast news* [Motion picture]. United States: Twentieth Century Fox Film Corporation.

Cameron, J. (Director). (1991). *Terminator 2* [Motion picture]. United States: TriStar Pictures.

Cameron, J. (Director). (1997). *Titanic* [Motion picture]. United States: Paramount Pictures.

Campion, J. (Director). (1996). *Portrait of a lady* [Motion picture]. United States: Gramercy Pictures.

Carpenter, J. (Director). (1978). *Halloween* [Motion picture]. United States: Compass International Pictures.

Carr, S. (Director). (2003). *Daddy day care* [Motion picture]. United States: Columbia Pictures.

Cattaneo, P. (Director). (1997). *The full monty* [Motion picture]. Great Britain: Channel Four Films.

Chaplin, C. (Director). (1936). *Modern times* [Motion picture]. United States: United Artists.

Cimino, M. (Director). (1978). *The deer hunter* [Motion picture]. United States: Universal Pictures.

Clayton, J. (Director). (1974). *The great Gatsby* [Motion picture]. United States: Paramount Pictures.

Clements, R., & Musker, J. (Directors). (1989). *The little mermaid* [Motion picture]. United States: Walt Disney Pictures.

Clements, R., & Musker, J. (Directors). (1992). *Aladdin* [Motion picture]. United States: Walt Disney Pictures.

Coen, J., & Coen, E. (Directors). (1987). *Raising Arizona* [Motion picture]. United States: Twentieth Century Fox Film Corporation.

Coen, J., & Coen, E. (Directors). (1990). *Miller's crossing* [Motion picture]. United States: Twentieth Century Fox Film Corporation.

Coen, J., & Coen, E. (Directors). (1996). *Fargo* [Motion picture]. United States: Gramercy Pictures.

Coen, J., & Coen, E. (Directors). (2000). *O brother, where art thou?* [Motion picture]. United States: Buena Vista Pictures.

Columbus, C. (Director). (1993). *Mrs. Doubtfire* [Motion picture]. United States: Twentieth Century Fox Film Corporation.

Columbus, C. (Director). (2001). *Harry Potter and the sorcerer's stone* [Motion picture]. United States: Warner Brothers.

Columbus, C. (Director). (2002). *Harry Potter and the chamber of secrets* [Motion picture]. United States: Warner Brothers.

Coppola, F. F. (Director). (1972). *The Godfather* [Motion picture]. United States: Paramount Pictures.

Coppola, F. F. (Director). (1974a). *The Godfather Part II* [Motion picture]. United States: Paramount Pictures.

Coppola, F. F. (Director). (1974b). *The conversation* [Motion picture]. United States: Paramount Pictures.

Coppola, F. F. (Director). (1979). *Apocalypse now* [Motion picture]. United States: United Artists.

Coppola, F. F. (Director). (1990). *The Godfather Part III* [Motion picture]. United States: Paramount Pictures.

Craven, W. (Director). (1996). *Scream* [Motion picture]. United States: Dimension Films.

Craven, W. (Director). (1997). *Scream 2* [Motion picture]. United States: Dimension Films.

Cuarón, A. (Director). (2004). *Harry Potter and the prisoner of Azkaban* [Motion picture]. United States: Warner Brothers.

Cunningham, S. S. (Director). (1980). *Friday the 13th* [Motion picture]. United States: Paramount Pictures.

Davies, T. (Director). (2000). *The house of mirth* [Motion picture]. United States: Columbia TriStar Films.

Demme, J. (Director). (1991). *The silence of the lambs* [Motion picture]. United States: Orion Pictures Corporation.

Demme, J. (Director). (1993). *Philadelphia* [Motion picture]. United States: TriStar Pictures.

Dindal, M. (Director). (2005). *Chicken little* [Motion picture]. United States: Walt Disney Pictures.

Donen, S. (Director). (1967). *Two for the road* [Motion picture]. United States: Twentieth Century Fox Film Corporation.

Donner, R. (Director). (1987). *Lethal weapon* [Motion picture]. United States: Warner Brothers.

Donner, R. (Director). (1989). *Lethal weapon 2* [Motion picture]. United States: Warner Brothers.

Donner, R. (Director). (1992). *Lethal weapon 3* [Motion picture]. United States: Warner Brothers.

Donner, R. (Director). (1998). *Lethal weapon 4* [Motion picture]. United States: Warner Brothers.

Eastwood, C. (Director). (1992). *Unforgiven* [Motion picture]. United States: Warner Brothers.

Eastwood, C. (Director). (1995). *The bridges of Madison County* [Motion picture]. United States: Warner Brothers.

Edwards, B. (Director). (1963). *The pink panther* [Motion picture]. United States: United Artists.

Eisenstein, S. M., & Aleksandrov, G. (Directors). (1925). *Potemkin (Bronenosets Potyomkin)* [Motion picture]. Soviet Union: Goskino.

Emmerich, R. (Director). (1998). *Godzilla* [Motion picture]. United States: TriStar Pictures.

Emmerich, R. (Director). (2004). *The day after tomorrow* [Motion picture]. United States: Twentieth Century Fox Film Corporation.

Ephron, N. (Director). (1993). *Sleepless in Seattle* [Motion picture]. United States: TriStar Pictures.

Eyre, C. (Director). (1998). *Smoke signals* [Motion picture]. United States: Miramax Films.

Fleming, V. (Director). (1939). *The wizard of Oz* [Motion picture]. United States: Metro-Goldwyn-Mayer (MGM).

Ford, J. (Director). (1939). *Stagecoach* [Motion picture]. United States: United Artists.

Frears, S. (Director). (1990). *The grifters* [Motion picture]. United States: Miramax Films.

Frears, S. (Director). (1996). *The van* [Motion picture]. United States: Fox Searchlight Pictures

Gabriel, M., & Goldberg, E. (Directors). (1995). *Pocahontas* [Motion picture]. United States: Walt Disney Pictures.

George, T. (Director). (2004). *Hotel Rwanda* [Motion picture]. United States: United Artists.

Geronimi, C. (Director). (1959). *Sleeping beauty* [Motion picture]. United States: Walt Disney Pictures.

Geronimi, C., & Jackson, W. (Directors). (1950). *Cinderella* [Motion picture]. United States: Walt Disney Pictures.

Geronimi, C., & Jackson, W. (Directors). (1953). *Peter Pan* [Motion picture]. United States: Walt Disney Pictures.

Gilbert, L. (Director). (1983). *Educating Rita* [Motion picture]. United States: Columbia Pictures.

Gillespie, J. (Director). (1997). *I know what you did last summer* [Motion picture]. United States: Columbia Pictures.

Gilliam, T. (Director). (1995). *Twelve monkeys* [Motion picture]. United States: Universal Pictures.

Greenaway, P. (Director). (1991). *Prospero's books* [Motion picture]. France: Miramax Films.

Hand, D. (Director). (1942). *Bambi* [Motion picture]. United States: Walt Disney Pictures.

Harlin, R. (Director). (1990). *Die Hard 2* [Motion picture]. United States: Twentieth Century Fox Film Corporation.

Hawks, H., & Rosson, A. (Directors). (1948). *Red river* [Motion picture]. United States: United Artists.

Heckerling, A. (Director). (1995). *Clueless* [Motion picture]. United States: Paramount Pictures.

Hellman, M. (Director). (1971). *Two-lane blacktop* [Motion picture]. United States: Universal Pictures.

Hiller, A. (Director). (1970). *Love story* [Motion picture]. United States: Paramount Pictures.

Hirschbiegel, O. (Director). (2004). *Downfall (Der untergang)* [Motion picture]. Germany: Constantin Film.

Hitchcock, A. (Director). (1946). *Notorious* [Motion picture]. United States: RKO Radio Pictures.

Hitchcock, A. (Director). (1954). *Rear window* [Motion picture]. United States: Paramount Pictures.

Hitchcock, A. (Director). (1959). *North by northwest* [Motion picture]. United States: Metro-Goldwyn-Mayer (MGM).

Hitchcock, A. (Director). (1960). *Psycho* [Motion picture]. United States: Paramount Pictures.

Hitchcock, A. (Director). (1963). *The birds* [Motion picture]. United States: Universal Pictures.

Hogan, P. J. (Director). (1997). *My best friend's wedding* [Motion picture]. United States: TriStar Pictures.

Hooper, T. (Director). (1974). *The Texas chainsaw massacre* [Motion picture]. United States: Bryanston Distributing Company.

Hopper, D. (Director). (1969). *Easy rider* [Motion picture]. United States: Columbia Pictures Corporation.

Hughes, J. (Director). (1984). *Sixteen candles* [Motion picture]. United States: Universal Pictures.

Huston, J. (Director). (1941). *The Maltese falcon* [Motion picture]. United States: Warner Brothers.

Huston, J. (Director). (1948). *Key Largo* [Motion picture]. United States: Warner Brothers.

Huston, J. (Director). (1985). *Prizzi's honor* [Motion picture]. United States: Twentieth Century Fox Film Corporation.

Iscove, R. (Director). (1999). *She's all that* [Motion picture]. United States: Miramax Films.

Jackson, P. (Director). (2001). *The lord of the rings: The fellowship of the ring* [Motion picture]. United States: New Line Cinema.

Jackson, P. (Director). (2002). *The lord of the rings: The two towers* [Motion picture]. United States: New Line Cinema.

Jackson, P. (Director). (2003). *The lord of the rings: The return of the king* [Motion picture]. United States: New Line Cinema.

James, S. (Director). (1994). *Hoop dreams* [Motion Picture]. United States: KTCA Television.

Jewison, N. (Director). (1987). *Moonstruck* [Motion picture]. United States: Metro-Goldwyn-Mayer (MGM).

Jordan, N. (Director). (1999). *The end of the affair* [Motion picture]. United States: Columbia Pictures.

Junger, G. (Director). (1999). *10 things I hate about you* [Motion picture]. United States: Buena Vista Pictures.

Kadár, J., & Klos, E. (Directors). (1965). *The shop on Main Street (Obchod na korze)* [Motion picture]. Czech Republic: Asociace Ceských Filmových Klubu (ACFK).

Kaufman, P. (Director). (1978). *Invasion of the body snatchers* [Motion picture]. United States: United Artists.

Kellogg, R., & Wayne, J. (Directors). (1968). *The green berets* [Motion picture]. United States: Warner Brothers/Seven Arts.

Kenan, G. (Director). (2006). *Monster house* [Motion picture]. United States: Sony Pictures Animation.

Kramer, S. (Director). (1960). *Inherit the wind* [Motion picture]. United States: Lomitas Productions Inc.

Kubrick, S. (Director). (1964). *Dr. Strangelove or: How I learned to stop worrying and love the bomb* [Motion picture]. United Kingdom: Columbia Pictures.

Kubrick, S. (Director). (1968). *2001: A space odyssey* [Motion Picture]. United States: Metro-Goldwyn-Mayer (MGM).

Kubrick, S. (Director). (1971). *A clockwork orange* [Motion picture]. United Kingdom: Hawk Films Ltd.

Kubrick, S. (Director). (1980). *The shining* [Motion picture]. United States: Warner Brothers.

Kubrick, S. (Director). (1987). *Full metal jacket* [Motion picture]. United States: Warner Brothers.

Lang, F. (Director). (1931). *M* [Motion picture]. Germany: Vereinigte Star-Film GmbH.

Lang, F. (Director). (1953). *The big heat* [Motion picture]. United States: Columbia Pictures

Lee, A. (Director). (1995). *Sense and sensibility* [Motion picture]. United States: Columbia Pictures.

Lee, S. (Director). (1989). *Do the right thing* [Motion picture]. United States: MCA/Universal Pictures.

Lee, S. (Director). (1991). *Jungle fever* [Motion picture]. United States: Universal Pictures.

LeRoy, M. (Director). (1931). *Little Caesar* [Motion picture]. United States: Warner Bros.

Levinson, B. (Director). (1988). *Rain man* [Motion picture]. United States: MGM/UA Distribution Company.

Levinson, B. (Director). (1991). *Bugsy* [Motion picture]. United States: TriStar Pictures.

Linklater, R. (Director). (2003). *School of rock* [Motion picture]. United States: Paramount Pictures.

Lounsbery, J., & Reitherman, W. (Directors). (1977). *The many adventures of Winnie the Pooh* [Motion picture]. United States: Walt Disney Pictures.

Lucas, G. (Director). (1973). *American graffiti* [Motion picture]. United States: Lucasfilm Ltd/Universal Pictures.

Luhrmann, B. (Director). (1996). *Romeo + Juliet* [Motion picture]. United States: Twentieth Century Fox Film Corporation.

Luske, H., & Sharpsteen, B. (Directors). (1940). *Pinocchio* [Motion picture]. United States: Walt Disney Pictures.

Lynch, D. (Director). (1986). *Blue velvet* [Motion picture]. United States: De Laurentiis Entertainment Group.

Lynch, D. (Director). (1990). *Wild at heart* [Motion picture]. United States: Samuel Goldwyn Company.

Lynch, D. (Director). (2001). *Mulholland Drive* [Motion picture]. United States: The Picture Factory.

Lyne, A. (Director). (1987). *Fatal attraction* [Motion picture]. United States: Paramount Pictures

Malick, T. (Director). (1973). *Badlands* [Motion picture]. United States: Warner Brothers.

Mazursky, P. (Director). (1982). *Tempest* [Motion picture]. United States: Columbia Pictures.

McGrath, D. (Director). (1996). *Emma* [Motion picture]. United States: Miramax Films.

McTiernan, J. (Director). (1988). *Die hard* [Motion picture]. United States: Twentieth Century Fox Film Corporation.

McTiernan, J. (Director). (1993). *Last action hero* [Motion picture]. United States: Columbia Pictures.

McTiernan, J. (Director). (1995). *Die hard with a vengeance* [Motion picture]. United States: Twentieth Century Fox Film Corporation.

McTiernan, J. (Director). (1999). *The Thomas Crown affair* [Motion picture]. United States: Metro-Goldwyn-Mayer Distributing Corporation (MGM).

Michell, R. (Director). (1999). *Notting Hill* [Motion picture]. United States: MCA/Universal Pictures

Minghella, A. (Director). (1996). *The English patient* [Motion picture]. United States: Miramax Films.

Minghella, A. (Director). (2003). *Cold mountain* [Motion picture]. United States: Miramax Films.

Montgomery, R. (Director). (1947). *Lady in the lake* [Motion picture]. United States: Metro-Goldwyn-Mayer (MGM).

Moore, M. (Director). (1989). *Roger and me* [Motion picture]. United States: Warner Brothers.

Moore, M. (Director). (2002). *Bowling for Columbine* [Motion picture]. United States: United Artists.

Moore, M. (Director). (2004). *Fahrenheit 9/11* [Motion picture]. United States: Lions Gate Films.

Mulligan, R. (Director). (1962). *To kill a mockingbird* [Motion picture]. United States: Universal International Pictures.

Myrick, D., & Sánchez, E. (Directors). (1999). *The Blair witch project* [Motion picture]. United States: Alliance Atlantis Communications.

Newell, M. (Director). (1994). *Four weddings and a funeral* [Motion picture]. United States: Gramercy Pictures

Newell, M. (Director). (1997). *Donnie Brasco* [Motion picture]. United States: TriStar Pictures.

Newell, M. (Director). (2005). *Harry Potter and the goblet of fire* [Motion picture]. United Kingdom: Warner Brothers.

Niccol, A. (Director). (1997). *Gattaca* [Motion picture]. United States: Columbia Pictures.

Nichols, M. (Director). (1967). *The graduate* [Motion picture]. United States: Embassy Pictures Corporation.

Nichols, M. (Director). (1988). *Working girl* [Motion picture]. United States: Twentieth Century Fox Film Corporation.

Nichols, M. (Director). (1996). *The birdcage* [Motion picture]. United States: United Artists.

Nolan, C. (Director). (2000). *Memento* [Motion picture]. United States: Newmarket Films.

Olivier, L. (Director). (1944). *Henry V* [Motion picture]. United Kingdom: Eagle-Lion Distributors Limited.

Pacino, A. (Director). (1996). *Looking for Richard* [Motion picture]. United States: Twentieth Century Fox Film Corporation.

Palma, B. D. (Director). (1983). *Scarface* [Motion picture]. United States: Universal Pictures.

Palma, B. D. (Director). (1998). *Snake eyes* [Motion picture]. United States: Paramount Pictures.

Peckinpah, S. (Director). (1978). *Convoy* [Motion picture]. United States: EMI Films Ltd.

Penn, A. (Director). (1967). *Bonnie and Clyde* [Motion picture]. United States: Warner Brothers.

Penn, A. (Director). (1969). *Alice's restaurant* [Motion picture]. United States: United Artists.

Petersen, W. (Director). (1981). *Das boot* [Motion picture]. West Germany: Neue Constantin Film.

Petersen, W. (Director). (1995). *Outbreak* [Motion picture]. United States: Warner Bros.

Pichel, I. (Director). (1932). *The most dangerous game* [Motion picture]. United States: RKO Radio Pictures.

Pollack, S. (Director). (1982). *Tootsie* [Motion picture]. United States: Columbia Pictures.

Pontecorvo, G. (Director). (1966). *The battle of Algiers* [Motion picture]. Algeria: Casbah Films.

Rafelson, B. (Director). (1981). *The postman always rings twice* [Motion picture]. United States: Paramount Pictures.

Raimi, S. (Director). (2002). *Spider-Man* [Motion picture]. United States: Sony Pictures.

Raimi, S. (Director). (2004). *Spider-Man 2* [Motion picture]. United States: Sony Pictures.

Ramis, H. (Director). (1993). *Groundhog day* [Motion picture]. United States: Columbia Pictures.

Redford, R. (Director). (1994). *Quiz show* [Motion picture]. United States: Buena Vista Pictures.

Reed, C. (Director). (1949). *The third man* [Motion picture]. United States: Selznick Releasing Organization.

Reiner, R. (Director). (1986). *Stand by me* [Motion picture]. United States: Columbia Pictures.

Reiner, R. (Director). (1989). *When Harry met Sally* [Motion picture]. United States: Columbia Pictures.

Resnais, A. (Director). (1955). *Night and fog (Nuit et brouillard)* [Motion picture]. France: Available from The Criterion Collection Web site: http://www.criterionco.com/asp/release.asp?id=197.

Riefenstahl, L. (Director). (1935). *Triumph of the will* [Motion picture]. Germany: Leni Riefenstahl-Produktion.

Romero, G. A. (Director). (1968). *Night of the living dead* [Motion Picture]. United States: Market Square Productions.

Ross, G. (Director). (1998). *Pleasantville* [Motion picture]. United States: New Line Cinema.

Ross, G. (Director). (2003). *Seabiscuit* [Motion picture]. United States: Universal Pictures.

Rozema, P. (Director). (1999). *Mansfield Park* [Motion picture]. United States: Miramax Films.

Scorsese, M. (Director). (1980). *Raging bull* [Motion picture]. United States: United Artists.

Scorsese, M. (Director). (1990). *Goodfellas* [Motion picture]. United States: Warner Bros.

Scorsese, M. (Director). (1991). *Cape Fear* [Motion picture]. United States: Universal Pictures.

Scorsese, M. (Director). (1995). *Casino* [Motion picture]. United States: MCA/Universal Pictures.

Scott, R. (Director). (1991). *Thelma and Louise* [Motion picture]. United States: Metro-Goldwyn-Mayer (MGM).

Scott, R. (Director). (2001). *Black Hawk down* [Motion picture]. United States: Columbia Pictures.

Scott, T. (Director). (1993). *True romance* [Motion picture]. United States: Warner Brothers.

Sears, T., & Creedon, R. (Directors). (1937). *Snow White and the seven dwarfs* [Motion picture]. United States: Walt Disney Pictures.

Sena, D. (Director). (1993). *Kalifornia* [Motion picture]. United States: Gramercy Pictures.

Shelton, R. (Director). (1992). *White men can't jump* [Motion picture]. United States: Twentieth Century Fox Film Corporation.

Singer, B. (Director). (1995). *The usual suspects* [Motion picture]. United States: Gramercy Pictures.

Siodmak, R. (Director). (1946). *The killers* [Motion picture]. United States: Universal Pictures.

Smith, J. N. (Director). (1995). *Dangerous minds* [Motion picture]. United States: Hollywood Pictures.

Sonnenfeld, B. (Director). (1997). *Men in black* [Motion picture]. United States: Columbia Pictures.

Spielberg, S. (Director). (1974). *Sugarland express* [Motion picture]. United States: Universal Pictures.

Spielberg, S. (Director). (1975). *Jaws* [Motion picture]. United States: Universal Pictures.

Spielberg, S. (Director). (1985). *The color purple* [Motion picture]. United States: Warner Brothers.

Spielberg, S. (Director). (1993). *Schindler's list* [Motion picture]. United States: Universal Pictures.

Spielberg, S. (Director). (1993). *Jurassic Park* [Motion picture]. United States: Universal Pictures.

Spielberg, S. (Director). (1998). *Saving Private Ryan* [Motion picture]. United States: DreamWorks Distribution LLC.

Spielberg, S. (Director). (2002a). *Minority report* [Motion picture]. United States: Twentieth Century Fox Film Corporation

Spielberg, S. (Director). (2002b). *Catch me if you can* [Motion picture]. United States: DreamWorks Distribution LLC.

Spottiswoode, R. (Director). (1997). *Tomorrow never dies* [Motion picture]. United States: United Artists.

Spurlock, M. (Director). (2004). *Super size me* [Motion picture]. United States: Samuel Goldwyn Films LLC.

Stallone, S. (Director). (1979). *Rocky II* [Motion picture]. United States: United Artists.

Stallone, S. (Director). (1982). *Rocky III* [Motion picture]. United States: MGM/UA Entertainment Company.

Stallone, S. (Director). (1985). *Rocky IV* [Motion picture]. United States: Metro-Goldwyn-Mayer (MGM).

Stone, O. (Director). (1986). *Platoon* [Motion picture]. United States: Orion Pictures Corporation.

Stone, O. (Director). (1989). *Born on the Fourth of July* [Motion picture]. United States: Ixtlan Corporation.

Stone, O. (Director). (1994). *Natural born killers* [Motion picture]. United States: Warner Brothers.

Sturges, J. (Director). (1960). *The magnificent seven* [Motion picture]. United States: United Artists

Tarantino, Q. (Director). (1992). *Reservoir dogs* [Motion picture]. United States: Miramax Films

Tarantino, Q. (Director). (1994). *Pulp fiction* [Motion picture]. United States: Miramax Films.

Tarantino, Q. (Director). (1997). *Jackie Brown* [Motion picture]. United States: Miramax Films.

Tass, N. (Director). (1986). *Malcolm* [Motion picture]. Australia: Cascade Films

Trousdale, G., & Wise, K. (Directors). (1991). *Beauty and the beast* [Motion picture]. United States: Walt Disney Pictures.

Truffaut, F. (Director). (1966). *Fahrenheit 451* [Motion picture]. United Kingdom: Anglo-Enterprise/Vineyard Films.

Turteltaub, J. (Director). (1995). *While you were sleeping* [Motion picture]. United States: Buena Vista Pictures.

Tykwer, T. (Director). (1998). *Run Lola run* [Motion picture]. Germany: X-Filme Creative Pools/Westdeutscher Rundfunk.

Wachowski, A., & Wachowski, L. (Directors). (1999). *The matrix* [Motion picture]. United States: Warner Brothers.

Wachowski, A., & Wachowski, L. (Directors). (2003). *The matrix reloaded* [Motion picture]. United States: Warner Brothers.

Wacks, J. (Director). (1989). *Powwow highway* [Motion picture]. United States: Warner Brothers.

Ward, D. S. (Director). (1989). *Major league* [Motion picture]. United States: Paramount Pictures.

Weir, P. (Director). (1998). *The Truman show* [Motion picture]. United States: Paramount Pictures.

Welles, O. (Director). (1941). *Citizen Kane* [Motion picture]. United States: RKO Radio Pictures/Mercury Productions.

Welles, O. (Director). (1947). *The lady from Shanghai* [Motion picture]. United States: Columbia Pictures.

Welles, O. (Director). (1948). *Macbeth* [Motion picture]. United States: Republic Pictures Corporation.

West, S. (Director). (1997). *Con air* [Motion picture]. United States: Buena Vista Pictures.

White, A. (Director). (2005). *The control room* [Motion picture]. United Kingdom: Agar House.

Wilder, B. (Director). (1944). *Double indemnity* [Motion picture]. United States: Paramount Pictures.

Wilder, B. (Director). (1950). *Sunset Blvd.* [Motion picture]. United States: Paramount Pictures.

Wilder, B. (Director). (1959). *Some like it hot* [Motion picture]. United States: United Artists.

Winner, M. (Director). (1978). *The big sleep* [Motion picture]. United States: United Artists.

Wiseman, F. (Director). (1994). *High school II* [Motion Picture]. United States: Zipporah Films.

Wiseman, F. (Director). (2002). *Domestic violence* [Motion Picture]. United States: Zipporah Films.

Woo, J. (Director). (1997). *Face/off* [Motion picture]. United States: Paramount Pictures.

Wright, J. (Director). (2005). *Pride and prejudice* [Motion picture]. United States: Focus Features/Universal Studios.

Wyler, W. (Director). (1939). *Wuthering Heights* [Motion picture]. United States: United Artists.

Yakin, B. (Director). (2000). *Remember the Titans* [Motion picture]. United States: Buena Vista Pictures.

Zeffirelli, F. (Director). (1968). *Romeo & Juliet* [Motion picture]. UK/Italy: B.H.E. Film-Verona Production-Dino De Laurentis Cinematografica S.P.A. Productions.

Zeffirelli, F. (Director). (1990). *Hamlet* [Motion picture]. United States: Warner Brothers.

Zemeckis, R. (Director). (1997). *Contact* [Motion picture]. United States: Warner Brothers.

Zinnemann, F. (Director). (1952). *High noon* [Motion picture]. United States: United Artists.

TELEVISION SERIES

Abascal, P., & Brown, R. W. (Directors). (1988–present). *America's most wanted* [Television series]. Los Angeles: 20th Century Fox Television.

Ackerman, A. (Director). (2001–2002). *The Ellen show* [Television Series]. New York: CBS Television.

Addiss, J., & Arnold, J. (Directors). (1959–1966). *Rawhide* [Television series]. New York: CBS Television.

Altman, R., & Katzin, L. H. (Directors). (1959–1973). *Bonanza* [Television series]. Burbank, CA: NBC Studios.

Amann, D. (Producer). (1993–2002). *The X-files* [Television series]. Los Angeles: 20th Century Fox Television.

Asher, W., Daniels, M., & Kern, J. (Directors). (1951–1957). *I love Lucy* [Television series]. New York: CBS Television/Desilu Productions, Inc.

Attanasio, P. (Creator). (1993–1999). *Homicide: Life on the street* [Television series]. Burbank, CA: NBC Studios.

Baumgarten, R. (Producer). (2005). *Mystery Theater: The Inspector Lynley Mysteries* [Television series]. Boston: WGBH.

Bochco, S., & Kozoll, M. (Creators). (1981–1987). *Hill Street blues* [Television series]. New York: NBC Television.

Brown, E., & Price, S. (Directors). (1992–present). *The tonight show with Jay Leno* [Television series]. Burbank, CA: NBC Studios.

Burnett, M. (Director). (2000–present). *Survivor* [Television series]. New York: CBS Television.

Burrows, J., Charles, G., & Charles, L. (Creators). (1982–1993). *Cheers* [Television series]. Hollywood, CA: Paramount Television.

Calderwood, D., & Kartun, A. (Directors). (1993–present). *Late night with Conan O'Brien* [Television series]. Burbank, CA: NBC Studios.

Carlin, S. (Producer). (1955–1958). *The $64,000 question* [Television series]. New York: CBS Television.

Cassidy, C. (Creator). (2004). *Girls in America* [Television Series]. San Francisco: Independent Television Service/Public Broadcasting System.

Castle, S. (Director). (2005–present) *In the mix: Hearing between the lines* [Television series]. New York: CastleWorks, Inc.

Chapman, G., Cleese, J., Idle, E., Jones, T., Palin, T., & Gilliam, T. (Creators). (1969–1974). *Monty Python's flying circus* [Television series]. London: British Broadcasting System.

Charlie Rose, Inc. (1991–present). *Charlie Rose* [Television series]. New York: WNET/Public Broadcasting System.

Chase, D. (Creator). (1999–present). *The Sopranos* [Television series]. New York: Home Box Office.

Crichton, M. (Creator). (1994–present). *ER* [Television series]. Los Angeles: Warner Brothers Television Network.

Daniels, G., & Judge, M. (Creators). (1997–present). *King of the hill* [Television series]. Los Angeles, CA: 20th Century Fox Television.

Davies, G., & Edlund, B. (Producers). (2002–2004). *Firefly* [Television Series]. Los Angeles: 20th Century Fox Television.

Davies, R. T. (Creator). (1990–2005). *Queer as folk* [Television series]. New York: Showtime Networks, Inc.

Devlin, D., Emmerich, R., Glassner, J., and others. (Producers), Waring, W., and others (Directors). (1997–present). *Stargate: SG-1* [Television series]. Century City, CA: MGM Television Productions.

Dolezal, R., & Rossacher, H. (2003). *Get up, stand up* [Television series]. New York: WNET/Public Broadcasting System.

Douthit, R. (Director). (1985–present). *Larry King live* [Television series]. Atlanta: Cable News Network.

Eastman, B. (Producer). (1989–1999). *Mystery theater: Poirot* [Television series]. Boston: WGBH.

Eaton, R. (Producer). (1980–2006) *Mystery theater* [Television series]. Boston: WGBH.

Ensler, J., & Karell, M. (Directors). (1999–2006). *The West Wing* [Television series]. Burbank, CA: NBC Studios.

Foley, J., & Grossack, R. (Directors). (1993–present). *The late show with David Letterman* [Television series]. New York: Worldwide Pants.

Froug, W. (Producer), (Serling, R., Writer). (1959–1964). *The twilight zone* [Television series]. New York: CBS Television.

Funk, D., Goodman, R., & Monemvassitis, K. (Directors). (1975–present). *Good morning America* [Television series]. New York: ABC News.

Groening, M. (Producer), Silverman, D. (Director). (1989–present). *The Simpsons* [Television series]. Los Angeles, CA: 20th Century Fox Television.

Hepworth, S., & Downing, H. (Directors). (2000–2006). *Big brother* [Television series]. London, UK: Channel 4 Television Corporation.

Holland, T., & Smith, J. (Creators). (1985–present). *East Enders* [Television series]. London: British Broadcasting System.

Hoppe, B., & Shaw, S. (2002). *Frontier house* [Television series]. New York: WNET/Public Broadcasting System.

Jacobs, D. (Creator). (1978–1991). *Dallas* [Television series]. Los Angeles: Lorimar Television.

Judge, M., & Kaplan, Y. (Directors). (1993–1997). *Beavis & Butthead* [Television series]. New York: MTV Animation.

Kelley, D. E. (Creator). (1994–2000). *Chicago hope* [Television series]. Los Angeles, CA: 20th Century Fox Television.

King, D. R. (Director). (1999–present). *The early show* [Television series]. New York: CBS News.

Klazura, G. (Director). (1991–present). *The Jerry Springer show* [Television series]. New York: NBC Television.

Kohan, D., & Mutchnick, M. (Creators). (1998–2006). *Will & Grace* [Television series]. New York: NBC Universal Television.

Lascelles, D. (Producer). (1987–2005). *Mystery theater: Inspector Morse* [Television series]. Boston: WGBH.

Leeson, M., Weinberger, E., & Cosby, B. (Creators). (1984–1992). *The Cosby show* [Television series]. New York: NBC Television.

Levinson, B. (Producer). (1993–1999). *Homicide: Life on the street* [Television Series]. New York: NBC Television.

Lurie, R. (Creator). (2005–2006). *Commander in chief* [Television Series]. Burbank, CA: ABC Television.

MacNeil/Lehrer Productions. (1975–present). *NewsHour* [Television series]. Washington, DC: WETA/Public Broadcasting System.

McCarthy, D. (Producer). (2000). *1900 house* [Television series]. New York: WNET/Public Broadcasting System.

Meston, J. (Creator). (1955–1975). *Gunsmoke* [Television series]. Universal City, CA: NBC Television.

Michaels, J., & Monemvassitis, K. (Directors). (1952–present). *Today show* [Television series]. New York: NBC News.

Michaels, L., (Creator). (1975–present). *Saturday night live* [Television series]. New York: NBC Television.

Milch, D. (Creator). (2004–present). *Deadwood* [Television series]. New York: Home Box Office.

Nava, G. (Creator). (2002–2004). *American family* [Television Series]. Los Angeles: KCET/Public Broadcasting Corporation.

Newman, S. (Creator). (1963–1989). *Dr. Who* [Television series]. London: British Broadcasting System.

Parker, T., Stone, M., & Stough, E. (Directors). (1997–present). *South Park* [Television series]. New York: MTV Networks/Comedy Central.

Priestley, J., Klein, J., Wasserman, S., and others (Producers). (1990–2000). *Beverly Hills 90210* [Television series]. Los Angeles, CA: Spelling Television.

Raymond, A., & Raymond, S. (Directors). (1974). *An American family* [Television series]. Washington, DC: Public Broadcasting System.

Roddenberry, G. (Creator). (1966–1969/1987–1994). *Star trek* [Television series]. Hollywood, CA: Paramount Television.

Russert, T. (Current Editor). (1947–present). *Meet the press* [Television series]. New York: NBC News.

Schieffer, B. (Current Host). (1954–present). *Face the nation* [Television series]. New York: CBS News.

Schulian, J., & Tapert, R. G. (Creators). (1995–2001). *Xena, warrior princess* [Television series]. New York: MCA Television.

Schwartz, J. (Creator). (2003–present). *The OC* [Television series]. Los Angeles: Warner Brothers Television Network.

Sherman, A. (Creator). (2000–present). *Gilmore girls* [Television series]. Los Angeles: Warner Brothers Television Network.

Skags, C., & Taylor, D. V. (Producers). (2001). *Local news* [Television series]. New York: WNET/Public Broadcasting System.

Star, D. (Creator). (1992–1999). *Melrose Place* [Television series]. Los Angeles: Fox Television Network.

Star, D. (Creator). (1998–2004). *Sex and the city* [Television series]. New York: Home Box Office.

Straczynski, J. M. (Creator). (1994–1998). *Babylon 5* [Television Series]. Los Angeles: Warner Brothers Television Network.

Whedon, J. (Creator). (1997–2003). *Buffy the vampire slayer* [Television series]. Los Angeles: 20th Century Fox Television.

Williams, M. (Creator). (1988–1997). *Roseanne* [Television series]. Studio City, CA: Carsey-Werner Company.

Wolf, D. (Creator). (1990–present). *Law & order* [Television series]. New York: NBC Universal Television.

Zuiker, A. E. (Creator). (2000–present). *CSI: Crime scene investigation* [Television series]. New York: CBS Television.

Print References

Abanes, R. (2005). *Harry Potter, Narnia, and the Lord of the Rings: What you need to know about fantasy books and movies.* Eugene, OR: Harvest House Publishers

Abercrombie, N., & Longhurst, B. (1998). *Audiences: A sociological theory of performance and imagination.* Thousand Oaks, CA: Sage.

Alcorn, M. W. (2002). *Changing the subject in English class: Discourse and the constructions of desire.* Carbondale: Southern Illinois University Press.

Altman, R. (1995). A semantic/syntactic approach to film genre. In B. K. Grant (Ed.), *Film Genre Reader II* (pp. 26–40). Austin: University of Texas Press.

Alvermann, D. E., Huddleston, A., & Hagood, M. C. (2004). What could professional wrestling and school literacy practices possibly have in common? *Journal of Adolescent & Adult Literacy, 47*(7), 532–540.

Anderson, D. R., Bryant, J., Wilder, A., Santomero, A., Williams, M., & Crawley, A. M. (2000). Researching *Blue's Clues*: Viewing behavior and impact. *Media Psychology, 2*(2), 179–194.

Anderson, L. H. (2002). *Fever 1793.* New York: Aladdin.

Anderson, M. T. (2002). *Feed.* Cambridge, MA: Candlewick Press.

Ang, I. (1991). *Desperately seeking the audience.* New York: Routledge.

Angell, M. (2004). *The truth about the drug companies.* New York: Random House.

Appleman, D. (2000). *Critical encounters in high school English: Teaching literary theory to adolescents.* New York: Teachers College Press.

Askew, K. M., & Wilk, R. R. (2002). *The anthropology of media.* London: Blackwell.

Attallah, P., & Shade, L. (2002). *Mediascapes: New patterns in Canadian communication.* Toronto: Nelson Press.

Austin, E. W., Chen, Y., Pinkleton, B. E., & Johnson, J. Q. (2006). Benefits and costs of Channel One in a middle school setting and the role of media-literacy training. *Pediatrics, 117*(3), 423–433.

Bailey, S. (2005). *Media audiences and identity: Self-construction and the fan experience.* New York: Palgrave.

Barron, N. (2004). *Anatomy of wonder: A critical guide to science fiction.* Westport, CT: Greenwood Publishing.

Bartel, J. (2004). *From A to Zine: Building a winning zine collection in your library.* Washington, DC: American Library Association.

Barthes, R. (1968). *Elements of semiology.* New York: Hill and Wang. First half available online. Retrieved March 15, 2006, from http://www.marxists.org/reference/subject/philosophy/works/fr/barthes.htm

Barton, M. (2004, May 21). Embrace the Wiki Way! Retrieved March 15, 2006, from http://www.mattbarton.net/tikiwiki/tiki-print_article.php?articleId=4

Baudrillard, J. (1998). *The consumer society: Myths and structures.* Thousand Oaks, CA: Sage.

Beach, R. (2004). Researching response to literature and the media. In A. Goodwyn & A. Stables (Eds.), *Learning to read critically in language and literacy* (pp. 123–148). Thousand Oaks, CA: Sage.

Beach, R., & Myers, J. (2001). *Inquiry-based English instruction: Engaging students in life and literature.* New York: Teachers College Press.

Beach, R., & O'Brien, D. (in press). Popular culture in the classroom. In D. Leu, J. Coiro, M. Knobel, & C. Lankshear (Eds.), *Handbook on new media literacies.* Mahwah, NJ: Erlbaum.

Beeman, W. O. (1997). *Performance theory in an anthropology program.* Retrieved March 16, 2006, from http://www.brown.edu/Departments/Anthropology/publications/PerformanceTheory.htm

Bell, A. (2005). *Creating digital video in your school: How to shoot, edit, produce, distribute and incorporate digital media into the curriculum.* Worthington, OH: Linworth.

Bennett, A., & Kahn-Harris, K. (Eds.). (2004). *After subculture: Critical studies in contemporary youth culture.* New York: Palgrave Macmillan.

Bennett, A., & Peterson, R. A. (Eds.). (2004). *Music scenes: Local, translocal, and virtual.* Nashville, TN: Vanderbilt University Press.

Bennett, T., Couldry, N., Herbert, D., Gillespie, M., & Livingstone, S. M. (2006). *Media audiences.* New York: McGraw-Hill.

Bennett, T., Grossberg, L., & Morris, M. (2005). *New keywords: A vocabulary of culture and society.* Malden, MA: Blackwell.

Berger, A. (2004). *Media analysis techniques.* Thousand Oaks, CA: Sage.

Bernadi, D. (Ed.). (2001). *Classic Hollywood, classic whiteness.* Minneapolis: University of Minnesota Press.

Bertens, H. (2004). *Literary theory: The basics.* New York: Routledge.

Bhabha, H. (1994). *The location of culture.* New York: Routledge.

Bignell, J. (2000). *Postmodern media culture.* Scotland: Edinburgh University Press.

Bird, E. (2003). *The audience in everyday life: Living in a media world.* New York: Routledge.

Bird, E., & Barber, J. (2002). Constructing a virtual ethnography. In M. Angrosino (Ed.), *Doing cultural anthropology: Projects for ethnographic data collection.* Prospect Heights, IL: Waveland.

Black, R. W. (2005). Access and affiliation: The literacy and composition practices of English language learners in an online fanfiction community. *Journal of Adult and Adolescent Literacy, 49*(2), 118–128.

Blomquist, D., & Zukin, C. (1997). Does public journalism work? The campaign central experience. Retrieved November 20, 2005, from the Pew Center for Civic Journalism website: http://www.pewcenter.org/doingcj/research/r_does.html

Blood, R. (2002). *The weblog handbook: Practical advice on creating and maintaining your blog.* Cambridge, MA: Perseus Publishing.

Bobo, J. (2003). The color purple: Black women as cultural readers. In W. Booker & D. Jermyn (Eds.), *The audience studies reader* (pp. 305–314). New York: Routledge.

Boese, C. (1998). *The ballad of the Internet nutball: Chaining rhetorical visions from the margins to the mainstream in the Xenaverse.* Dissertation, Rensselear Polytechnic University. Retrieved March 20, 2006, from http://www.nutball.com/dissertation/index.htm

Bolter, J. D., & Grusin, R. (2000). *Remediation: Understanding new media.* Cambridge, MA: MIT Press.

Bonilla-Silva, E. (2001). *White supremacy and racism in the post–Civil Rights era.* Boulder, CO: Lynne Rienner Publishers.

Bordwell, D. (1991). *Making meaning: Inference and rhetoric in the interpretation of cinema.* Harvard University Press.

Bordwell, D., & Thompson, K. (2003). *Film art: An introduction* (7th ed.). New York: McGraw-Hill.

Borjesson, K. (Ed.). (2005). *Feet to the fire: The media after 9/11, top journalists speak out.* New York: Prometheus Books.

Borzekowski, D. L. G., & Robinson, T. N. (2005). The remote, the mouse, and the no. 2 pencil: The household media environment and academic achievement among third grade students. *Archives of Pediatrics & Adolescent Medicine, 159,* 607–613.

Bourdieu, P. (1977). *Outline of a theory of practice.* Cambridge, UK: Cambridge University Press.

Boyd, D. (2006). *Identity production in a networked culture: Why youth heart MySpace.* Paper presented at the American Association for the Advancement of Science. Retrieved March 30, 2006, from http://www.danah.org/papers/AAAS2006.html

Breton, S., & Cohen, R. (2003). *Shooting people: Adventures in reality TV.* London: Verso.

Brighouse, H. (2005). Channel One, the anti-commercial principle, and the discontinuous ethos. *Educational Policy, 19*(3), 528–549.

Brooker, W. (Ed.). (2002). *The audience studies reader.* New York: Routledge.

Brookes, R. (2001). Sport. In G. Creeber (Ed.), *The television genre book* (pp. 87–89). London: British Film Institute.

Brunsdon, C., D'Acci, J., & Spigel, L. (1997). *Feminist television criticism: A reader.* New York: Oxford University Press.

Buckingham, D. (1996). *Moving images: Understanding children's responses to television.* New York: Manchester University Press.

Buckingham, D. (2003). *Media education: Literacy, learning and contemporary culture.* Malden, MA: Polity.

Burke, J. (2002). *Tools for thought: Helping all students read, write, speak, and think.* Portsmouth, NH: Heinemann.

Butler, J. (1999). *Gender trouble: Feminism and the subversion of identity.* New York: Routledge.

Califano, J. A., & Sullivan, L. W. (2006, June 29). The flavor of marketing to kids. *The Washington Post,* p. A27.

Carey-Webb, A. (2001). *Literature & lives: A response-based, cultural studies approach to teaching English.* Urbana, IL: National Council of Teachers of English.

Cary, S. (2004). *Going graphic: Comics at work in the multilingual classroom.* Portsmouth, NH: Heinemann.

Center for Media Design. (2005). *Concurrent media exposure.* Retrieved September 25, 2005, from the Center for Media Design, Ball State University Web site: http://www.bsu.edu/cmd/insightresearch/

Center on Alcohol Marketing and Youth. (2002). *Youth exposure to alcohol ads on television.* Washington, DC: Author.

Center on Alcohol Marketing and Youth. (2003). *Drops in the bucket, alcohol industry "responsibility": Advertising on television in 2001.* Washington, DC: Author.

Chang, J. (2005). *Can't stop won't stop: A history of the hip hop generation.* New York: St. Martin's Press.

Choi, C. C., & Ho, H. (2002, July/August). Exploring new literacies in online peer-learning environments. *Reading Online, 6*(1). Retrieved January 5, 2005, from http://www.readingonline.org/newliteracies/lit_index.asp?HREF=choi/index.html

Chomsky, N. (2002). *Media control: The spectacular achievements of propaganda.* New York: Seven Stories Press.

Christakis, D. A., Zimmerman, F. J., DiGiuseppe, D. L., & McCarty, C. A. (2004). Early television exposure and subsequent attentional problems in children. *Pediatrics, 113*(4), 708–713.

Christian-Smith, L. (1990). *Becoming a woman through romance.* New York: Routledge.

Clark, A. (2003). *Natural-born cyborgs: Minds, technologies, and the future of human intelligence.* New York: Oxford University Press.

Cook, G. (2001). *The discourse of advertising.* New York: Routledge.

Cortes, C. E. (2000). *The children are watching: How the media teach about diversity.* New York: Teachers College Press.

Costanzo, W. (2004). *Reading the movies: Twelve great films and how to teach them.* Urbana, IL: National Council of Teachers of English.

Cowan, P. (2004). Devils or angels: Literacy and discourse in lowrider culture. In J. Mahiri (Ed.), *Literacy in the lives of urban youth* (pp. 47–74). New York: Peter Lang.

Creeber, G. (Ed.). (2001). *The television genre book.* London: British Film Institute.

Currie, D. (1999). *Girl talk: Adolescent magazines and their readers.* Toronto: University of Toronto Press.

Dalton, M. M., & Linder, L. R. (Eds.). (2005). *Sitcom reader, America viewed and skewed.* Albany, NY: State University of New York Press.

Dayan, D., & Katz, E. (1992). *Media events: The live broadcasting of history.* Cambridge, MA: Harvard University Press.

De Zengotita, T. (2005). *Mediated: How the media shapes your world and the way you live in it.* New York: Bloomsbury.

Deleuze, G. (1989). *Cinema 2: The Time-image.* Minneapolis: University of Minnesota Press.

Dennison, B. A., Erb, T. A., & Jenkins, P. L. (2002). Television viewing and television in bedroom associated with overweight risk among low-income preschool children. *Pediatrics, 109*(6), 1028–1035.

Digital Media Center. (2005). *Using wikis in the classroom.* University of Minnesota. Retrieved March 15, 2006, from http://dmc.umn.edu/etf/wikis.pdf

Dine, G., & Humez, J. M. (Eds.). (2002). *Gender, race, and class in media: A text-reader.* Thousand Oaks, CA: Sage.

Dovey, J. (2001). Reality TV. In G. Creeber (Ed.), *The television genre book* (pp. 134–137). London: British Film Institute.

Draper, N. (2002, July 8). Video use in schools challenged: Do teachers rely too heavily on tapes and DVDs? One school board is taking a look. *Minneapolis Star Tribune,* p. 1A.

Ebersbach, A., Glaser, M., & Heigl, R. (2005). *Wiki: Web collaboration.* New York: Springer-Verlag.

Ede, L., & Lundsford, A. (1990). *Singular texts plural authors.* Carbondale: Southern Illinois University Press.

Education Service Center Region XV. (2006). *Viewing and representing: Media literacy in Texas.* Retrieved June 30, 2006, from http://www.netxv.net/pm-view.php?page=108/

Ellsworth, E. (1997). *Teaching positions: Difference, pedagogy, and the power of address.* New York: Teachers College Press.

Emery, S., et al. (2005). Televised state-sponsored anti-tobacco advertising and youth smoking beliefs and behavior in the United States, 1999–2000. *Archives of Pediatric Adolescent Medicine, 159,* 639–645.

Emmons, M. (2002, June 23). A question of culture: UC-Santa Cruz student examines the drive behind NASCAR fans' loyalty. *San Jose Mercury News,* p. 3C.

Entman, R., & Rejecki, A. (2000). *The Black image in the White mind.* Chicago: University of Chicago Press.

Ewen, S. (1999). *All consuming images: The politics of style in contemporary culture.* New York: Basic Books.

Ewen, S. (2001). *Captains of consciousness: Advertising and the social roots of the consumer culture.* New York: Basic Books.

Fairclough, N. (1995). *Media discourse.* London: Arnold.

Fairclough, N. (2003). *Analysing discourse: Text analysis for social research.* New York: Routledge.

Feagin, J. R., & O'Brien, E. (2003). *White men on race: Power, privilege, and the shaping of cultural consciousness.* Boston: Beacon Press.

Featherstone, M., & Wernick, A. (Eds.). (1995). *Images of aging: Cultural representations of later life.* New York: Routledge.

Ferdig, R. E., & Trammell, K. D. (2004). Content delivery in the "blogosphere." *THE Journal.* Retrieved March 14, 2006, from http://www.thejournal.com/articles/16626

FIND/SVP. (2004). *Rethinking the television ad.* New York: Author.

Foust, J. C. (2005). *Online journalism: Principles and practices of news for the Web.* Scottsdale, AZ: Holcomb Hathaway.

Frank, T. (2004). *What's the matter with Kansas? How conservatives won the heart of America.* New York: Metropolitan Books.

Freccero, C. (1999). *Popular culture: An introduction.* New York: New York University Press.

Freedman, J. L. (2002). *Media violence and its effects on aggression: Assessing the scientific evidence.* Ontario: University of Toronto Press.

Freedom House. (2005). *Freedom of the press 2005: A global survey of media independence.* Washington, DC: Author. Retrieved December 12, 2005, from http://www.freedomhouse.org/media/pressrel/042705.htm

Gallagher, M. (2001). *Gender setting: New agendas for media monitoring and advocacy.* New York: Zed Books.

Garber, M., Matlock, J., & Walkowitz, R. (Eds.). (1993). *Media spectacles.* New York: Routledge.

Garfield, C. F., Chung, P. J, & Rathouz, P. J. (2003). Alcohol advertising in magazines and adolescent readership. *Journal of the American Medical Association, 289,* 2424–2429.

Gee, J. P. (1996). *Social linguistics and literacies: Ideology in discourses.* Philadephia: Falmer.

Gee, J. P. (2003). *What video games have to teach us about learning and literacy.* New York: Palgrave Macmillan.

Gerster, C., & Zlogar, L. W. (Eds.). (2005). *Teaching ethnic diversity with film: Essays and resources for educators in history, social studies, literature and film studies.* Jefferson, NC: McFarland & Company.

Giannetti, L. (2004). *Understanding movies* (10th ed.). Upper Saddle River, NJ: Prentice Hall.

Giblin, J. C. (1997). *When plague strikes: The black death, small pox, AIDS.* New York: HarperTrophy.

Gibson, S. (2006). Using WebQuests to support the development of digital literacy. In L.T.W. Hin & R. Subramaniam (Eds.), *Handbook of research on literacy and technology at the K–12 level* (pp. 322–336). Hershey, PA: Idea Group Reference.

Gillmor, D. (2004). *We the media: Grassroots journalism by the people, for the people.* Retrieved November 20, 2005, from the O'Reilly Media website: http://www.oreilly.com/catalog/wemedia/book/index.csp

Gilroy, P. (2004). *Postcolonial melancholia.* New York: Columbia University Press.

Ginsburg, F., Abu-Lughod, L., & Larkin, B. (2002). *Media worlds: Anthropology on new terrain.* Berkeley: University of California Press.

Giroux, H. (2001). *The mouse that roared: Disney and the end of innocence.* New York: Rowman & Littlefield.

Giroux, H. (2004). *The abandoned generation: Democracy beyond the culture of fear.* New York: Palgrave.

Gitlin, T. (2001). *Media unlimited: How the torrent of images and sounds overwhelms our lives.* New York: Henry Holt.

Glazer, S. (2005, September 18). Manga for girls. *The New York Times,* pp. 16–17.

Glogoff, S. (2005). Instructional blogging: Promoting interactivity, student-centered learning, and peer input. *Innovate: Journal of Online Education, 1*(5). Retrieved October, 10 2005, from http://www.innovateonline.info/index.php?view=login&id=126&next=index.php%3Fview%3Darticle%7Cid%3D126%7Caction%3Darticle

Goffman, I. (1988). *Gender advertisements.* New York: HarperCollins.

Golden, J. (2001). *Reading in the dark: Using film as a tool in the English classroom.* Urbana, IL: National Council of Teachers of English.

Golden, J. (2006). *Reading in the reel world: Teaching documentaries and other non-fiction texts.* Urbana, IL: National Council of Teachers of English.

Goldhaber, M. (1997). The attention economy and the net. *First Monday.* Retrieved from http://www.firstmonday.dk/issues/issue2_4/goldhaber

Goldman, R. (1992). *Reading ads socially.* New York: Routledge.

Gosney, J. W. (2004). *Blogging for teens.* Boston: Thompson Course Technology.

Gough, P. (2004, April 22). Consumers respond favorably to product placement of brands in TV, movies. *Media Daily News,* p. 2.

Graff, K. (2003, February 1). References on the Web: Graphic novels. *Booklist.* Retrieved March 15, 2006, from http://www.ala.org/ala/booklist/speciallists/speciallistsandfeatures3/referenceonweb/graphicnovels.htm

Graydon, S. (2003). *Made you look: How advertising works and why you should know.* Toronto, CA: Annick Press.

Graydon, S. (2004). *In your face: The culture of beauty and you.* Toronto, CA: Annick Press.

Green, P. (2005). *Primetime politics: The truth about conservative lies, corporate control, and television culture.* Lanham, MD: Rowman & Littlefield.

Greene, K., & Kramar, M. (2005). Predicting exposure to and liking of media violence: A uses and gratifications approach. *Communication Studies, 56*(1), 71–93.

Greider, K. (2003). *The big fix: How the pharmaceutical industry rips off American consumers.* Washington, DC: Publicaffairs.

Grindstaff, L. (2002). *The money shot: Trash, class, and the making of TV talk shows.* Chicago: University of Chicago Press.

Grossberg, L., Wartella, E., & Whitney, D.C. (1998). *MediaMaking: Mass media in a popular culture.* Thousand Oaks, CA: Sage.

Gunter, B. (2003). *News and the net.* Mahwah, NJ: Lawrence Erlbaum.

Hall, S. (1993). Encoding, decoding. In S. During (Ed.), *The cultural studies reader* (pp. 90–103). New York: Routledge.

Hall, S. (Ed.). (1997). *Representation: Cultural representations and signifying practices.* Thousand Oaks, CA: Sage.

Hammett, R. F., & Barrell, B. R. C. (2002). *Digital expressions: Media literacy and English language arts.* Calgary, Alberta: Detselig Enterprises.

Harrington, C. L., & Bielby, D. (1995). *Soap fans: Pursuing pleasure and making meaning in everyday life.* Philadelphia: Temple University Press.

Harris, C., & Alexander, A. (Eds.). (1998). *Theorizing fandom: Fans, subculture and identity.* Cresskill, NJ: Hampton Press.

Hartley, J. (2002). *Communication, cultural and media studies: The key concepts.* New York: Routledge.

Hill, B. (2006). *Blogging for dummies.* New York: Wiley Publishing.

Hills, M. (2002). *Fan cultures.* London: Routledge.

Hine, C. M. (2000). *Virtual ethnography.* Thousand Oaks, CA: Sage.

Hirsch, M., & Kacandes, I. (Eds.). (2005). *Teaching the representation of the Holocaust.* New York: Modern Language Association.

Hobbs, R. (2006). *Reading the media in high school.* New York: Teachers College Press.

Hobbs, R., & Frost, R. (1999). Instructional practices in media literacy and their impact on students' learning. *New Jersey Journal of Communication, 6*(2), 123–148.

Hobbs, R., & Frost, R. (2003). Measuring the acquisition of media literacy skills. *Reading Research Quarterly, 38*(3), 330–355.

Hocks, M. E. (2003). Understanding visual rhetoric in digital writing environments. *College Composition and Communication, 54*(4), 629–656.

Hogan, M. (2001). Parents and other adults: Models and monitors of healthy media habits. In D. Singer & J. Singer (Eds.), *Handbook of children and the media* (pp. 663–680). Thousand Oaks, CA: Sage.

Holland, N. (1998). *Reading and identity.* Retrieved March 1, 2006, from http://www.clas.ufl.edu/users/nnh/rdgident.htm

hooks, b. (1996). *Reel to real: Race, sex, and class at the movies.* New York: Routledge.

hooks, b. (2000). *Where we stand: Class matters.* New York: Routledge.

Howard, I. (2002). *On party, gender, race and class, TV news looks to the most powerful groups.* Retrieved January 5, 2005, from the Power Sources website: http://www.fair.org/extra/0205/power_sources.html.

Huisman, R., Murphet, J., Dunn, A., & Fulton, H. (Eds.). (2005). *Narrative and media.* New York: Cambridge University Press.

Hull, G. (2003). At last: Youth culture and digital media: New literacies for new times. *Research in the Teaching of English, 38*(2), 229–233.

Hunt, R. (2002). Making student writing count: The experience of "from the page to the stage." In G. Tucker & D. Nevo (Eds.), *Atlantic universities' teaching showcase 2001: Proceedings* (pp. 121–130). Halifax: Mount St. Vincent University.

Hyde, J. S. (2005). The gender similarities hypothesis. *American Psychologist, 60*(6), 581–592. Retrieved November 13, 2005, from http://www.apa.org/journals/releases/amp606581.pdf

Jackson, Z. A. (2003). Connecting video games and storytelling to teach narratives in first-year composition. *Kairos 7*(3). Retrieved April 25, 2006, from http://english.ttu.edu/kairos/7.3/binder2.html?coverweb/jackson/index.htm

Jameson, F. (1991). *Postmodernism, or, the cultural logic of late capitalism.* London: Verso.

Jenkins, H. (1992). *Textual poachers: Television fans and participatory culture.* New York: Routledge.

Jenkins, H. (1997). "Never trust a snake!": WWF wrestling as masculine melodrama. In A. Barker & T, Boyd (Eds.), *Out of bounds: Sports, media and the politics of identity* (pp. 48–80). Bloomington: Indiana University Press.

Jenkins, H. (2004a). Media literacy goes to school. Retrieved December 5, 2005, from http://educationarcade.org/node/58

Jenkins, H. (2004b). Game design as narrative architecture. In N. Wardrip-Fruin & P. Harrigan (Eds.), *First person: New media as story, performance, and game* (pp. 118–130). Cambridge: MIT Press. Retrieved from http://www.electronicbookreview.com/v3/servlet/ebr?essay_id=jenkins&command=view_essay

Jhally, S. (1995). *Dreamworlds II* [video]. Northhampton, MA: Education Media Foundation.

Jhally, S. (1997). *Advertising & the end of the world* [video]. Northhampton, MA: Education Media Foundation.

Johnson, S. (2005). *Everything bad is good for you: How today's popular culture is actually making us smarter.* New York: Riverhead Books.

Jonassen, D., & Stollenwerk, D. (2000). *Computers as mindtools for schools: Engaging critical thinking.* New York: Pearson.

Kane, M. J., Griffin, P., & Messner, M. (Creators). (2002). *Playing unfair: The media image of the female athlete* [DVD]. Northhampton, MA: Education Media Foundation.

Kaplan, E. A. (Ed.). (2000). *Feminism and film.* New York: Oxford University Press.

Kellner, D. (2000). Beavis and Butt-Head: No future for postmodern youth. In H. Newcomb (Ed.)., *Television: The critical view* (pp. 319–329). New York: Oxford University Press.

Kendall, D. (2005). *Framing class: Media representations of wealth and poverty in America*. Lanham, MD: Rowan & Littlefield.

Kenny, R. F. (2004). *Teaching TV production in a digital world*. Westport, CT: Libraries Unlimited.

Kilbourne, J. (1995). *Slim hopes: Advertising & the obsession with thinness* [video]. Northhampton, MA: Education Media Foundation.

Kilbourne, J. (1999). *Can't buy my love*. New York: Simon & Schuster.

Kilbourne, J. (Creator) (2000). *Killing us softly, 3* [video]. Northhampton, MA: Education Media Foundation.

Kirsch, S. J. (2004). *Children, adolescents, and media violence: A critical look at the research*. Thousand Oaks, CA: Sage.

Klein, N. (2000). *No logo: Taking aim at the brand bullies*. New York: Picador.

Kline, D., & Burstein, D. (2005). *Blog!: How the newest media revolution is changing politics, business, and culture*. New York: CDS Books.

Knowledge Networks/SRI. (2003). *How children use™ media technology*. Menlo Park, CA: Author.

Kramer, S., Vittinghoff, N., & Gentz, N. (Eds.). (2006). *Globalization and media studies: Cultural identity and media representations*. Albany, NY: State University of New York Press.

Krause, S. D. (2004). When blogging goes bad: A cautionary tale about blogs, email lists, discussion, and interaction. *Kairos, 9*(1). Retrieved March 21, 2006, from http://english.ttu.edu/kairos/9.1/binder.html?praxis/krause/index.html

Krcmar, M., & Vieira, E. T. (2005). Imitating life, imitating television: The effects of family and television models on children's moral reasoning. *Communication Research, 32*(3), 267–294.

Kress, G. (2003). *Literacy in the new media age*. New York: Routledge.

Kress, G., & van Leeuwen, T. (1996). *Reading images: The grammar of visual design*. New York: Routledge.

Krueger, A. B. (2005, August 18). Fair? Balanced? A study finds it does not matter. *The New York Times*, p. C–2.

Kubey, R., & Baker, F. (1999, October 27). Has media literacy found a curricular foothold? *Education Week, 19*, 56.

Kurtz, H. (2005, November 8). His night in the sun: After 25 years, Ted Koppel is leaving the show that did it his way. *The Washington Post*, p. C–1. Retrieved November 10, 2005, from http://www.washingtonpost.com/wp-dyn/content/article/2005/11/07/AR2005110701686.html

Lacan, J. (1977). *The four fundamental concepts of psychoanalysis*. London: Hogarth Press.

Lacey, N. (2000). *Narrative and genre: Key concepts in media studies*. New York: Palgrave.

Landis, L. (2002). *Media representations of the elderly in films*. Minneapolis: University of Minnesota.

Landow, G. (2006). *Hypertext 3: Critical theory and new media in an era of globalization*. Baltimore: Johns Hopkins University Press.

Langer, J., & Close, E. (2001). *Improving literary understanding through classroom conversation*. Albany, NY: National Research Center on English Learning & Achievement.

Lankshear, C., & Knobel, M. (2003). *New literacies, changing knowledge and classroom learning*. Philadelphia: Open University Press.

Larson, S. G. (2005). *Media & minorities: The politics of race in news and entertainment*. Lanham, MD: Rowman & Littlefield.

Lee, C. D. (2001). Is October brown Chinese? A cultural modeling activity system for underachieving students. *American Educational Research Journal, 38*(1), 97–142.

Lemke, J. (2003). *Towards critical multimedia literacy*. Retrieved April 20, 2006, from http://www.personal.umich.edu/~jaylemke/webs/nrc_2003.htm

Lenhart, A., & Madden, M. (2005). *Teen content creators and consumers*. Retrieved November 3, 2005, from the Pew Internet and American Life Project website: http://www.pewinternet.org/PPF/r/166/report_display.asp

Lenhart, A., Madden, M., & Hitlin, P. (2005). *Teens and technology: Youth are leading the transition to a fully wired and mobile nation*. Retrieved October 8, 2005, from the Pew Internet and American Life Project website: http://www.pewinternet.org/PPF/r/162/report_display.asp

Lewis, C., & Fabos, B. (2005). Instant messaging, literacies, and social identities. *Reading Research Quarterly, 40*(4), 470–501. Retrieved December 12, 2005, from http://www.reading.org/Library/Retrieve.cfm?D=10.1598/RRQ.40.4.5&F=RRQ-40-4-Lewis.html

Lidchi, H. (1997). The poetics and the politics of exhibiting other cultures. In S. Hall (Ed.), *Representation: Cultural representations and signifying practices* (pp. 151–221). Thousand Oaks, CA: Sage.

Lieberman, T. (2000). *Slanting the story: The forces that shape the news*. New York: New Press.

Liebes, T., & Katz, E. (1994). *The export of meaning: Cross-cultural readings of Dallas*. New York: Polity Press.

Lind, R. A. (2003). *Race/gender/media: Considering diversity across audience, content, and producers*. Boston: Allyn & Bacon.

Lindquist, J. (2002). *A place to stand: Politics and persuasion in a working-class bar*. New York: Oxford University Press.

Linn, S. (2004). *Consuming kids: The hostile takeover of childhood*. New York: New Press.

Lynch, W., Maciejewski, P. K., & Potenza, M. N. (2004). Psychiatric correlates of gambling in adolescents and young adults grouped by age at gambling onset. *Archives of General Psychiatry, 61*, 1116–1122.

Maira, S., & Soep, E. (Eds.). (2005). *Youthscapes: The popular, the national, the global*. Philadephia: University of Pennsylvania Press.

Malbon, B. (1998). The club: Clubbing, consumption, identity and the spatial practices of every-night life. In T. Skelton & G. Valentine (Eds.), *Cool places: Geographies of youth cultures* (pp. 266–286). New York: Routledge.

Malpas, S. (2005). *The postmodern*. New York: Routledge.

Mandese, J. (2004, April 5). *Video games emerge as "No. 4" medium, displace print among young guys*. Retrieved from MediaPost's MediaDailyNews website: http://www.mediapost.com/dtls_dsp_news.cfm?newsId=245176

Manly, L. (2005, October 2). On television, brands go from props to stars. *The New York Times*, p. 3-1.

Manovich, L. (2001). *The language of the new media*. Retrieved from the MIT Press website: http://mitpress.mit.edu/lnm

Marling, K. A. (1996). *As seen on TV: The visual culture of everyday life in the 1950s*. Cambridge, MA: Harvard University Press.

Martin, B. (2000). After viewing: Reflections on responding to films in the classroom. *California English*, pp. 32–39.

Martino, W., & Mellor, B. (2000). *Gendered fictions*. Urbana, IL: National Council of Teachers of English.

Mason, P. (Ed.). (2004). *Criminal visions: Media representations of crime and justice*. Portland, OR: Willan Publishing.

Mazzarella, S. R. (Ed.). (2005). *Girl wide web: Girls, the Internet, and the negotiation of identity*. New York: Peter Lang.

McCloud, S. (1994). *Understanding comics: The invisible art*. New York: Harper.

McKinley, E. G. (1997). *Beverly Hills, 90210: Television, gender, and identity*. Philadelphia: University of Pennsylvania Press.

McRobbie, A. (2005). *The uses of cultural studies: A textbook*. Thousand Oaks, CA: Sage.

Meloni, J. C. (2006). *Blogging in a snap*. Indianapolis, IN: Sams Publishing.

Mellor, B., & Patterson, A. (2001). *Investigating texts: Analyzing fiction and nonfiction in high school*. Urbana, IL: National Council of Teachers of English.

Merrill, J. C., Gade, P. J., & Blevens, F. R. (2001). *Twilight of press freedom: The rise of people's journalism*. Mahwah, NJ: Lawrence Erlbaum.

Miller, D. (1997). Consumption and its consequences. In H. Mackay (Ed.), *Consumption and everyday life* (pp. 13-64). Thousand Oaks, CA: Sage.

Miller, M. (1990). *Seeing through movies*. New York: Pantheon.

Miller, M. (1997). *How to be stupid: The lessons of Channel One*. EXTRA! Retrieved January 5, 2005, from http://www.fair.org/extra/9705/ch1-miller.html

Miller, T. (2001). The action series. In G. Creeber (Ed.), *The television genre book* (pp. 17–19). London: British Film Institute.

Mindich, D. T. Z. (2004). *Tuned out: Why Americans under 40 don't follow the news*. New York: Oxford University Press.

Modleski, T. (1988). *The women who knew too much: Hitchcock and feminist theory*. New York: Methuen.

Moeller, S. (2004, April 21). How the media blew the Iraq story. *Newsday*, p. A–4.

Monaco, J. (2000). *How to read a film: Movies media, multimedia*. New York: Oxford University Press.

Moore, A. (2004). *Hey kidz, buy this book: A radical primer on corporate and governmental propaganda and artistic activism for short people*. Brooklyn, NY: Soft Skull Press (Free download for educational purposes: http://www.anneelizabethmoore.com).

Moore, J. (1998). Street signs: Semiotics, Romeo and Juliet, and young adult literature. *Theory into Practice, 37*, 211–219.

Moores, S. (2003). *Interpreting audiences: The ethnography of media consumption*. Thousand Oaks, CA: Sage.

Morgan, M. C. (2004). NotesTowardsARhetoricOfWiki/Intro. Bemidji State University. Retrieved March 15, 2006, from http://biro.bemidjistate.edu/cgi/notebook.pl?NotesTowardsARhetoricOfWiki/Intro

Morrell, E. (2002). Toward a critical pedagogy of popular culture: Literacy development among urban youth. *Journal of Adolescent & Adult Literacy, 46*(1), 72–77.

Moxley, J., Morgan, M. C., Barton, M., & Hanak, D. (2005). For teachers new to wikis. Retrieved March 15, 2006, from http://writingwiki.org/default.aspx/WritingWiki/For Teachers New to Wikis.html

Mulvey, L. (1975). Visual pleasure and narrative cinema. *Screen, 16*(3), 6–18.

Murray, J. (1998). *Hamlet on the holodeck*. Cambridge: MIT Press.

Myers, G. (1999). *Ad worlds: Brands, media, audiences*. New York: Oxford University Press.

Myers, J., & Beach, R. (2004). Constructing critical literacy practices through technology tools and inquiry. *Contemporary Issues in Technology and Teacher Education, 4*(3). Retrieved January 4, 2005, from http://www.citejournal.org/vol4/iss3/languagearts/article1.cfm

Nadel, A. (2005). *Television in black-and-white America: Race and national identity*. Lawrence: University Press of Kansas.

National Center for Education Statistics. (2004). *Trends in educational equity of girls & women: 2004*. Washington, DC: U.S. Department of Education Institute of Education. Retrieved July 1, 2006 from http://nces.ed.gov/pubs2005/2005016.pdf

National Federation of State High School Associations. (2003). *Survey resources: Participation sets record for fifth straight year*. Indianapolis, IN: Author. Retrieved July 2, 2006, from http://www.nfhs.org

Navarro, M. (2005, November 6). The prime time of the telenovela: A global audience for campy drama shows its force. *The New York Times*, p. 1.

Nealon, J., & Giroux, S., (2003). *The theory toolbox: Critical concepts for the humanities, arts, and social sciences*. New York: Rowland and Littlefield.

Nichols, B. (2001). *Introduction to documentary*. Bloomington: Indiana University Press.

Nichols, J., & McChesney, R. W. (2005). *Tragedy & farce: How the American media sell wars, spin elections, and destroy democracy*. New York: The New Press.

Nightingale, V. (1996). *Studying audiences: The shock of the real*. New York: Routledge.

Nixon, S. (1997). Exhibiting masculinity. In S. Hall (Ed.), *Representation: Cultural representations and signifying practices* (pp. 291–336). Thousand Oaks, CA: Sage.

Obermiller, C., Spangenberg, E., & MacLachlan, D. (2005). Ad skepticism: The consequences of disbelief. *Journal of Advertising, 34*(3), 7–17.

O'Brien, D. (2003, March). Juxtaposing traditional and intermedial literacies to redefine the competence of struggling adolescents. *Reading Online, 6*(7). Retrieved January 5, 2005, from http://www.readingonline.org/newliteracies/lit_index.asp?HREF=obrien2/

O'Brien, D. G., & Bauer, E. (2005). New literacies and the institution of old learning. *Reading Research Quarterly, 40*(1), 120–131.

O'Brien, D. G., Beach, R., & Scharber, C. (in press). "Struggling" middle schoolers: Engagement and literary competence in a reading–writing intervention class. *Reading Psychology*.

O'Brien, T. (1995). *In the lake of the woods*. New York: Penguin.

Ogdon, R. (2001). Why teach popular culture? *College English, 63*(2), 500–516.

Ohmann, R. (2003). *Politics of knowledge: The commercialization of the university, professions, & print culture*. Middletown, CT: Wesleyan University Press.

O'Shaughnessy, J., & O'Shaughnessy, N. J. (2004). *Persuasion in advertising*. New York: Taylor & Francis.

Patterson, N. (2000). Weaving middle school webs: Hypertext in the language arts classroom. *Kairos, 5*(1). Retrieved

March 4, 2006, from http://english.ttu.edu/kairos/5.1/binder.html?coverweb/patterson/home.html

Penley, C., Parks, L., & Everett, A. (2003). Log on: The oxygen media research project. In A. Everett & F. Caldwell, *New media: Theories and practices of digitextuality* (pp. 225–242). New York: Routledge.

Pipher, M. B. (1994). *Reviving Ophelia: Saving the selves of adolescent girls.* New York: Putnam.

Polanksy, J., & Glantz, S. (2004). *First-run smoking presentations in U.S. movies 1999–2003.* Retrieved from http://repositories.cdlib.org/ctcre/tcpmus/Movies2004/

Postman, N. (1985). *Amusing ourselves to death: Public discourse in the age of show business.* New York: Viking.

Potkewitz, H. (2005, August 1). Big media paying big to find kids. *Los Angeles Business Journal.* Retrieved November 10, 2005, from http://www.labusinessjournal.com/article.asp?aID=160434202.7060305.1176071.9719163.4442175.654&aID2=90458

Project on Disney. (1995). *Inside the mouse: Work and play at Disney World.* Durham, NC: Duke University Press.

Quart, A. (2003). *Branded: The buying and selling of teenagers.* New York: Basic Books.

Quindlen, A. (1996). The glass half empty. In J. B. Gordon & K. Kuehner (Eds.), *NTC's anthology of nonfiction* (pp. 349–351). Lincolnville, IL: NTC Publishing Group.

Rabinowitz, P., & Smith, M. W. (1998). *Authorizing readers: Resistance and respect in the teaching of literature.* New York: Teachers College Press.

Radway, J. (1991). *Reading the romance: Women, patriarchy, and popular literature.* Chapel Hill: University of North Carolina Press.

Raynor, P., Wall, P., & Kruger, P. (2004). *Media studies: The essential introduction.* New York: Routledge.

Real, M. (1996). *Exploring media culture.* Thousand Oaks, CA: Sage.

Reinartz, T. J. (2004). Computer mediated literacy practices through communities of practice: An activity theory analysis. Unpublished dissertation, University of Minnesota.

Restak, R. (2003). *The new brain: How the modern age is rewiring your mind.* New York: Rodale Press.

Rice, J. (2003a). The 1963 hip-hop machine: Hip-hop pedagogy as composition. *College Composition and Communication, 54*(3), 453–471.

Rice, J. (2003b). The handbook of cool. *Kairos, 7*(2). Retrieved April 15, 2006, from http://english.ttu.edu/kairos/7.2/binder.html?sectiontwo/rice

Richardson, W. (2006). *Blogs, wikis, podcasts and other powerful web tools for the classroom.* Thousand Oaks, CA: Corwin Press.

Robinson, T., Wilde, M. L., Navracruz, L. C., Haydel, K. F., & Varady, A. (2001). Effects of reducing children's television and video game use on aggressive behavior, *Archives of Pediatric Adolescent Medicine, 155*(1), 17–23.

Robson, D. (2006). *Female and male athletes in the media: Are they portrayed equally?* Retrieved March 30, 2006, from http://www.bodybuilding.com/fun/drobson42.htm

Roediger, D. R. (2002). *Colored white: Transcending the racial past.* Berkeley, CA: University of California Press.

Rohde, T. (1996). "I love you; let's pray" The business and "ministry" of the Christian romance novel. Unpublished paper, University of Minnesota.

Romano, T. (2000). *Blending genre, altering style: Writing multi-genre papers.* Portsmouth, NH: Heinemann.

Said, E. (1978). *Orientalism.* New York: Penguin.

Sargent, J. D., Beach, M. L., Dalton, M. A., Ernstoff, L. T., Gibson, J. J., Tickle, J. J., et al. (2004). Effect of parental R-rated movie restriction on adolescent smoking initiation: A prospective study. *Pediatrics, 114,* 149–156.

Schechner, R. (2003). *Performance studies: An introduction.* New York: Routlege.

Schechter, D. (2006). *When news lies: Media complicity and the Iraq War.* New York: Select Books.

Schirato, T., & Webb, J. (2004). *Understanding the visual.* Thousand Oaks, CA: Sage.

Scholes, R., Comley, N. R., & Ulmer, G. L. (2001). *Text book: Writing through literature.* Boston: Bedford/St. Martin's.

Schor, J. (2004). *Born to buy: The commercialized child and the new consumer culture.* New York: Scribner.

Schrøder, K., Drotner, K., Kline, S., & Murray, C. (2003). *Researching audiences.* London: Arnold.

Schwartz, D. (1998). *Contesting the Super Bowl.* New York: Routledge.

Schwarz, G., & Brown, P. U. (2005). *Media literacy: Transforming curriculum and teaching, 104th Yearbook.* Chicago: National Society for the Study of Education.

Scott, A. O. (2002, June 16). A hunger for fantasy, a movie empire to feed it. *The New York Times,* pp. 1, 26.

Seelye, K. Q. (2005, November 8). Newspaper daily circulation down 2.6%. *The New York Times,* p. C–8.

Selfe, C. L. (2004). *Video games, narrative theory, and aggressive behavior: An exploration of cause, effect, and responsibility.* Houghton, MI: Department of Humanities, Michigan Technological University.

Shaffer, D. W., Squire, K. R., & Gee, J. P. (2005). Video games and the future of learning. *Phi Delta Kappan, 87*(2), 105–111.

Shannon, P., & Crawford, P. (1998). Summers off: Representations of teachers' work and other discontents. *Language Arts, 75*(4), 255–264.

Shapiro, S. M. (2005, January 2). The war inside the Arab newsroom. *The New York Times Magazine,* pp. 27–33, 48, 54.

Sharman, D. C. (2005, November 15). Study: Online newspapers flourish. *ZDNet News.* Retrieved November 20, 2005, from http://news.zdnet.com/2100-9588_22-5953393.html

Shary, T. (2002). *Generation multiplex: The image of youth in contemporary American cinema.* Austin: University of Texas Press.

Shattuc, J. (2001). The confessional talk show. In G. Creeber (Ed.), *The television genre book* (pp. 84–87). London: British Film Institute.

Shuart-Faris, N., & Bloome, D. (Eds.). (2005). *Use of intertextuality in classroom and educational research.* Greenwich, CT: Information Age Publishing.

Siegel, M. (2006). *False alarm: The truth about the epidemic of fear.* New York: John Wiley.

Sifry, M. (2004, November 22). The rise of open-source politics. *The Nation, 279*(17), 14–20. Retrieved December 23, 2004, from http://www.thenation.com/doc.mhtml?i=20041122&s=sifry

Simon, R. K. (1999). *Trash culture: Popular culture and the great tradition.* Berkeley: University of California Press.

Sink, S. (2001). Doing visual ethnography: Images, media and representation in research. Thousand Oaks, CA: Sage.

Spiegelman, A. (1996). *The complete Maus: A survivor's tale.* New

York: Pantheon.

Spring, J. (2003). *Educating the consumer-citizen: A history of the marriage of schools, advertising, and media.* Mahwah, NJ: Erlbaum.

Spurlock, M. (2005). *Don't eat this book.* New York: Putnam.

Squire, K. (2005). Changing the game: What happens when video games enter the classroom? *Journal of Online Education, 1*(6). Retrieved October 10, 2005, from http://www.innovateonline.info/index.php?view=article&id=82

Staiger, J. (2005). *Media reception studies.* New York: New York University Press.

Staubhaar, J., & LaRose, R. (2004). *Media now: Understanding media, culture, and technology.* Belmont, CA: Wadsworth/Thomson.

Stern, S. R. (2005). Messages from teens on the big screen: Smoking, drinking, and drug use in teen-centered films. *Journal of Health Communication, 10*(4), 331–347.

Sternheimer, K. (2003). *It's not the media: The truth about pop culture influence on children.* Boulder, CO: Westview.

Stokes, J. (2003). *How to do media and cultural studies.* Thousand Oaks, CA: Sage.

Stone, J.C. (2005, December 1). *Popular websites in adolescents' out-of-school lives: Critical lessons on literacy.* Paper presented at the National Reading Conference, Miami.

Strasburger, V., & Wilson, B. (2002). Ten arguments in favor of solutions. In V. Srasburger & B. Wilson (Eds.), *Children, adolescents & the media* (pp. 368–421). Thousand Oaks, CA: Sage.

Street, B. (Ed.). (2004). *Literacies across educational contexts: Mediating learning and teaching.* Philadelphia: Caslon Publishing.

Stroupe, C. (2000). Visualizing English: Recognizing the hybrid literacy of visual and verbal authorship on the Web. *College English, 62*(5), 607–632.

Subervi, F. (2005, May 13). *Latinos and media project.* Paper presented at the meeting of the National Association of Hispanic Journalists.

Swiss, T. (2005). *Rock autobiographies: Popular music.* New York: Cambridge University Press.

Talan, J. (2004, December 28). Alcohol abuse among young girls on the rise, AMA warns. *Newsday,* p. 3C.

Tannen, D. (1999). *The argument culture: Stopping America's war of words.* New York: Ballantine.

Teasley, A. B., & Wilder, A. (1997). *Reel conversations: Reading films with young adults.* Portsmouth, NH: Boyton/Cook Publishers.

Thomas, A. (2004). Digital literacies of the cybergirl. *E-Learning, 1*(3), 358–382.

Thompson, C. (2005, August 7). The Xbox auteurs. *The New York Times Magazine,* p. 21.

Thussu, D., & Freedman, D. (Eds.). (2003). *War and the media: Reporting conflict 24/7.* Thousand Oaks, CA: Sage.

Thwaites, T., Davis, L., & Mules, W. (2002). *Introducing cultural and media studies: A semiotic approach.* New York: Palgrave.

Tincknell, E. (2005). *Mediating the family: Gender, culture and representation.* London: Arnold.

Travis, M. (1998). *Reading cultures: The construction of readers in the twentieth century.* Carbondale, IL: Southern Illinois University Press.

Turkle, S. (1995). *Life on the screen: Identity in the age of the Internet.* New York: Simon & Schuster.

Turkle, S. (1996). Parallel lives: Working on identity in virtual space. In D. Grodin & T. Lindlof (Eds.)., *Constructing the self in a mediated world* (pp. 156–175). Thousand Oaks, CA: Sage.

United States Census Bureau. (2000). *United States census 2000.* Washington, DC: Author. Retrieved July 1, 2006, from http://www.census.gov/

Vasquez, V. (2005). Creating opportunities for critical literacy with young children: Using every issues and everday text. In J. Evans (Ed.)., *Literacy moves on: Popular culture, new technologies, and critical literacy in the elementary classroom* (pp. 83–105). Portsmouth, NH: Heinemann.

Vera, H., & Gordon, A. (2003). *Screen saviors: Hollywood fictions of whiteness.* Lanham, MD: Rowman & Littlefield.

Walsh, D. (1994). *Selling out America's children: How America puts profits before values—and what parents can do.* New York: Fairview Press.

Warlick, D. (2005). *Classroom blogging: A teacher's guide to the blogosphere.* Napa, CA: Lulu Press.

Welsh, J. (2000). Action films: The serious, the ironic, the postmodern. In W. Dixon (Ed.), *Film genre 2000: New critical essays* (pp. 161–176) Albany: State University of New York Press.

Wenner, L., & Gantz, W. (1998). Watching sports on television: Audience experience, gender, fanship, and marriage. In L. Wenner (Ed.), *Mediasport* (pp. 233–251). New York: Routledge.

Wiggins, G., & McTighe, J. (2005). *Understanding by design* (expanded 2nd ed., e-book: Adobe Reader download). Alexandria, VA: American Society for Curriculum Development.

Wilferth, J. (2003). Private literacies, popular culture, and going public: Teachers and students as authors of the electronic portfolio. *Kairos, 7*(2). Retrieved March 5, 2006, from http://english.ttu.edu/kairos/7.2/ binder.html?sectionone/wilferth

Wilke, M. (2002, May 13). *Are gay stereotypes gaining ground and losing bite?* Retrieved November 13, 2005, from http://www.commercialcloset.org/cgi-bin/iowa/?page=column&record=58

Wilson, C. C., Gutierrez, F., & Chao, L. (2003). *Racism, sexism, and the media: The rise of class communication in multicultural America.* Thousand Oaks, CA: Sage.

Wolfreys, J. (2001). *Introducing literary theories.* Edinburgh: Edinburgh University Press.

Worsnop, C. M. (2000). Assessment in media education. *Reading Online, 4*(5). Retrieved October 10, 2005, from http://www.readingonline.org/newliteracies/lit_index.asp?HREF=/newliteracies/worsnop/index.html

Wysocki, A. (2004). The sticky embrace of beauty. In A. Wysocki, J. Johnson-Eilola, C. L. Selfe, & G. Sirc, *Writing new media: Theory and applications for expanding the teaching of composition* (pp. 147–197). Logan: Utah State University Press.

Young, W. H., & Young, N. K. (2004). *The 1950s: American popular culture through history.* Westport, CT: Greenwood Press.

Zetti, H. (2004). *Sight sound motion: Applied media aesthetics.* New York: Wadsworth.

Index

About the Author

Richard Beach is Professor of English Education at the University of Minnesota. He is the author of 17 books, including the co-authored *Inquiry-Based English Instruction: Engaging Students in Life and Literature; Teaching Literature to Adolescents; Engaging Students in Digital Writing;* and *High School Students' Competing Social Worlds: Negotiating Identities and Allegiances Through Responding to Multicultural Literature.* He conducts research on responses to literature/media and is a former president of the National Conference on Research in Language and Literacy.